The Slapstick Camera

THE SUNY SERIES

HORIZONS OF CINEMA

MURRAY POMERANCE | EDITOR

The Slapstick Camera

Hollywood and the
Comedy of Self-Reference

Burke Hilsabeck

Cover: Buster Keaton in *The Cameraman* (1928), directed by Edward Sedgwick and Buster Keaton. Credit: MGM/Photofest © MGM

Published by State University of New York Press, Albany

© 2020 State University of New York

All rights reserved

Printed in the United States of America

No part of this book may be used or reproduced in any manner whatsoever without written permission. No part of this book may be stored in a retrieval system or transmitted in any form or by any means including electronic, electrostatic, magnetic tape, mechanical, photocopying, recording, or otherwise without the prior permission in writing of the publisher.

For information, contact State University of New York Press, Albany, NY
www.sunypress.edu

Library of Congress Cataloging-in-Publication Data

Names: Hilsabeck, Burke, 1978– author.
Title: The slapstick camera : Hollywood and the comedy of self-reference / Burke Hilsabeck.
Description: Albany : State University of New York Press, [2020] | Series: SUNY series, horizons of cinema | Includes bibliographical references and index.
Identifiers: LCCN 2019011272 | ISBN 9781438477312 (hardcover : alk. paper) | ISBN 9781438477305 (pbk. : alk. paper) | ISBN 9781438477329 (ebook)
Subjects: LCSH: Comedy films—United States—History and criticism. | Motion pictures—Philosophy. | Motion pictures—Production and direction—United States. | Television comedies—United States—History and criticism.
Classification: LCC PN1995.9.C55 H55 2020 | DDC 791.43/617—dc23
LC record available at https://lccn.loc.gov/2019011272

10 9 8 7 6 5 4 3 2 1

Contents

List of Illustrations	vii
Acknowledgments	ix
Introduction: The Comedy of Self-Reference	1
1 Slapstick Spectators: *Tillie's Punctured Romance* (1914)	15
2 Buster Keaton's Theory of Film	27
3 Redeeming Vision: Charlie Chaplin	53
4 Bodies of Silence, Bodies of Sound: The Marx Brothers	79
5 Hollywood, Television, and the Case of Ernie Kovacs	101
6 *Nouvelles Blagues*: Jerry Lewis	125
Epilogue: The Apotheosis of Failure: *Jackass*	163
Notes	177
Bibliography	191
Index	201

Illustrations

Figure 1.1	"A Thief's Fate" (*Tillie's Punctured Romance*)	20
Figure 1.2	Distracted spectatorship (*Tillie's Punctured Romance*)	23
Figure 2.1	Failure (*The Cameraman*)	38
Figure 2.2	Mastery (*The Cameraman*)	38
Figure 2.3	Buster and the screen (*Sherlock Jr.*)	45
Figure 2.4	Waking up to and turning away from the image of reality (*Sherlock Jr.*)	49
Figure 2.5	Waking up to and turning away from the image of reality (*Sherlock Jr.*)	49
Figure 3.1	Fantasy at the threshold of the screen (*City Lights*)	65
Figure 3.2	Sight and screen (*City Lights*)	66
Figure 3.3	The screen as surveillance and wall (*Modern Times*)	73
Figure 4.1	The grotesque body (*Duck Soup*)	98
Figure 5.1	Olsen and Johnson in the projection booth (*Hellzapoppin'*)	103
Figure 5.2	"Die Morität von Mackie Messer" as "seen" through an oscilloscope (*The Ernie Kovacs Show*, January 23, 1962)	118
Figure 5.3	Turning the oscilloscope to milk (*The Ernie Kovacs Show*, January 23, 1962)	122
Figure 6.1	Rick Todd (Dean Martin) and the Trim Maid (*Artists and Models*)	127

Figure 6.2	Eugene Fullstack (Jerry Lewis) and his "Bat Lady" comic books (*Artists and Models*)	128
Figure 6.3	The Trim Maid spits the pages of Eugene's comic books (*Artists and Models*)	128
Figure 6.4	Accidental abstraction (*Artists and Models*)	129
Figure 6.5	The space of continuity (*The Ladies Man*)	139
Figure 6.6	Televised simultaneity (*The Ladies Man*)	143
Figure 6.7	The house as set (*The Ladies Man*)	144
Figure 6.8	Mis-extended duration: a gag about gags (*The Errand Boy*)	148
Figure 6.9	The sausage factory (*Tout Va Bien*)	156
Figure 6.10	A second horizontality (*Tout Va Bien*)	159

Acknowledgments

Earlier versions of two sections of this book have been previously published. Part of chapter 3, "Redeeming Vision: Charlie Chaplin," is included in *The Philosophy of War Films* (2014, ed. David Larocca). A section of chapter 6, "*Nouvelle Blagues*: Jerry Lewis," appeared first in *LOLA* (as "Modernism from Clement Greenberg to Frank Tashlin") and then in *Modernist Cultures* 11.2 (as "Frank Tashlin's Jackson Pollock").

People sometimes say that the completion of a feature film is a small miracle. The same holds true for any academic monograph. Like most scholarship, this book is the result of the support of several institutions; more importantly, it owes its existence to the kindness and conversation of my friends, mentors, and colleagues.

The Slapstick Camera began as a dissertation in the Department of English Language and Literature at the University of Chicago. It was shaped especially by my dissertation committee and mentors James Lastra and James Chandler, and from conversations with James Conant. Thank you too to the members of the Mass Culture Workshop, from whose conversation I learned to navigate a new discipline.

At Oberlin College, I spent untold hours at the Black River Cafe with William Patrick Day, whose insight and patience were instrumental in transforming an awkward dissertation into a somewhat less awkward book. The book also benefited from conversations in Oberlin with Grace An and Geoff Pingree, and from the support of the dean's office, and Pablo Mitchell in particular. A Grant-in-Aid provided me with an opportunity to work at the Margaret Herrick Library, whose staff was both helpful and gracious. Thanks go too to my many wonderful students at Oberlin, some of whose insights appear within. I think especially of Joshua Blankfield and Isabella Miller.

At the University of Northern Colorado, the book received the gracious support of the dean's office. It would not have been completed without the help of Laura Connolly and Chris Marston and a Faculty Reassignment Award that allowed me to continue to work while caring for my infant daughter. Thank you too to my colleagues in the English department at UNC, who have been supportive at every turn.

Like many others, I owe a debt of gratitude to the inimitable Murray Pomerance, who is patient, exuberant, and always happy to pick up the phone. Murray showed me the ropes. At SUNY Press, James Peltz is a model director—both supportive and attentive to detail. Thank you too to the two anonymous readers whose input was both generous and detailed and whose model I hope to emulate in my own service to the profession.

The attentive reading of many friends and colleagues shaped the form and content of this book, identifying errors of omission and sharpening my ear. Thanks go to Kenneth Chan, Doron Galili, Akiva Gottlieb, Katie Lennard, Daniel Morgan, Andrew Ritchey, Matthew Solomon, and Alberto Zambenedetti. What errors remain are certainly mine alone.

As I worked on this book, the conversation of dear friends gave me both pleasure and courage. Among many such friends, I think especially of Andy Broughton, Sarah Cornish, Neal Fisher, David Hahn, David Hoffman, Dana Kletter, Benjamin Landry, Marianna Ritchey, Sara Schaff, Brian Short, Daniel Torday, and John Zahl.

A friend once told me that all academic work falls into two categories, labors of ego and labors of love. Perhaps the two cannot be fully separated, but I try my best to walk in the latter. This book works through a style of comedy that I came to love as a child. My feeling for the Marx Brothers, for Laurel and Hardy, and for Buster Keaton and Charlie Chaplin I owe to my grandfather, the late Robert Burke Hilsabeck, and to the laughter and friendship of my brother Geoffrey.

To that end, I still remember the evening, as a child of nine or ten, when my father returned from the video store with a videocassette copy of *A Night at the Opera*. In this and in many other things, it was my great good fortune to be raised by Steven and Alison Hilsabeck, educators, thinkers, and exemplary parents.

And finally, thank you Elizabeth—poet, mother, helpmeet *ne plus ultra*.

Introduction

The Comedy of Self-Reference

FOR MANY YEARS, I HAVE BEEN interested in the intelligence of slapstick comedy. For a mode of performance and filmmaking whose predicates are idiocy and failure, many slapstick comedies have a surprising ability to turn themselves inward and think—dumb movements suddenly shouldered with a philosophical cast. So much comedy involves the attempt to solve a physical problem that suddenly takes on psychological, and sometimes metaphysical, consequences: What's the best way to jump off this moving train? How do we get a piano up this flight of stairs? Can one put together a Sears home without instructions?[1] At times, this metaphysical impulse reaches toward the medium in which it is voiced. It is difficult not to be impressed by the way in which Buster Keaton rides the cow catcher of an antique train, for instance, but it can be stupefying to see that the track and its train stand as a metaphor for the cinema itself, photograph after photograph pulled across the sprockets of the projector like coal cars over railroad ties.

In the case of Keaton's *The General* (1927), this self-reference is elegant metaphor, but a remarkable number of comedies turn the camera more literally upon the technologies and the ontology of the cinema. Keaton's own *Sherlock Jr.* (1924), for instance, tells the story of a projectionist who falls asleep before his machine. It includes an extended meditation about the viewer's relationship to the plane of the film screen and about the fact that the film image is projected before its viewers as a necessary condition of its illusion. Several decades later, Jerry Lewis's *The Ladies Man* (1961), a movie that is in part about the making of television, is not only concerned with the temporality of narrative cinema (the relationship between the recorded and the live image, say) and the means by which such images are produced, but the ways in which space, time, and characterization may be utilized to create new kinds of formal coherence. These are just a few examples of a distinctly comic form of self-reference that traverses studios, directors, and stars and that involves, in its various manifestations, investigations of the technologies of the cinema itself; of the particular narrativity of the studio-era film; of the place, nature, and transformation of the human body onscreen; of the stylistic conventions and industrial processes behind the production of the Hollywood cinema; and of the nature and effects of its photographic basis.

Although his work appears only intermittently in what follows, my interest in this subject and much of the method of this book derive from the writing of the late Stanley Cavell. Late in *The World Viewed*, in a chapter about the ways in which the cinema might be said to exhibit itself and about the relation between this exhibition and the condition of modernism, Cavell pursues a series of examples of self-reference: Cary Grant stepping out of role, in *His Girl Friday* (1940), to refer to Ralph Bellamy by name; the *mise-en-abyme* structure of Ole Olsen and Chic Johnson's *Hellzapoppin'* (1941); Buster Keaton's magnificent step into montage in *Sherlock Jr.*[2] The issue of self-reference also lies at the beating heart of Cavell's later books on film, as in his claim that the blanket that both separates and conjoins Clark Gable and Claudette Colbert in their motor cabin in *It Happened One Night* (1934) can be understood as a figure for the film screen, or that Gable's character acts as a kind of director.[3] This blanket, Gable acting as a director of Colbert's "star," the photos that mark the end of *The Philadelphia Story* (1940)—for Cavell, these images suggest that "film exists in a state of philosophy," that it "is inherently self-reflexive, takes itself as an inevitable part of its craving for speculation."[4]

When I first encountered it, the idea that the action of self-reference took a particular generic and affective form in Hollywood made muddy the picture of studio-era cinema with which I was most familiar. Was there a distinct sort of self-reference, almost a modernist spirit, present in the products of the Hollywood studio system? What did this self-reference suggest for the ways in which we might interpret these films? Was there was something about the form and address of studio-era cinema that gave it a particular relation to the comic? At the end of the passage on self-reference in *The World Viewed*, Cavell gives his observation a final turn, tying it to his larger project of situating the cinema within the history and experience of skepticism: "This comedy of self-reference satirizes the effort to escape the self by viewing it, the thought that there is a position from which to rest assured once and for all of the truth of your views."[5] Were these films really capable of giving voice to the metaphysical?

The Slapstick Camera is an attempt to articulate this voice by directing some of Cavell's procedures and insights into the cinema toward a series of films to which he never dedicated sustained attention but which do very much give voice to the metaphysical. One of the book's central commitments is to Cavell's sense that there is properly no theory without first acts of aesthetic judgment, or, to use an old-fashioned word, criticism. As he says in *Pursuits of Happiness*, "If we are to find a way to speak of [the] conditions of viewing film as transcendental, we must equally find a way to speak of them as empirical, for certainly they are only to be discovered empirically, or rather discovered in what I call acts of criticism."[6] Here, the idea of the transcendental stands in for the ambitions of theory, the desire to move between the particular and the general. Although it may only matter to Cavell's most devoted readers, the distinction between theory and criticism maps onto the distinction between criteria and judgment that he makes in his work on Wittgenstein, where the underlying structure of ordinary language is understood as existing within, and not antecedent to, its intelligible use. In the realm of aesthetics, then, the word *theory* signifies the articulation of what Cavell calls the "possibilities" of an artistic medium, where these possibilities exist within or through acts of criticism and not as the ground from which criticism is undertaken. The intelligibility of any theory, in this sense, actually rests upon the agreement produced by individual acts of criticism. This book attempts to follow this insight by attempting to let individual acts of criticism tell us something about the films under aesthetic consideration.

Each of the films at issue in this book displays and articulates an interest in its medium, from the transitional feature *Tillie's Punctured Romance* (Sennett, 1914) and its concern about the nature of early film narrative to the Marx Brothers' *Monkey Business* (McLeod, 1931) and its account of Hollywood film sound to Jerry Lewis's *The Patsy* (1964) and its little excursus on the end of the Hollywood star system. Unlike the films that Cavell takes up in *Pursuits of Happiness* and *Letter from an Unknown Woman*, however, these comedies do not constitute the members of a genre or subgenre. Producers and audiences did not place these films into a distinct category nor did these filmmakers or performers understand themselves as working within a distinct generic tradition (as they did with, say, the "war musical"). It also seems dubious to think of them as a genre that has become visible in retrospect, like *film noir* or Cavell's own "comedies of remarriage." It is perhaps more accurate to call slapstick comedy a *mode* of performance and filmmaking into which all sorts of genres may slip: just as a single scene in *The Winter's Tale* might be called "pastoral," a single scene (even an isolated moment of performance) in *Bringing Up Baby* might be understood as "slapstick."[7] To be sure, for a period of time, the slapstick comedy was a genre, that is to say, a film comedy that was characterized, from beginning to end, by the tone and manner of slapstick, but producers tended simply to call these films "comedies" and let reviewers employ the descriptors "slapstick" and "knockabout" as (usually pejorative) modal terms.

Instead of serving as members of a coherent generic family, then, the comedies in this book are united by their use of a device that is recurrent within slapstick comedy considered as both genre and mode—the staging and acknowledgment of the medium itself. I call this a device and not a type of gag insofar as it can license, in cases such as *Sherlock Jr.* and *The Cameraman* (1928), the entire plot of a feature-length film, but—as most of the other examples within this book suggest—is more commonly employed to structure individual gags, like Harpo's lip-sync turn as Maurice Chevalier in *Monkey Business*, or single sequences, such as the film-within-a-film of *Tillie's Punctured Romance*. More fascinatingly, this device is not always used for the production of humor, as is the case at the conclusion of Chaplin's *City Lights* (1931). Using what is undoubtedly an unfunny term, then, I follow Cavell and call this device the comedy of self-reference, both in order to give the phenomenon a name and to distinguish it from the concept of self-reflexivity, toward which it bears some resemblance (even, in small measure, a history) but which is a mostly unproductive way of thinking about film comedies that were produced for mass audiences.

Where did slapstick comedy get its brain? Although the device of self-reference originated in part from the stage traditions from which film comedians drew, the specific formal problems that these performers faced as they sought to transpose their acts from stage to screen further help to explain the presence and nature of this self-reference and its interest in the medium of film. The self-reference of some slapstick comedy was the result of a combination of preexisting generic norms (e.g., audience address in the vaudeville act; an expectation of travesty) *and* practical problems involved in producing successful gags for the screen. Almost of necessity, many film comedians had to work on creative problems that were more like those of engineering than like those of the established arts, a fact that is visible in what Hilde D'Haeyere has called Keystone's "meta-movies," films such as *Mabel's Dramatic Career* (1913), which was shot within the actual Keystone facilities replete with its own sets, cameras, and craftspeople.[8] The adaptation of a literary or stage work to the cinema—as in, say, D. W. Griffith's adaptation of the stage play *The Two Orphans* as *Orphans of the Storm* (1921)—may have called for an understanding of how certain effects might be translated to the silent screen, an understanding of what might be added to or subtracted from the action of the original play, and so forth, but to produce the montage sequence in *Sherlock Jr.*, Keaton actually called in a team of surveyors who plotted his movements down to the "fraction of an inch."[9] Like much classical film theory, then, these comedies ask, what can the cinema *do*?

Of course, the work of a filmmaker like Cecil DeMille also involved such an interest, even similar problems of engineering (e.g., the production of the set for *The Ten Commandments* [1923], with its seventy-foot cranes, its massing and ordering of figures on this stage), but in DeMille's case this interest worked in service of the maintenance of a different mode of audience address, one that relied more fully upon the maintenance of a coherent story world, however much it was also interested in breaking with that story to give space to spectacle. Unlike the melodrama, slapstick in its purest instances is always and everywhere an environment of distance, a fact that aligns it with the domains of film theory and philosophy of film. If *The Ten Commandments* depicts melodramatic turns of fate as if realistically, the comedies under consideration do not depict accidents, per se, as much as they depict *images of* accidents. The irony and audience address of slapstick comedy often focalizes, or makes visible, the problems of its production. These problems may remain hidden (i.e., Keaton doesn't stop *Sherlock Jr.* to say how he produces a given trick), but the problems are frequently displayed *as* problems. In other words, the presence of the gag is always in a sense also about the staging of the gag. As Kenneth Burke once wrote, "The comic frame should enable people to be observers of themselves."[10] Slapstick comedy takes place at this level of remove, the position of ironic awareness or intelligence, the sense that what is before us is everywhere a performance.

As it turns out, the idea that these comedies somehow refer to and reflect upon the cinema itself is an old one. For many early film theorists, slapstick was not a marginal case but rather a privileged site for the articulation of the specificity of the cinema. A remarkable number of early theorists prized the slapstick comedy for its utilization of techniques, motifs, and possibilities that were understood as unique to the cinema or as harbingers of more sophisticated, medium-specific future practices. Simultaneously "primitive" and wholly "new," a form that was connected to the deep history of the theater but was also exemplary of new practices and new aesthetics, slapstick film comedy served to place the cinema within and beyond various histories of the arts. In this sense, the slapstick comedy allowed these writers to conceptualize what they understood to be distinct about the cinema in historical terms, with slapstick functioning both as a placeholder for the patrimony of folk history (a link to the past) and as a kind of spur toward the future practice of a modernist mass culture (an image of the future).

As early as *Visible Man* (1924), for instance, the critic Béla Balázs wrote of Chaplin that his "difficult but victorious struggle with practical objects is rooted in a grotesque and mocking indignation about our tool-based civilization and its estrangement from nature." Chaplin's relationship to these objects represented, for Balázs, "a childlike humanity," one that gave Chaplin "a view of the world that becomes poetic in films. This is the poetry of ordinary life, the inarticulate life of ordinary things," a life "which only children and tramps with time on their hands care to linger over."[11] Balázs's lyricism is not unusual in the European reception of Chaplin, but what is less familiar is the suggestion that Chaplin, even slapstick comedy itself, might articulate something about the cinema's specificity. "It is precisely this lingering process," he continues, "that yields the richest film poetry."[12] Like many other writers of the era, Balázs used the figure of Chaplin to place the cinema within the rhetoric of medium-specificity, a rhetoric that worked to justify the cinema's inclusion within the broader realm of the arts but also to articulate Balázs's unique project of "an inspiring theory that will fire the imagination of future seekers for new worlds and creators of new arts."[13]

Visible Man is by some accounts the inaugural instance of film theory, but almost a decade earlier, Hugo Munsterberg had employed the figure of slapstick to recount his own history of the medium. Writing in William Randolph Hearst's *The Cosmopolitan*, he used comedy as a kind of hinge between the explication of a form that he believed to be specific to the cinema and the suitability of this form for what he called "an artistic plot," a higher form of cinema that would fully realize the medium's potential. Notably for the future history of slapstick comedy, the form in question is something like the cinema's ability to join together disparate spaces. "The moving pictures," Munsterberg wrote, "allow a rapidity in the change of scenes which no stage manager could imitate":

> At first, these possibilities were used only for humorous effects. We enjoyed the lightening quickness with which we could follow the eloper over the roofs of the town, up-stairs and down, into cellar and attic, and jump with him into the motor-car and race over the country roads, changing the background a score of times in a few minutes, until the culprit falls over a bridge into the water and is caught by the police. This slap-stick humor has not disappeared, but the rapid change of scenes has meanwhile been put into the service of much higher aims. The true development of an artistic plot

has been brought to possibilities which the real drama does not know by allowing the eye to follow the hero and heroine continuously from place to place.[14]

Munsterberg employed an imaginary "slap-stick" chase film to describe what would later be called continuity (alongside a normative claim that this continuity should be used in service of character-driven narrative) but in order to make this point, he had to acknowledge the apparent *incoherence* of slapstick continuity, an incoherence he attributes to its speed, or what he calls its "lightening quickness" and "rapid change of scenes." In Munsterberg's account, the humor of this movie derives from its ability to make visible one way in which the technology itself works. This rhetorical move aligns Munsterberg's account with the sense in which the early cinema participated in what the historian Neil Harris called the "operational aesthetic," a style or mode of presentation that encouraged "a delight in observing process," highlighted the ways in which a technology might be seen to function, and taught its spectators to "absorb knowledge."[15] In short, "slap-stick humor" serves here to explicate possibilities or effects that are specific to the medium.

Munsterberg's interest in "slap-stick" is particularly early, but the sense in which the physical comedy is of heuristic value in accounting for the specificity of the cinema, and the stronger claim that these comedies are something like purer instances of cinema, would become common to theorists and filmmakers as geographically and temporally diverse as René Clair, Lev Kuleshov, Rudolf Arnheim, Walter Benjamin, André Bazin, and Sigfried Kracauer. For decades after in the domain of film theory, the slapstick comedy worked as shorthand for a style and form that was uniquely cinematic, hence Clair's sense that "the film comedy is the type of film in which the cinema has best succeeded in being itself," or Kracauer's early privileging of the slapstick comedy because of its utilization of one "characteristic of camera reality," the "fortuitous," a motif that he believed was assigned "a major role . . . in a truly cinematic genre, the American silent film comedy."[16]

By the time that Bazin composed "Theater and Cinema" in 1951, the idea that the slapstick comedy was somehow distinctly cinematic was so entrenched in his readers' minds that he used this idea to provocatively stage his claim that the specificity of the cinema might be located not in styles and forms that possess *no* theatrical origins but in those that productively develop to "maturity" ideas that originated on the stage:

> Certain dramatic situations, certain techniques that had degenerated in the course of time, found again, in the cinema, first

> the sociological nourishment they needed to survive and, still better, the conditions favorable to an expansive use of their aesthetic, which the theater had kept congenitally atrophied. In making a protagonist out of space, the screen does not betray the spirit of farce, it simply gives to the metaphysical meaning of Scarpin's stick its true dimensions, namely those of the whole universe. . . . [T]he grafting together of cinema and comedy-theater happened spontaneously and has been so perfect that its fruit has always been accepted as the product of pure cinema.[17]

For Bazin, slapstick comedy did not simply utilize the capacity of the cinema to reproduce or re-present the spaces of the physical world (in "The Virtues and Limitations of Montage," his example of this action is Chaplin stuck in a lion's cage in *The Circus* [1928]) but uses this capacity in order to extend "the spirit of farce" into the realm of the metaphysical, Scarpin's stick of the *commedia dell'arte* metastasizing into the objects of the world itself.

This sort of ontological inquiry more or less disappeared with the institutionalization of cinema studies in the 1960s and 70s. Critical theory inserted a new sort of distance between itself and its object, one that moved away from questions of practice and progress. In distinction to its privileged place in classical film theory, slapstick comedy all but disappears from these later texts. There are several reasons for this, but paramount among them is the turn away from questions concerning the progress of the medium. Many classical film theorists were exercised by formal and ontological questions such as, "How does the cinema make meaning?" and "What separates the cinema from the other arts?" The first question necessitated strict attention to individual texts with an eye toward guiding future practice, and the second was concerned with movement within and between the arts. Slapstick was an interesting case for both forms of inquiry: its irony and formalism made vivid the sorts of questions faced by filmmakers as they produced new works that drew upon the resources and possibilities of the medium. More obviously, slapstick texts are, in an important sense, superficial: their meaning would appear to reside almost entirely upon their surfaces; their pleasures seem to derive primarily from their form. This makes them difficult—although certainly not impossible—to read symptomatically. They rather actively resist the assignation of depth and surface out of which psychoanalytic, feminist, semiotic, and Marxist forms of film theory and criticism are formed. Shot through with formal and ideological ambivalence, it is difficult to turn them into "good" or "bad" objects.

This meant that, in the decades that followed, slapstick comedy fell between the fence posts of a more rigorous historical poetics, including accounts of the so-called classical film, on the one hand, and a series of genres that were put forth as exceptions to this classical film, on the other. Thus, in their groundbreaking *The Classical Hollywood Cinema: Film Style and Mode of Production to 1960*, David Bordwell, Janet Staiger, and Kristin Thompson bracketed the distinct formal qualities of the physical comedy (alongside those of the musical) by declaring that they were explicable as the result of "generic motivation," while at the same time the genre failed to merit inclusion in the "body genres" that Linda Williams opened up for serious study in her influential 1991 essay.[18] The physical comedy's exclusion from the concerns of Bordwell, Thompson, and Stagier is a result of peculiarities in both its formal structure and its unique early production history, which was distinct from that of the emerging dramatic film and which did not share its drive toward narrative coherence that would allow for the industrial organization of Hollywood. Its exclusion from Williams's body genres, on the other hand, was the result not of a spectacle-driven indifference to narrative but to a particular spectatorial position. The genres in which Williams was most interested involve sympathy on the part of the spectator: she cries with the jilted lover of the "weepie," she screams with the victim of the horror film, she reaches orgasm with the porn star. Slapstick comedy involves no such mimicry; its interest is in the ironic distance between viewer and actor, and more broadly, between ideal and reality.

Scholarship that has sought to connect the creation and development of the cinema to the broader environment of industrial modernity has shifted this interest in formal and ideological unity and stressed instead the multiple and contradictory qualities of popular cinema. Studies of spectatorship have worked against the implication that the popular cinema created uniform reception practices, and these accounts documented the ways in which spectators of the popular cinema shaped its products to their own ends, creating sites for the formation of counterpublics and alternate ways of seeing. Much of this work has recognized that the physical comedy, which was birthed in the early, demotic days of the cinema before the formation of the studio system, has traditionally been home to both nonstandardized production processes and the expression of ideological difference. This scholarship has argued that the physical comedy was uniquely capable of reflecting certain features of industrial modernity, like the creation of new patterns of visual and auditory attention and the new existence of mechanized work processes. This is literally the case in celebrated films like the aptly named *Modern Times* (Chaplin, 1936), but it is apparent also in less self-conscious filmmaking of the sort described by a Keystone publicity man: "Rough workers . . . like things that go bang."[19]

Finally, much of the most exciting new work on slapstick comedy has explored and recuperated the work of female comedians, whose presence has been suppressed both in the production practices of Hollywood and in its scholarly histories.[20] For all of the remarkable performances that the studio system produced (and despite the romance with which it is still publicly invested), the Hollywood studios very much foreclosed upon the diversity of the nineteenth-century American stage and provided only limited opportunities for comedians who were not white and male. This is one reason why female performances of the comedy of self-reference appear in interstitial sites: in the transitional era before the codification of narrative and stylistic norms that eventually attended the formation of studio system (e.g., Marie Dressler and Mabel Normand); in the world of early television, a "feminine" medium that pulled from the ranks of contemporary vaudeville performers (e.g., Lucille Ball and Gracie Allen); and in the more diffuse and less ideologically constrained realm of contemporary television and Internet video (e.g., Tina Fey, *Broad City*). The relative absence of female-produced comedy of self-reference in the studio era also reflects a salient fact about this form of irony: it is much more readily available to performers and filmmakers whose bodies, by virtue of their privilege, do not immediately signify difference. Buster Keaton's body may be the principle interest of his movies, and his movies may imagine him as distinct or even alienated from his peers, but the meaning of his body is almost always understood as separate from the social and material worlds that produced it, *individual*, even authorial, not burdened with the meaning of otherness.

Given its interest in articulating the work of these comedians as theory and, more specifically, as a kind of theory that possesses a historical orientation, I have sometimes thought of this book as a series of sketches toward a historical ontology of Hollywood film, one that calls back to the tradition of classical film theory and its interest in the nature and identity of the medium. The question "What sort of thing is cinema?" can seem both naive and unanswerable. Certainly, one wants to say, there is no single *thing* that cinema is; it is, after all, unknowable apart from the institutional, economic, and aesthetic contexts out of which it emerged and through which it continues to grow. Philosophical writing on cinema and photography sometimes seems ignorant of these charges, from the ideas, for instance, that (fictional) films are not artworks insofar as they are not in and of themselves representations but are instead photographs of representations, or that objects are literally visible "through" the photographs in which they appear.[21] The former insistence about the non-art status of films is at odds with the fact that many individual movies have been taken exactly as art, from the European art cinema of the 1960s to the gallery film; the latter sense of photographic transparency is seemingly blind to the cultural and institutional contexts through which this understanding of photographs came into being. That is, these ideas can seem both to spare themselves the trouble of situating their claims historically and to contradict various common sense ideas about the nature of the cinema.

But ontological inquiry into film need not contradict common sense; perhaps more importantly, it need not be ahistorical. As Amie Thomasson has argued, artworks may be the kinds of things the natures of which are inextricable from the ordinary beliefs and practices that surround them.[22] In other words, they might not be entities about which truth claims are discoverable; what they are may instead rely upon our (usually implicit) assumptions about their very natures. And as Cavell's body of writing on the cinema has stressed, our assumptions and interest in the nature of a medium become visible in acts of criticism, judgments that can be agreed upon or refused by viewers. That is, the ontology of the cinema rests upon the categories of sense that we bring to it. It takes a community of artists and readers to bring the possibilities of a medium into being.

A historical ontology, then, would acknowledge the fact that what the cinema is has changed and will continue to change across time as its material and technological bases shift, as it comes into contact with new cultures and ways of taking it as an object, and in concert with its economic and industrial foundations. (As any art historian is well aware, what counted as the activity and products of painting in medieval Florence is not isomorphic with what counted as the activity and products of painting in twentieth-century Manhattan. The beliefs and practices that surrounded these "art worlds" are separated by great gulfs of religious belief, institutional support, technology, and style. Yet they are also not radically *dis*continuous: the Arts and Crafts movement is inconceivable without its picture of the Middle Ages.) The simple fact that our designations for these objects bear some sense of consistency suggests the need for historically inflected ontological inquiry, for a style of inquiry that respects the historicity of individual art forms but which at the same time strives to describe them in their coherence. Curiously, through its production of images of its medium, slapstick film comedy provides us with a route into this inquiry.

At stake in the relation between slapstick comedy and the Hollywood studio system, then, is what we could call its difference—from melodrama, from more naturalistic forms of filmmaking, from other modes of performance. This book often sets these comedies against one particular model of a classical Hollywood cinema in order to broaden our sense of what these films are capable of, how they amount to a kind of philosophical practice—just as Cavell did for the "comedy of remarriage" and the "drama of the unknown woman" and just as William Rothman has done for Hitchcock (and indeed other filmmakers and genres).[23] If this sort of classical filmmaking stresses character psychology and narrative coherence, many slapstick film comedies give the appearance of doing so while preserving a sense that the comedian him or herself is not a well-rounded or realistic character and while charting new courses for the forms that individual films might take.

In fact, many of these slapstick comedies put a wrench in critical models that narrow the reach and possibilities of both classical and modernist cinemas. The slapstick comedy is above all a middle case, and its products suggest that generic difference is inadequately accounted for in the most global accounts of the Hollywood studio era. Jerry Lewis's interest in innovation, for example, is evident both in the technological sophistication with which he worked (apparent in his creation of the video assist) and in the stylistic peculiarities of his films, from their willingness to forgo the realistic depiction of space to their almost experimental interest in duration to their odd and persistent self-reference. Lewis's interest in, or articulation of, the breakdown in conviction that was present in older forms is apparent in and modulated through his peculiar anxiety and almost anti-intentional behavior, a form of behavior and clowning that is frequently staged alongside or within spaces that disclose the ontology of the cinema and its problematic relationship to other media, as in the extended business that occurs in relationship to the staging and production of live television in *The Ladies Man*.

For these reasons, this book calls back to the discourse of classical film theory by arguing that many of these comedies are themselves concerned with the ontology of film. The book works with supposition that, by moving diachronically across the studio era, we might be able to form a coherent, if also slant, account of that cinema, one that is told from the surprising perspective of the slapstick clown. As the sequence of chapters suggests, the device of self-reference was realized most fully by comedians who possessed substantial control over the production of their films and who often directed their own work. The exceptions here are directors such as Mack Sennett and Frank Tashlin who themselves had distinct comedic sensibilities, and performers like the Marx Brothers, who did not direct their own work but who fashioned many of their own jokes and gags.

Chapter 1, "Slapstick Spectators: *Tillie's Punctured Romance* (1914)," describes the formal and stylistic transformations occasioned by Mack

Sennett's burlesque of D. W. Griffith's *A Drunkard's Reformation* (1909) and it explores the particular place of this burlesque within the larger narrative economy of the nascent feature-length film, arguing that Sennett's film provides us with one account of the narrativity of the cinema of the teens.

Chapter 2, "Buster Keaton's Theory of Film," takes the book into the 1920s, developing the theoretical purchase of slapstick comedy by reading two of Keaton's feature films, *Sherlock Jr.* (1924) and *The Cameraman* (1928). The chapter argues that the automatism at the heart of Keaton's physical gags should be read as metonymic for the automatism of the cinema itself. That is, I argue that we might read Keaton as articulating an ontology of the cinema that proceeds from a sense of the cinema as constitutively automatic. After looking at some of the historical context behind this interest in automatism, I suggest that Keaton's work is legible as having articulated a sense of realist automatism, an idea that is apparent in Keaton's distinct relationship to the camera and to the screen.

Chapter 3, "Redeeming Vision: Charlie Chaplin," argues for the understanding of Wittgenstein's concept of aspect perception as a means for understanding the relationship between visual perception and ethical value. This allows me to locate a parallel concept in Chaplin's films of the teens and twenties by paying attention to the ways in which Chaplin asks his audiences to, in Wittgenstein's phrasing, see one thing "as" another. The chapter then turns to Chaplin's work of the early thirties, paying close attention to how Chaplin developed a style of comedy that attempted to resist the coming of synchronized sound. The chapter concludes with readings of *City Lights* (1931) and *Modern Times* (1936) as describing a melancholic relationship between the experience of the cinema as a series of views and an ethics of intimacy.

Chapter 4, "Bodies of Silence, Bodies of Sound: The Marx Brothers," moves the book's claim forward to the dawn of synchronized sound, situating the Marx Brothers' Paramount films (1929–33) alongside the industrial development of technologies of sound representation. In the early days of synchronized sound, the Hollywood studios dealt not simply with technical issues about how to properly equip their stages and theaters but with the issue of defining the nature of film sound itself. They sought to teach their audiences how to hear film sound, which was radically different than that of live theater. I argue that we should understand the Marx Brothers' Paramount films as parodies of this attempt at self-definition, even as they put forth their own account of the relationship between sound and image through a series of gags that incorporate and instantiate the technologies associated with the phonograph, radio, and the telephone. The chapter concludes this reading of the Marx Brothers' relation to technologies of sound synchronization by reflecting upon the relationship between Harpo's embodied silence and the films' general verbal excess, setting the odd construction of Harpo's silence against accounts of the classicized Hollywood body.

Chapter 5, "Hollywood, Television, and the Case of Ernie Kovacs," looks at the comedy of self-reference during the two decades during which the industry achieved its most stable form, with brief accounts of *Hellzapoppin'* (1941), animation at Warner Bros., Bob Hope and Bing Crosby, and The Three Stooges. It then looks closely at Ernie Kovacs's pioneering work on network television, and its distinct interest in the fact and nature of this new medium, paying special attention to Kovacs's presentation of the synchronization of sound and image in his ABC specials of 1961 and 1962.

Chapter 6, "*Nouvelle Blagues*: Jerry Lewis," engages with Jerry Lewis's comedy, reading its firmly intermedial inheritance as deriving from his relation to the aesthetics and ontology of live television. The chapter analyzes Lewis's self-directed work in light of its engagement with the qualities of the televisual and as representing a distinct, almost modernist break with the formal conventions of studio-era Hollywood cinema. In Lewis's films, the cinema—now at the end of the studio system and in competition with television—is a site of productive performance as well as the cause of an inevitable isolation. The chapter closes by analyzing the formal ideas that Lewis brings to bear upon this tension, highlighting their affinities with the more political modernism of Jean-Luc Godard.

Finally, an epilogue takes a speculative look at recent work in slapstick comedy and its relationship to video. As a case study, it considers the *Jackass* television series and features, placing the series and the films in the historical context of the genre and arguing that the gag-structure and larger affect of their comedy is specific to their origin in video. It concludes by suggesting that the representation and meaning of the human body is radically changed in the medium of video, where not its grace but its pain is taken as the index of its reality.

1

Slapstick Spectators

Tillie's Punctured Romance (1914)

THE FORM AND MANNER OF COMEDY that we now call slapstick originated in popular stage entertainments, stretching as far back as the Italian *commedia dell'arte* but more immediately in pantomime, minstrelsy, burlesque, medicine shows, English music hall, circus, and vaudeville. Indeed, when one considers slapstick historically, one is struck by the fact that what are now remembered as the great silent comedies of the 1920s are belated and deracinated instances of a form of comedy that thrived more fully in certain corners of the nineteenth-century and early twentieth-century stage, places where the gag did not have to continually reconcile itself to the demands of narrative. The fact that the feature-length silent comedies that are well remembered today are not the full flowering of a preceding stage tradition but rather a kind of erasure of the stylistic and even ideological diversity of multiple stage traditions is apparent in the relative absence of female performers and actors of color. The great Marie Dressler, considered below, became a film star in her own right, but only by shifting the generic tense of her work, as in her great success in the comic melodrama *Min and Bill* (1930).[1] And we might not remember Bert Williams as a slapstick clown, but his work in pantomime and, more generally, in the peculiar form of black minstrelsy was understood by his contemporaries to be the very pinnacle of stage comedy.

In each of these theatrical contexts, and again in the cinema itself, slapstick was both style and form—a manner of performance, derived from pantomime and from the need for "business" on the comic stage, and the various forms that have housed this manner, from the minstrel and burlesque *olio* to the variety act structure of the vaudeville show. In these cases, slapstick performance was not subordinated to narrative form, as it would be in the studio-era Hollywood film, but functioned instead within a larger economy of spectacle and affect. The structure of the vaudeville bill, for instance, took into account the unstable nature of audience attention as it organized itself around the production of affect: opening and closing acts typically did not rely upon dialogue so that they could accommodate the filling and emptying of the theater; the fifth and eighth acts—the act before intermission and the penultimate act, respectively—were showstoppers toward which the rest of the program built.[2] In cases where slapstick performance occurred within the constraints of narrative, it did so in contexts that were formally and ideologically distinct from that of the "legitimate" stage, as in the afterpiece of the minstrel show or in the travesty portion of the burlesque program. Although the vaudeville act allowed for the direct acknowledgment of the audience (and hence an acknowledgment of that form), burlesque was almost entirely self-referential, taking part in a wide-ranging travesty of not simply the legitimate theater but also middle-class social mores. All of which is to say that the self-reference that is present in the slapstick film comedy has origins that should be understood through these earlier stage traditions.

The Keystone Film Company's *Tillie's Punctured Romance* was produced on the very cusp of the studio era, making it much closer to these stage forms than the other films considered below. It was, for this reason, concerned with questions about the nature of film spectatorship as well as the form and status of what would become the industry's core product, the feature-length narrative film.[3] As Keystone's first feature-length film, *Tillie's Punctured Romance* was a vehicle for the comedian Marie Dressler, who was then famous on the Broadway stage. The film co-starred Mabel Normand and a young (and not yet world famous) Charles Chaplin. The film is of particular interest for the study of slapstick comedy, and indeed for the generic differentiation of the studio-era cinema more generally, because it represented the first attempt to situate the distinct formal and stylistic features of the physical comedy within the narrative constraints demanded of the feature film. It is in this sense a bridge between earlier stage comedy and the more well-remembered features of Keaton, Chaplin, Lloyd, and Langdon. Contemporary reviews of the film as well as Keystone's promotional materials were highly conscious of this fact. Keystone's one-page advertisements, for instance, claimed that the film represented "THE IMPOSSIBLE ATTAINED," the phrase staking the claim that Mack Sennett was the first producer to successfully—and improbably—cram a whiz-bang mode of comedy into the pendulous form of the feature film.

Prior to founding the Keystone Film Company, Sennett himself worked at Biograph, first as an actor and later as director of the company's comedy unit. At Biograph, he undertook a kind of apprenticeship under D. W. Griffith, whom he later referred to as "my day school, my adult education program, my university."[4] At Biograph, Sennett worked on many of the short subjects that he would later travesty in his own studio, from *The Lonely Villa* (1909), which became *Help! Help!* (1912), to *The Fatal Hour* (1908), which became *At Twelve O'Clock* (1913), to the films below, Griffith's *A Drunkard's Reformation* (1909) and the six-reel *Tillie's Punctured Romance*. Sennett's "burlesques on melodrama" at Keystone (the phrase was used by the studio in its promotional materials), and their signature style, were tremendously successful. They formed a major part of Keystone's output and helped to define the studio's style and to articulate its distinct appeal to a largely working-class audience. Their movement is from a Griffithian melodrama that drew heavily from the popular stage to broad comic travesty, which in turn drew from stage traditions of vaudeville, minstrelsy, and burlesque.

Sennett's travesties of specific Biograph shorts are of further historical and theoretical interest because of the influence that Griffith's films exerted upon the formation of Hollywood film style and form. Asking how and to what effect the travesty of *A Drunkard's Reformation* that is interpolated in *Tillie's Punctured Romance* transformed its source, and how it is placed within the structure of the larger, six-reel feature, actually reveals something about this broader history of style and form. A better account of the nature of this movement between source film and travesty, and of the reception of both films, provides a way to better understand the Hollywood feature-length film in general as well as help to articulate what I will call the "gesture of display" that characterizes this travesty and which provides some purchase for thinking more deeply about the mode of slapstick comedy.

Griffith's ten-minute film contains thirty-three shots: the opening seven establish the relations between a family of three, the husband and father of which is the titular drunkard. The following twenty-four shots—which take up about two-thirds of the running time of the film—consist of the father and his daughter at a stage adaptation of Emile Zola's *L'Assommoir* during which he is convinced, by virtue of his viewing of the play, to abstain from drink. The final two shots see the father and daughter return home to the mother, the father's request for forgiveness, and a concluding tableau of the happy family gathered before a glowing hearth.

Griffith structures the middle, play-within-a-film sequence entirely by means of an alternation between the drama onstage and a medium long shot of the father and daughter in the audience. The drama here is not that of the stage performance, but rather that of the father's reformation, which unfolds in concert with the action of the play. After an initial establishing shot of the theater, this alternation is uninterrupted between shots nine and thirty-one (except by title cards). As Tom Gunning has argued, the sequence takes a proto-shot-reverse-shot form: the film figures each action frontally and in staging that marks the father as part of a larger audience, but makes clear, both by means of a rope that separates the spectators from the stage and by its foregrounding of the father and daughter and the bright whites of their costumes, that we are to read the play's action through, or alongside, these spectators, and through the father specifically.[5] (It is internal to the message of Griffith's film that the father is not filmed in relative isolation, as he would have been as the continuity system became more codified just a few years later, but is instead shown to be part of a larger audience.)

A Drunkard's Reformation is a privileged moment for the *embourgoisement* of the cinema. The film is foundational to Gunning's account of Griffith's creation of the "narrator system" and the particular stylistic and ideological constellation of a mode of filmmaking that would eventually be understood as classical. The film was one of the very first films approved by the National Board of Censorship, which had been created in the wake of New York City's shuttering of the nickelodeons in 1908. The censorship board was embraced by the Motion Picture Patents Company as a means for ensuring the political stability of film exhibition and for advancing its appeal to middle-class patrons.

In Gunning's influential argument, *A Drunkard's Reformation* does not simply function as a moralizing tale about the evils of drink but actually advocates for the value of motion pictures as themselves reformist. He argues that Griffith uses this alternation to depict a psychological change in an individual character and, consequently, to carry the ideological claim that the cinema might be used in the service of this reform, rather than simply in service of suspense. That is, *A Drunkard's Reformation* advances, in almost self-conscious fashion, a particular idea about the form, style, and even audience of the cinema. As would become clear in Griffith's later features, the cinema is equated here with the narrative and affect of melodrama, which is in turn underwritten stylistically by what would become the continuity system.

This implies a fascinating question: What becomes of this sequence and its particular ideological charge as it is transformed by Sennett into the target of travesty? There is little in the historical record to suggest the origins of the story of *Tillie's Punctured Romance*, which was supposed to be a loose adaptation of Dressler's successful stage comedy *Tillie's Nightmare*. Several historians have suggested that the plot of *Tillie's Punctured Romance* (and there isn't much of it) bears some resemblance to the story that was told in the hit song from Dressler's play, "Heaven Will Protect the Working Girl." In broad strokes, the story of Sennett's film is this: Tillie, a girl from the country, is persuaded by Chaplin's tramp (here, "The Stranger") to elope to the big city. Upon their arrival, The Stranger and his female accomplice (Mabel Normand, "The Other Woman") steal all of Tillie's money. Tillie is left to fend for herself until her wealthy uncle apparently dies in a mountain climbing accident, at which time she inherits his fortune. Reading about this, The Stranger finds his way back into her graces in order to marry her and make off with the inheritance. It is eventually discovered, however, that the uncle did not die. Upon his return, the uncle sends Tillie and The Stranger out of his home, but not before Tillie discovers Chaplin lavishing his attentions on The Other Woman. In the end, neither Tillie nor The Stranger nor The Other Woman is left with anything, with the exception of a potential friendship between Dressler and Normand, who are united in their rejection of Chaplin's advances.

The film's comedy is so broad, however, that to describe the film's story in this way is, in an important sense, to misrepresent it. The humor and indeed the appeal of *Tillie's Punctured Romance* derives from its exuberant, partially improvised performances and from the film's almost antinomian relationship to other stage and film texts. The voluminous Dressler, for instance, plays a "country girl" who is a burlesque version of the petite and virginal figure familiar from the contemporary stage (and who would soon find her onscreen articulation in the waif-like figure of Lillian Gish). And Chaplin's Stranger is familiar as the villain of the melodramatic stage, but whose lack of graces (and of adequate clothing) figure him not with the false suavity of this villain but as an almost *lumpen* and fundamentally unserious con artist.[6]

Much of the film's eighty-five minutes consists of calculated digressions from this basic plot. These digressions are used for multiple comic purposes and bear different relationships to the story. For instance, several minutes are set aside for Dressler's famous drunk dancing routine (a staple of stage performances of *Tillie's Nightmare*), which is of some importance for setting up her relationship to the wealthy uncle. (His character reference appears to release her from the jailing that was the result of her dancing.) Alternately, the opening reel in which Dressler's and Chaplin's characters are introduced to each other contains several minutes of violent slapstick that bears only a tenuous relation to the development of their relationship.

Sennett interpolates his travesty of Griffith into the third reel, where it is sandwiched between Tillie's release from jail and her taking a job as a waitress. The story of *Tillie's Punctured Romance* relies throughout on its viewers' familiarity with the plots of melodramas, such that the sequence at first appears to set the stage for a change in fortune in which Chaplin and Normand are set upon by the police and are perhaps driven to repent. Indeed, after a title card that calls to mind Griffith and Biograph ("A MOVING PICTURE STRANGELY SHOWS THEM THEIR OWN GUILT AND ITS POSSIBLE CONSEQUENCES"), they take their seats in the cinema next to a man who turns out to be a cop. What follows is a five-minute sequence in which Chaplin and Normand watch this film-within-the-film (a crime melodrama called "A Thief's Fate" that is mysteriously identified by its title card as a Keystone "farce comedy"), signal to each other their own resemblance to the characters onscreen, disrupt other patrons in the theater, and leave (Figure 1.1).

Figure 1.1. "A Thief's Fate" (*Tillie's Punctured Romance*).

In an important sense, the joke lies in the fact that Sennett's travesty bears *no* narrative relationship to the rest of the film. The film-within-the-film is supposed, like Griffith's stage play, to cause The Stranger and The Other Woman to reflect upon their own misdeeds, which are mirrored exactly in the story of "A Thief's Fate." But it is less that they are not persuaded by the similarity between their actions and the story onscreen and more that they seem unable to form the moral judgment that formed the heart of Griffith's drama, despite the fact that their comic business in the audience shows them to grasp the similarities between themselves and the characters onscreen. (Normand compares the villain's moustache to Chaplin's and even goes as far as to mouth "That's you" in reference to him; in a further moment of meta-diegetic complexity, the villain's female accomplice is referred to, in a title card, as "the other woman.") As Rob King has written, "What they have learned from the film is the imminent possibility of being caught, not the moral consequences of their wrongdoing—and, as their continued misdeeds will prove, this hardly counts as 'reformation.'"[7] What is more, they are not caught: they simply watch the movie and leave.

In both style and form, this sequence in *Tillie's Punctured Romance* displays a greater complexity of form and technological accomplishment than *A Drunkard's Reformation*. While Griffith's film is built of a simple alternation between the action onstage and the father and daughter in the audience that is bookended by long shots of the theater itself, Sennett's sequence folds a third term—the image of the theater—into the alternation between film and its spectators. This third term introduces a note of ironic distance into the sequence that is, for obvious reasons, not present in Griffith's film. This alternation (1-2-3-1-2-3 rather than 1-2-1-2) figures the spectatorship of both the film-within-the-film and indeed *Tillie's Punctured Romance* itself not as demanding a quiet, rapt absorption and identification but as energetic and distracted, and non- or antipsychological. And the film represents this affective constellation quite literally in the persons of Chaplin and Normand, who are shown to be unable to keep their viewing to themselves and to pay close attention to the images onscreen.

Furthermore, as perhaps befits the transformation of the stage adaptation of *L'Assommoir* into the fictional film "A Thief's Fate," there is much greater complexity to the representation of the text-within-the-film. While Griffith utilizes the movement of curtains in order to mark the beginning, ending, and act breaks of the play (further retaining a separation between the play and its audience by means of ropes that indicate the outline of the stage), Sennett allows "A Thief's Fate" to partially stand of its own accord. The interior film contains multiple camera distances, an insert of a letter that is part of the film's action, and even continuity between two different spaces onscreen. Unlike Griffith's play, "A Thief's Fate" is shown to exist both within the larger space of the theater and to serve as its own (albeit parodic) intertext.

The relative complexity of Sennett's film certainly has to do with the remarkable leap in and codification of film form and technology that had occurred in the five years that separates the two films, but it has also to do with the semantic and ideological character of the travesty itself. Instead of considering Sennett's film a potshot at a former mentor, or as a means for securing the generic distinction of Keystone's particular brand of physical comedy, we might understand Sennett's travesty as working to establish an alternative style and form, as constructing an appeal to a different audience, and as reflecting upon a different form of spectatorship.

In this sense, a further point of comparison is between the audiences of the two sequences and hence the sort of spectatorship for which each can be said to advocate. Griffith's film depicts an audience that is largely composed of respectable-seeming, middle-class women. (The two other men in his audience seem not to be the single, working-class men who frequented the burlesque stage but well-dressed men of the middle class, each of whom seems to be accompanied by a woman.) The individuals in Griffith's audience enact a restrained, if also openly affective spectatorship that reflected contemporary norms for middle-class spectatorship in the theater and hence suggested, for the benefit of the censorship board and industry interests, that film spectatorship could and should be made in its image. In this sense, the film's pedagogical message stretches beyond the father's internalization of the "moral" narrator that Gunning describes in order to also suggest, rather impressively, that such reform and internalization relied not simply upon changes in film form and style but upon changes in practices of film spectatorship.

In Sennett's film, this audience, and the behavior of Chaplin and Normand, have an entirely different character. The audience for "A Thief's Fate" is composed mostly of unaccompanied men, albeit in tidy, middle-class costumes. And while these spectators *attempt* the sort of serious, absorbed, potentially normative spectatorship that lies at the heart of Griffith's film, they are prevented from doing so by Chaplin and Normand's more distracted behavior. The two comedians speak volubly with each other about the content of the film, move their bodies in ways that prevent the people behind them from seeing the screen, and engage in improvised "business" with their clothing and with a frustrated policeman to their left (Figure 1.2). If Griffith's film triangulates, with remarkable concision, a psychological and reformist style of storytelling, a nascent form of continuity, and a restrained, middle-class kind of spectatorship,

Figure 1.2. Distracted spectatorship (*Tillie's Punctured Romance*).

Sennett's sequence does something like its opposite: the travesty itself has an antipsychological quality just as it represents an ironic and distracted form of spectatorship.

In this sense, the movement from Griffith to Sennett has implications for our understanding of the nature of the feature-length Hollywood film. *Tillie's Punctured Romance* is sometimes referred to as the "first feature-length slapstick comedy." The designation is something of an anachronism. While the word *slapstick* was in popular use at the time (primarily as a pejorative marker that distinguished between low and genteel forms of comedy), the film's promotional materials (and its more sympathetic reviewers) did not use it, referring to Sennett's film simply as a "comedy." (As the title of "A Thief's Fate" suggests, Sennett himself sometimes used the word *farce*, which retained a perhaps proudly pejorative connotation.) More interestingly for the subject at hand, advertisements within exhibitor's magazines of the time refer to *Tillie's Punctured Romance* as, simply, "a six reel [sic] comedy," stressing not the distinct generic status of the film but rather its novel combination of genre and length, a combination that had previously been considered oxymoronic.[8]

While it makes sense to question the sense in which the film counts as the first *slapstick* feature, there is no doubt that the production and release of the film constitutes an important moment in the history both of comedies to follow as well as in the development of the feature-length film as the primary industrial commodity of the studio system. If we take into account the relationship that Sennett's travesty bears to the broader narrative of *Tillie's Punctured Romance*, it is clear that while the sequence relies upon what might be called the situation of these two characters, its inclusion in the film serves both as an occasion for comic fun ("business" on the meta-diegetic level) and, most likely, as a means of padding the running time of the film. That is, if we understand Sennett not as seeking to produce a slapstick film within the constraints of feature-film narrative (slapstick forming an ambiguous and contradictory relationship to this narrativizing impulse) but as trying to produce this comedy in the context of industrial demand for multiple-reel films (as trade advertisements and popular criticism of the film imply was the case), then the sequence takes on a different character. The travesty of Griffith becomes a semiautonomous unit of filmic meaning that has been imported, more or less whole, from the tradition of one- and two-reel comedies that previously comprised Keystone's entire output. If Sennett's travesty of *The Lonely Villa* (*Help! Help!*) had served as sufficient structure for a single-reel film, *Tillie's Punctured Romance* interpolates this structure into the larger form of the multiple-reel film not in order to serve its story but as an attraction within it. The film does suggest that audience interest in a six-reel feature could not be sustained without a larger narrative, but Sennett seems to have taken this demand for narrative in a rather loose sense, using the broader narrative, as one reviewer of the time put it, as "a framework upon which the members of the cast hang innumerable laugh-provoking mannerisms and carelessly accomplished, but exceedingly clever, feats."[9]

Now, this operation of travesty might help us to see something about the classical film and its narration. Bordwell, Thompson, and Staiger stake their understanding of a specifically classical Hollywood cinema on a functionalist understanding of filmmaking, one in which the different techniques and devices of the studio era are understood as working within a single, coherent system of filmmaking.[10] But their account of Hollywood cinema misses much about individual films like *Tillie's Punctured Romance* and consequently, much about the nature of the studio-era film more generally. Bordwell, Thompson, and Staiger are certainly capable of recognizing the intertextuality that is present in *Tillie's Punctured Romance* and of charting the place of this travesty within the larger structure of Sennett's film (which it ascribes to the rather broad concept of generic motivation). But what their account struggles to account for is both the tone of the film (and of the action of travesty specifically) and the particular self-consciousness—about its intertextuality, about its depictions of film narrative, style, and spectatorship—at work here.

This is to say that one way to read Sennett's travesty, and its place within the larger form of *Tillie's Punctured Romance*, is as a gesture toward the act of narration itself. Much as certain films do not simply utilize the particular codes of continuity but rather thematize and interrogate them (the obvious example here is Hitchcock, but this sort of display is present much earlier), Sennett's travesty does not simply participate within broader systems of genre, narrative, and continuity, it actually displays and in this sense might be understood to theorize these relations through the action of travesty.

In *Tillie's Punctured Romance*, the history of comic self-reference is present in kernel: the travesty of other forms and styles (here in the context of a parody of a single text); the articulation of—even a kind of claim for—a distanced and ironic form of spectatorship that creates room for reflection upon form and style; and an ambivalent relationship to the narrative norms of the studio system, hence, the production of moments of excess in which the ontology of the studio-era cinema comes into focus. Here, the action of travesty gives a figure-ground constellation to our sense of the Hollywood cinema by setting its travesty against a background of new norms of style and form. As the next chapter will describe, in Keaton's work, this interest in self-reference and the declaration of the medium goes partly underground, never fully buried by the burdens of narrative integration and surfacing repeatedly in moments of stylistic, technical, and physical virtuosity.

2

Buster Keaton's Theory of Film

LIKE OTHER SLAPSTICK COMEDIES that were concerned with dangerous surprises, experiences of shock and stimulation, and the cause-and-effect structures of machines, Buster Keaton's films responded to a new self-consciousness about the mechanization of human life. People in the United States and Western Europe witnessed an explosion of new machine technologies in the late nineteenth and early twentieth centuries as a result of the accelerating pace of industrialization. And these new technologies resulted in new forms of experience, from unfamiliar patterns of labor in automated workspaces such as those of the Ford Motor Company, to increased numbers and kinds of street accidents as trolleys and automobiles whipped down roads previously reserved for people and horses, to new aesthetic practices like the cinema that were understood as part of this larger machine age.

Unsurprisingly, these changes, and the nature and potential of the relationship between human beings and machines, were of interest to filmmakers across the world. While Keaton was busy wringing comedy from construction cranes, crossing gates, and cast iron fences, Dziga Vertov was piecing together a vision of the cinema as reconciling people to the life of machines in Soviet Russia ("In revealing the machine's soul, in causing the worker to love his workbench, the peasant his tractor, the engineer his engine—we introduce creative joy into all mechanical labor, we bring people into closer kinship with machines, we foster new people");[1] Louis Aragon was proclaiming the radical aesthetic importance of décor ("Before the appearance of the cinematograph hardly any artist dared use the false harmony of machines and the obsessive beauty of commercial inscriptions, posters, evocative lettering, really common objects, everything that celebrates life");[2] Fritz Lang was imagining a highly mechanized, dystopian future for Germany and the world in *Metropolis* (1927); and Luis Buñuel was praising Keaton as "the great specialist against all sentimental infection," in part because of his ability to assume the features and responses of an automaton—the machine man.[3]

While Keaton himself did not document or even understand the affinities between his films and those of his more self-consciously modernist peers, his films stand firmly within this larger tradition and consciousness of a machine age and culture. His movies articulate the fraught relationship between the human, to whom the figure of Buster stands in a metonymic relation, and a world that has become mechanized and automatic. Buster always moves about in a less-than-human environment, one that is scaled toward its machines rather than the people who must move within it. Even in the absence of actual machines, the physical environments and broad, type-like characters of Keaton's films—from the crowded streets and relentless policemen of *Cops* (1922) to the gale force winds and cyclonic father of *Steamboat Bill Jr.* (1928)—function by means of grand and implacable laws that assert a rigorous discipline upon Buster and his movements. In this sense, Keaton's films collapse "thick" descriptions of human behavior into humorously simple accounts of human beings that function as automatisms. And it is for this reason that the narratives of Keaton's films, and many of the individual gags that make up these films, consist of running attempts on Buster's part to adapt to the mechanics of these inhospitable environments and to harmonize himself with the automatic behaviors of both machines and other people.[4] Their thrills lie in a question: Will Buster succeed?

Much scholarship has read Keaton's work as having depicted the possibility that machines might be adapted to the ends not of a larger mechanized society but of the individual. We could call this the "heroic reading" of Keaton's films. It understands his comedy to enact a restoration of the machine to a place recognizable to human activity and intention. As Nöel Carroll has written, "Whenever machines appear in Keaton's work, Keaton, the director, clearly loves them. He does not fear them, nor does he encourage viewers to. He relishes playing with the mechanisms, exploring them, and sometimes even inventing them."[5] Keaton's mature work, Carroll believes, has nothing of the fear and cynicism that stalk the discourse of Henry Ford and Frederick Taylor in Europe; rather, Keaton "celebrates machines as extensions of our human powers. One finds no trepidations concerning the tendencies of modern industry to enslave and dehumanize labor."[6] Michael North has described Keaton's work in similar terms, reading a kind of heroism into the progressive mechanization of Buster himself. If Buster grows increasingly machine-like over the course of a particular film, North writes, he also employs "something like genius to adapt to the mindlessness of machinery. When Keaton reinvents himself as a machine part, he also restores our sense of machines as inventions, whose automatism is nothing more than the fit expression of the original idea that set the parts in motion."[7] In North's reading, Buster is a new hero, a man who takes on the aspect of the machine in order to remind his audience of their rightful place toward it.

Other scholarship has stressed the alienation, even the victimhood, of Keaton's comedy. Gilberto Perez located a firmly ahistorical Buster, a man who was a kind of beautiful alien condemned to life in a universe that cannot do justice to his spirit: "While on earth, he tried his best to do as earthlings do, and thereby made us aware of the peculiar systems by which we rule our lives."[8] Perez saw the rhythms and stories of Keaton's work as dictated not by an individual overcoming of the power of the machine, but by their automatism and force. *The Navigator* (1924) and *The General* (1926) "enact not so much a human as a mechanical drama, a drama in which, if Buster is the protagonist, the machine is not only the main scene of action but the main force actuating the proceedings."[9] Tom Gunning has put Keaton's comedy firmly in the context of Taylor and Ford, writing that "if Keaton recurringly shows the masterful cleverness of a mischievous boy engineer, he also frequently displays the distracted consciousness of a victim."[10] And he reminds us of the places in Keaton's films in which Buster becomes not a hero but the victim of a vast environment of impersonal forces, Keaton's comedy relying upon a Copernican displacement of the human being to make way for the machine tool.[11]

Hero, celebrant, alien, victim: if the larger dispute about Buster's relationship to machines is difficult to adjudicate, it is in part because Keaton's work displays both a remarkable richness of tone as well as a distinct ambivalence, an ambivalence that I want to suggest extends to his understanding of the cinema itself. Keaton's films reduce our world to the status of a machine, and they almost always depict this fate as contradiction. The absurd home of *The Electric House* (1922), for instance, imagines domestic life as overcome, both joyously and threateningly, by its devices. The giant steamship of *The Navigator* is, for a time, the only home its couple knows; and that movie asks the question whether romance is possible in a world that can admit only of mechanism. And while *Seven Chances* (1925), unusually for Keaton's features, does not center around a single machine or set of machines, it does imagine its world and the people who populate this world as unthinking, predictable, and reflexive—that is, automatic. The stakes of these movies rest upon Buster's ability to adapt with physical and emotional grace to an environment that is by definition mechanical and automated.

Keaton's films in this sense compare the automatisms of machines to various automatisms of human behavior and extend their ambivalence to the realm of the social. At the end of *The General*, for example, Buster sits on his locomotive's coupling rod. He has won not only a lieutenant's uniform but romance, and he desperately wants to kiss the woman who sits next to him. Yet every time he leans toward her a soldier walks by and he is forced to salute. The frequency of Buster's salutes increases, eventually culminating in the march of an entire camp of soldiers. Buster, of course, gives up: he leans in and kisses the girl while at the same time maintaining a free hand with which he mechanically salutes the passing soldiers. *The General* thus enjoins salute and coupling rod, human activity and the movement of a machine. Typically for his films, Buster's arm does not simply visually function like a part of a machine; the social activity of salutation is itself figured as an automatism, a routine that is maintained despite its manifest absurdity. Each term reflects upon the other: the locomotive emphasizes the unthinking quality of these behaviors, and these behaviors emphasize a basic and fraught kinship between human beings and their machines.

I want to suggest that Keaton's thematization of the automatic, and more specifically, the ambivalence with which he moves within and adapts to a world that is mechanical and automatic, should be understood as constituting a theoretical relationship to that world. His movies amount to a series of images that we can understand as a theory of film. In what follows, I try to bring this theory into focus in two ways, first by placing Keaton's films within a larger conversation that surrounded industrial mechanization and automation, and then by looking closely at how Keaton himself thinks of the cinema as part and parcel of this universe of mechanization and automation. Just as Keaton's gags tend to pivot around the automatic behavior of people and objects—of bathers and locomotives, brides and rowboats—his films manage to conflate this simplified human behavior with the idea that photographs and the cinema itself involve the automatic registration of the physical world. Keaton's films, in this sense, enjoin us to compare automatisms of gag and medium, an idea borne out most fully in *The Cameraman* (1928) and *Sherlock Jr.* (1924).

Early theories of film were particularly interested in the fact that the film camera was a machine. At the center of "The Work of Art in the Age of Its Mechanical Reproducibility," for instance, Walter Benjamin assigned this automatic nature a liberating function, the mechanical nature of moving pictures having done away, once and for all, with the mystical haze that surrounded the painted picture. André Bazin would later claim that the automatic nature of the photographic process had powerful psychological effects; photography, he said, satisfies "our appetite for illusion by a mechanical reproduction in the making of which man plays no part."[12] Siegfried Kracauer's sense of what he called the "inherent affinities" of film—their natural relation to certain objects and ways of being—is concerned with the ways in which the film camera both indexes and mirrors "physical reality" as such. The idea in all of these accounts, however disparate they may be in other respects, is that the interpretive sense that we attach to a given photograph or film is related to the automatic way in which its image has been produced. For Keaton too, as I will argue, the meaning of the film image, and its particular relation to fantasy, is underwritten by the fact that the camera registers the profilmic world as if automatically.

But to better understand the theoretical purchase of these films, it is helpful to look beyond the realm of classical film theory, which did not properly exist in the busiest years of Keaton's career, and turn instead to the discourse that surrounded the automation of labor at that time. This is important because what I am calling Keaton's theory of film thinks of the cinema as merely one machine amid a greater "empire of machines" (as one writer put it), a world in which not just labor and domestic tasks but indeed all human relations and the human sensorium itself were undergoing a profound transformation. Keaton's particular picture of the cinema, with its emphasis on the reality of the screened image, and the viewer's and performer's ambivalent relationship to that reality, derives from a sense of the cinema as transforming perception and fantasy in these ways.

At the same time that Keaton was leaving the vaudeville stage to apprentice with Fatty Arbuckle, or putting together his remarkable series of silent feature-length films, a great volume of writing—from regional trade papers like *The Louisiana Planter and Sugar Manufacturer*, to periodicals for the educated middle class like *Scientific Monthly* and *Yale Review*, to organs of the academic social sciences like the *American Journal of Sociology*—sought to answer a fundamental question about the relationship between human beings and machines. As an advertisement for one popular book put it: "Master or servant—which shall it be?"[13] The discourse surrounding automation consists of dystopian polemic about this invading empire of machines, reasoned calls to restore the balance between the human hand and its machine counterpart, and the outright celebration of the abundance that machine production was bringing into American homes. Whether through frightened polemic or exuberant apology, however, writers of the era were conscious of existing not only within a world in which labor was constrained by the spatial, aural, and rhythmic extensions of machines but one in which machines and the machine process had created entire urban conglomerations like Detroit, the "motor city"; birthed new social structures such as the evening shift and the factory school; and produced a "jazz culture" in which the forces of mechanization were shifting the aesthetics of everyday life toward experiences of standardization, industrial noise, and the programmed thrill.

Within this brave new world, these writers, like Keaton himself, understood the cinema as one machine among many, part of a larger movement that brought ordinary people into contact with the forces of modernization. A social scientist of the era, for instance, lists data for the production of film stock alongside those of automobiles, passenger planes, monthly magazines, radios, stamps, and telephones.[14] A polemicist argues that if the steel industry built Pittsburgh, then the cinema built Hollywood.[15] A management specialist stresses the physical and sensory difference of the modern environment, within which he includes the cinema: "The environment of the typical city and shop-worker is man made—paved streets, rented houses, municipal water and lighting, commercialized amusements, the artificial thrill of the melodrama on stage and the movie screen."[16] And an educator suggests that if automated work exists for the less intelligent portion of the population, then the cinema—that "modern universal drama of the screen where, more emphatically even than in modern industry, the moron seems to have come at last into a real kingdom"—is their leisure.[17] As the economic historian Gerben Bakker recently put it, the cinema "industrialized entertainment by automating it, standardizing it, and making it tradable."[18] It represented the automation of an activity that was previously "rival" and "labor-intensive," changing, as much theory of the period points out, the relationship between performer and audience, even the performer and his or her self. The cinema represented a distinctly mechanized form of culture, one that was consciously produced for mass consumption, like Ford automobiles and "Grand Rapids furniture."

If morons were to automated labor what filmgoers were to the cinema, there was also an understanding that the cinema was fitted to the sensorium of labor under this automation. Hyacinthe Dubreuil's *Robots or Men?* (1930), a first-person account of a French laborer's experiences in the American factory system, was translated and published in the United States under the auspices of the Taylor Society; unsurprisingly, it champions the efficiency and fairness of American factory management, especially in the booming auto industry of Detroit. But his appreciation for the system stops at the cultural corollary of automated work. Among other stories of life outside of the factory, Dubreuil recounts a trip to a Detroit cinema, and he links the phenomenon of moviegoing to the dulling noise of factory work:

> Following my companions from the factory into the little Detroit motion picture shows, I understand better the taste they display for the "silent art." I could not have been persuaded to go to a lecture instead. I even found during this entire time that my taste for reading diminished considerably, and I believe the direct cause was this factory noise, which created in me a sort of inaptitude for the particular work represented by attentive and, if I may say so, serious reading.[19]

In Dubreuil's telling, the constant whir and excitation of machines, and the standardization of goods that they produce, led to a fundamentally altered culture of stimulation and entertainment. Or as Kracauer had suggested more hopefully three years earlier, the cinema—and slapstick comedy in particular—served a compensatory function in this environment, matching the rhythms and noise of the assembly line with both the silence and thrill of the moving image.[20]

To better place Keaton in this discourse, I want to look briefly at "The American Automatic Tool," an article that appeared in *The Journal of Political Economy* in 1919, just as Keaton began to make short films with Fatty Arbuckle. "The American Automatic Tool" poses a question that surfaces repeatedly throughout periodicals of the era: How are we to harness the power of automation without at the same time forcing the worker to serve, as its author puts it, "as but a cog in the functioning of the Iron Man?"[21] The author of "The American Automatic Tool" was Ernest F. Lloyd, a retired manager of a private utility and manufacturer of machines for the refinement and distribution of natural gas. The question of automation had come into focus for him not simply because of his work as a manufacturer, but because of what was then his privileged geographic position for thinking through these ideas: he lived in southeastern Michigan under an economy that was then booming from the success of the auto industry. Lloyd was an almost nineteenth-century American figure, not unlike Keaton himself. A businessman, an untrained engineer, and, eventually, a trained political economist, he made a small fortune from the fruits of automation and then sought to reflect theoretically about the relation of human labor to what Thorstein Veblen had fifteen years earlier called "the machine process."

Lloyd's essay provides us with a clear definition of automation as it was understood at the time, or what he thinks of as the principle of automatism:

> Automatism in machinery is the incorporation into a tool or machine of a function that previously resided in the operator of the tool. Thus the capacity to do a certain work becomes a function of the tool itself, one to which it conforms without direction by the attendant. An automatic tool is a self-functioning mechanism.[22]

Lloyd's account stresses a historical relation between the activity of the automatic tool and that of the human hand (or the human hand working in concert with a nonautomatic tool, a tool "whose principal purpose," as he puts it, "is to strengthen the arm of the worker"). Automatic tools, in Lloyd's account, *substitute* themselves for human workers, displacing functions that were formerly interior to individual people ("in the operator") onto the outward, dumb form of the machine itself (what he calls its function).

In Lloyd's account, it is in effecting the substitution of machine for man that the machine process seeks to reduce "the human element," thereby posing a problem for the experience of work itself:

> It is difficult to make clear in words the utter detachment of the operator from any control over that which the tool does to the thing which he has placed in it. Of a truth, he becomes only an animated derrick. Put in, take out, put in, take out, for sixty minutes each hour, eight hours each day, six days each week, fifty-two weeks each year, under the always imperative condition that he synchronize the movements of his own body with the predetermined speed and cycle of the tool. The automatic tool thus attains its highest effectiveness when the human element in its operation has reached the irreducible minimum.[23]

In one sense, Lloyd's worker is simply "an attendant" to his machine. But he is also the recipient of an overwhelming discipline, one that is repetitive (even standardized like the products that the worker consumes in his off hours) and one that requires, as Lloyd later puts it, "adaptability, strength, deftness, or endurance" in order to keep pace with the work and the machine out of which that work unfurls.[24]

Lloyd's worker is above all an ambivalent figure, a man who is both "an animated derrick" and at the same time a hero who adjusts himself to the cadences and demands of the machines with which he works. He has lost the satisfactions of handwork, of a direct relation between his work and its product—vanishing qualities that Veblen had described as "manual dexterity, the rule of thumb, and the fortuitous conjecture of the seasons"—but his new work still requires physical feats of "adaptability, strength, deftness, or endurance."[25] The setting for this ambivalence is clear: he must meet the demands of the Iron Man while retaining his personhood. The literature on automation of the era returns over and over to this challenge, conjuring images of men grown angry and lazy from their daily fraternity with machines and others of well-adjusted workers who know how and when to daydream on the job. The reigning question is how to acclimate workers to these machines such that they retain what one writer calls their "human relationships."

It was within this context that Keaton's commerce with machines, his repurposing of their rhythms and the progressive and alienating mechanization of his own person, received their specific charge. In Lloyd's descriptions of the worker and the automatic tool, it is not difficult to discern the figure of Buster, an "animated derrick" who must "synchronize the movements of his own body with the predetermined speed and cycle of the tool" and do so with "strength, deftness [and] endurance." In Keaton's films, the fraught human relationship to the mechanical and automated world and the porous boundary between them extends to the figure of Buster himself, whose very being seems to take on, most often melancholically, the automatic nature of the mechanisms among which he cavorts.

Indeed, the ambivalence here helps to contextualize the nineteenth-century and often rural settings of so many of Keaton's films, which look back nostalgically upon a time prior to this machine age and the comedy of which very much champions the artisan-tinkerer who had not yet been absorbed into the larger machine process. Many of these films imagine the worker of the twenties in the clothes and mien of the century past, a man who must place and understand himself within a larger mechanistic field but whose inventiveness and pluck in such a context is still legible and effective. Indeed, such confusion of temporal registers is common to the era's visualization of itself. As Terry Smith has observed, "modernity, between the wars, exists essentially in the play of flow and blockage between imagined futures and echoing pasts."[26] That is, the question "Master or servant, robots or men?" itself has a temporal register, carrying with it the burden of the imagination of the future in the light of a vanishing past.

Like the worker that Lloyd conjures in his essay, Buster is *both* a heroic specimen whose adaptability and deftness with machines stakes the human claim in that relationship *and* an empty automaton at the mercy of a grand field of mechanized forces. Such a rhetorical strategy is very much in keeping with much American cinema of the studio era, which frequently reflects underlying social concerns and forces without at the same time endorsing specific, let alone radical, solutions to these problems. In true Hollywood form, Keaton's films are legible both as resistant to the dehumanizing forces of mechanization and as celebrations of a larger machine culture. They figure the human being as cast adrift within a world of "comic geometry," one built of a vast "confluence of intricate angles and intersections," while also insisting upon the possibility of re-scaling these machines to the foundations of human purpose.[27]

Furthermore, like Lloyd's worker whose labor requires that he put aside "his human relationships," Buster's adaptations to the lives of these machines inevitably require his alienation from the people around him. It is common for his films to proceed from this sense of alienation (in the ritual of engagement in *Seven Chances*, for instance, or in the behaviors of his in-laws in *One Week* [1920]) to the apparently successful achievement or resumption of a romantic relationship. Yet in almost all of these instances this romance is ironized (think, for example, of the joint tombstones that are the final image of *College* [1927]), its viability called into question by the fact that Buster has himself become a kind of machine, a device who cannot actually imagine the physical and emotional rigors of married life.

∽

If for many writers of the twenties the defining question of "the automatic tool" or the "machine process" is the human relationship to this machine, or the character of labor in conflict with automation, this is also a ruling question for Keaton's films, within which the people around Buster are shown to function automatically, without thought or creative endeavor, and where what is at stake for Buster himself is the maintenance and survival of his personhood in relationship to the physical and emotional discipline that these mechanisms and mechanical environments demand of their operators and inhabitants. Keaton's films, in this sense, collapse thick descriptions of human behavior into humorously simple images of what we might call, after Ernest Lloyd, automatisms.

Yet if Keaton's films are concerned with the relationship between the automatisms of machines and those of human beings, they also think of the cinema itself as constitutively automatic, part and parcel of a mechanized and automated world. Most of Keaton's feature-length films consist of Buster's confrontation with and eventual mastery of a single, complex machine, frequently one of transport: *The Navigator* concerns his relationship to an empty ocean liner, *Steamboat Bill Jr.* a steamboat, *The General* a locomotive. But on two separate occasions—in *Sherlock Jr.* and then in *The Cameraman*—Keaton staged a confrontation with one particular machine (properly speaking, one set of machines)—the cinema itself. Like his relationship with these other, mostly nineteenth-century machines of transport, Buster's relationship to the technologies of film is profoundly ambivalent. In order to master these machines, Buster must in a sense become them, thereby sacrificing a part of himself in the process. If a sense of automatism pervades the human behavior around Buster and his clowning, these films connect this automatism of behavior to a larger automatism of the medium of cinema, in the process providing an account of the viewer's relationship to the film screen.

In *The Cameraman*, Buster is a hapless photographer who buys an old Pathé film camera in order to impress a secretary at the MGM news desk. Much of the film is taken up with the comic staging of his inability to serve as a proper cameraman. In an early sequence, he shoots a day's footage on the city streets only to discover that it is hopelessly garbled montage. As occurs in his other feature-length films, he eventually proves his mastery of the machine, managing to film evidence of his heroism in a boating accident, saving his secretary girlfriend from drowning, and even securing himself a job as an MGM cameraman. In both moments—his failures with the Pathé and his eventual mastery of the camera and its codes—*The Cameraman* provides us with the images that Keaton has shot with his camera, which move in the first case from a kind of accidental city symphony with superimpositions and film played in reverse to, in the second case, highly legible, indeed newsworthy, images of his heroism with the boat (Figures 2.1 and 2.2 on page 38).

As is the case in Keaton's other films, where Buster enacts the progressive control of a single machine, these images would seem to depict a movement from failure to mastery. *The Cameraman*, however, encounters a further difficulty with the usual narrative from failure to mastery. Whereas it is more or less clear what constitutes the mastery of, say, a locomotive, it is less clear what constitutes mastery of the film camera. Mastery of the camera involves mastery not simply of a machine, but of a series of cultural codes. *The Cameraman* raises the issue of how to demonstrate this special kind of mastery, given the fact that, by the conventions of the studio-era cinema at least, it is impossible to simultaneously show Buster shooting film, rescuing his love interest, and projecting the image of this rescue before an audience. In *The Cameraman*, this movement is also

Figure 2.1. Failure (*The Cameraman*).

Figure 2.2. Mastery (*The Cameraman*).

represented as a semiotic transformation: from an opaque, heterogeneous image that recalls work of the avant-garde (and the city symphony film in particular) to one that is transparent, homogeneous, even classical in construction. That is, in *The Cameraman*, the mastering of the machine in question—the Pathé camera—is represented as the mastery of the norms of the studio cinema itself. The mastery of the camera *is* the successful adoption of these norms.

Indeed, by the codes of the studio-era cinema, the first image is illegible. It depicts several crowds of people in four overlapping long shots. Their faces are indistinguishable, zones of white in a landscape defined by its dark overcoats, moving automobiles, and dark facades. The image has an undefined temporality (the suggestion is that each of the four "scenes" was filmed by the same camera at different points in time), and its individual actors are not recognizably individual. Furthermore, they have no apparent bearing on the events depicted. The image is also recognized within the story as having been produced by an inept handling of the camera that has resulted from Buster's inadequate identification with that machine (Buster has inadvertently produced multiple exposures of the same film), much as the ocean liner running aground in *The Navigator* or the failed athletic feats in *College* (1927) were understood, within the stories of those films, to be failures related to Buster's insufficient identification with those machines (and hence subject to later corrections on his part).

The second image, on the other hand, is supremely legible. Unlike the image of the crowds, this image privileges bodies and faces as vehicles for story information. It makes sense both temporally (the image depicts two individuals engaged in a single event at a single time in the past) and diegetically (we understand that these individuals caused this event to occur and we understand the place of this event within the larger narrative of the film). Put another way, the visual intelligibility of this image corresponds to the intelligibility of its narrative—made evident here in an image of Buster's heroism. It is, in this sense, resolutely classical. By managing to secure Buster a position in the MGM News department, it is also understood as having been produced by more expert handling of the camera.

We might wish to extend the heroic reading to *The Cameraman* and argue that the film depicts the domestication of the film camera in Buster's hands, just as *The General* and *The Navigator* depicted his eventual mastery of those technologies of transportation. *The Cameraman* presents itself as a particularly nice candidate for such a reading because it thematizes this domestication as the movement from the nonclassical to the classical, from an image that is looked at to an image that is looked through. In doing so, it would conjoin our critical reading to the ways in which much Hollywood cinema wishes to be read: a mastery of the camera becomes the mastery of a certain aesthetic form. It would also square nicely with the fact that *The Cameraman* was the first feature that Keaton made as part of the studio system at MGM, and the film could be seen to depict Keaton's absorption into that mode of production, which upended the more artisanal production practices that Keaton and other silent comedians had previously enjoyed.[28]

But the heroic reading and its attendant themes of domestication and the meaningful achievement of form founder on one important fact: this legible, transparent image has been produced not by Buster, but by a monkey. *The Cameraman* reveals the monkey's presence on the beach by means of the tracking shot that ends the boating sequence. After saving Sally, Buster runs to a drugstore for medical supplies. While he is gone, Harold—a successful MGM cameraman after Sally's affections—returns to her on the beach and, seeing that she has no memory of his having left her to drown, allows her to believe that he, not Buster, has accomplished her rescue. The two walk off, and Buster returns to an empty beach. As he kneels in the sand, the camera tracks back to show the monkey standing next to the Pathé. (Notably, Buster does not take in this fact.) Until the camera tracks back, the two cameras (intra- and extra-diegetic) are identically positioned, a fact later confirmed in the MGM screening room, and in this sense, the action lays bare the process by which our image—the transparent, legible image that is *The Cameraman*—has been produced. It has been produced, we could say, by a bunch of monkeys.

Both the humor and the sadness of this moment lie in the fact that this self-consciously classical image of abandonment and rescue is the product not of human but of half-human hands, which is to say of the involuntary behavior against which Buster has had to struggle throughout the film, here made visible in the figure of the monkey. In this sense, the monkey depicts the space between human being and machine. Neither human nor machine, he figures the place where the involuntary behavior of the person meets the automatic process of the mechanism. In doing so, he lays bare a problem with critical descriptions of Keaton's movement between human and machine worlds and the failure of these accounts to describe the ambivalence that accompanies this movement. Against Carroll's sense of Keaton's "concrete intelligence" and North's idea of his restoration of the machine to its proper, human scale, the monkey's presence suggests that the film camera in particular is a site of ambivalence. Unlike the nineteenth-century technologies of transport that form the basis of so much of Keaton's comedy, the camera and its automatic image prove resistant to miniaturization. That this ambivalence gathers so densely around an image of the camera is evidence for the idea that the camera's automatism is not simply a mechanical fact about that machine but has something to do with our uses for it.

The ambivalence that surrounds the monkey has much to do with his place in the hierarchies of classical narrative and the relationship of this narrative to acts of parody.[29] David Bordwell has characterized "canonic narration" as ending "with a decisive victory or defeat, a resolution of the problem and a clear achievement or nonachievement of goals." And he has gone on to argue that in "classical fabula construction, causality is the prime unifying principle."[30] As others have argued, this way of thinking isn't very helpful for thinking about the particular tone of an image or performance; this is a particular problem when it comes to film parody, which can include the presence of classical narrative strategies without insisting upon their dominance.[31] A related problem for Bordwell's description is that his formalist vocabulary is at least to some degree genre-dependent. The idea that a film such as *The Cameraman* has a *fabula* in the same sense as a film like *The Docks of New York* (to pick a film released the same year) is to take the tone of, well, parody. While it makes potential sense to ask of both films what has happened off-camera, *The Cameraman* is plain about its stress on what happens *on*-camera. You might find yourself asking about George Bancroft's past as a dockworker, but if your friend asked this about Sally the Secretary, you might wonder about her basic competence as a filmgoer.

While *The Cameraman* is not a straightforward parody of a specific film or film genre, it is not difficult to hear, in the pitched irony of its ending, a parodic rejection of the basic ends of classical narration. The achievement of a monkey can hardly be considered "decisive" in Bordwell's sense, and the resolution of Buster's problem—his ineptitude with both Sally and the Pathé—is openly ironized in the monkey's ability to produce this classical, transparent image. The goals of classical narration are further ironized in the final moments of the film, which show Buster and Sally walking hand-in-hand through a ticker tape parade for Charles Lindbergh, but which Buster mistakenly understands as a spontaneous celebration of his luck in winning the job and the girl. That it is a parade for Lindbergh is another point of irony. It was the year prior to the release of *The Cameraman* that Lindbergh completed his transatlantic flight, a feat that raised the same questions as Keaton's films. As the historian John William Ward once put it, "Was the flight the achievement of a heroic, solitary, unaided individual? Or did the flight represent the triumph of the machine?"[32] But in the context of a movie about moviemaking, the irony further derives from the camera's power to produce meaning in the absence of the human hand, which is to say, from the camera's unique status as a machine that manufactures meaning.

That *The Cameraman* intersperses this image of Buster and Sally with archival footage of an actual parade for Lindbergh imbues the film's conclusion with several questions: What is the relationship between the "real," archival image and the image that was created in service of this fictional film? How do we explain the differences in meaning that the documentary and fictional images produce? And how is it that the latter is able to fold the former into itself? The images were produced by similar processes; both achieve a distance from the human hand. Yet *The Cameraman* imagines this distance as a kind of loss. Unlike Keaton's earlier films, it analogizes the separation of the hand from the image as the separation of the person from others. This is Keaton's sense of the automatism of the cinema: rather than the analogical world-image produced by the "pencil of nature," it is the strictures of transparency, legibility, and causality that are automatic, involuntary. With its quiet parody of the production process, *The Cameraman* allegorizes these stylistic codes and questions their relation to the medium. Its humor acknowledges an ethical fact: that it is our behavior, not simply the camera itself, that is automatic.

∽

In order to move forward into a discussion of *Sherlock Jr.*, I want to take up one final and counterintuitive idea of automatism—its articulation in the work of Stanley Cavell. If in the era of Keaton, automatism was popularly understood as "the incorporation into a tool or machine of a function that previously resided in the operator of the tool," and if this idea takes a different turn in early theories of photography and film, there are two additional senses of the word in Cavell's argument. The first is the idea of automatisms as forms or guarantors of meaning. Cavell links these forms to the material basis of the cinema, but he does not identify them with that basis:

> These mechanisms [the camera and projector] produce the physical or material basis of the medium of film, which I am articulating as successions of automatic world projections. What gives significance to features of this physical basis are artistic discoveries of form and genre and type and technique, which I have begun calling automatisms.[33]

In this passage and elsewhere in *The World Viewed*, the relationship between the definition of the medium as consisting of "successions of *automatic* world projections" and the *automatisms* of "form and genre and type and technique" is left radically open-ended.[34] Nevertheless, Cavell's suggestion is that the automatic nature of the camera and the projector (film's "mechanisms") alters the ways in which its forms (its genres, types, and techniques) produce meaning. We could say that Cavell's account acknowledges that the material world has some say in the grammatical structure of understanding itself. This idea of the material world impinging upon structures of meaning is something like a definition of modernism. Its suggestion is not that the material world had no say in the forms of artistic meaning that preceded the existence of mechanisms such as the camera and the projector, but that the modern position is one in which the relationship between material and meaning is a subject of intense interest, as well as one in which this relationship is called explicitly into question. In other words, it is one feature of modernist artworks that they take this relation as unsettled.

The second sense of automatism in Cavell is more difficult to parse, and that is the idea of movie viewing as making automatic *the condition of viewing as such*. Cavell begins his description of the automatism of the film camera by connecting it to what he calls our "wish to view the world itself":

> To say that we wish to view the world itself is to say that we are wishing for the condition of viewing as such. That is our way of establishing our connection with the world: through viewing it, or having views of it. Our condition has become one in which our natural mode of perception is to view, feeling unseen. We do not so much look at the world as look *out at* it, from behind the self. . . . Viewing a movie makes this condition automatic, takes the responsibility for it out of our hands. Hence movies seem more natural than reality.[35]

What is "the condition of viewing" and how does the cinema make this condition automatic? Relating the medium of film to his larger interest in the problematic of skepticism, Cavell conceives of this condition as a kind of metaphysical distance. As people who have lost a natural relation to the world and its object, we have the need to see the world as both visible and not our own, not, that is, the product of our senses but independent of them. The condition of movie viewing literalizes this fantasy. It figures our ability to *take* a view of the world, hence *The Cameraman*'s thematization of *looking through* and *looking at*. To look through the image is to take it as a stable view of the world as such; to look at it is to be thrown back on one's own perceptions, to destroy the distance that enables the fantasy of viewing the world unseen. Another way of saying this is that it is the cinema's distance from the world that creates a conviction in that world's reality. *The Cameraman* understands that this distance and conviction is related to the ways in which images are not embodied in and of themselves but come to life through the uses toward which they have been put, and thus that the world's presence onscreen takes an ethical cast.

In closing on *Sherlock Jr.*, I want to suggest that we think of this sense of, or interest in, the presence of the world—both its registration, or the automatic ways in which it is recorded, and the projection of this registration onscreen, its configuration within a medium—as a form of realism. To be sure, Keaton's movies are unlikely candidates for this designation: they are not about the ordinary concerns of common people, and—especially in the case of *Sherlock Jr.*, which turns on a series of camera tricks—they are not concerned with mimicking the texture of everyday life. But this sense of Keaton's films as realist in orientation arises if we can see that the idea of the cinema as automatic has consequences for its way of relating to and picturing the world itself. As this chapter has rehearsed, Keaton's theory of cinema is indebted to, even structured by means of, the figure of the mechanism. Automatisms of the camera, of the projected image, and of convention all place the human subject—as both performer and viewer—in a charged and complex relationship to the camera and the projected image, one that is characterized by contact with what I will call an image of reality—that is, not reality itself but its representation, an image with which to consider the concept in the first place. *Sherlock Jr.* specifically articulates a sense of how the automatism of the cinema itself—its automatic registration of the world, its ability to function without the direct input of the human hand—comes to affect or determine its ontology—the ways in which its images reflect back and upon the world as such and hence upon our being in it.

The film concerns the plight of a young projectionist and aspiring detective who pines for a neighborhood girl. After work one day, he brings her a box of chocolates. A local "Sheik"—a taller, older man who also desires this girl—thwarts the Projectionist's advances by stealing the girl's father's watch and then pinning the crime on Buster. Disappointed, the father banishes the Projectionist from his house, while the girl tells him she no longer wishes to see him. Dejected, Buster returns to his job and falls asleep at his projector.

What follows is a dream sequence in which Buster leaves his body and enters a film ("Hearts and Pearls") that he is in the process of projecting. The actors in this film are replaced by figures from the frame narrative, where Buster's ineptitude consists of his inward, or internalized, inability to master his inner desires and needs. He climbs out of his body in the projection booth (in double exposure) and then appears before the screen in the auditorium below (Figure 2.3). As he tries to enter the home in which the Girl and the Sheik are locked in some unspecified melodramatic conflict, the film cuts, causing Buster (whose location in the graphic plane of the screen does not change) to fall. Buster then encounters a series of different physical situations as this interior film cuts from scene to scene: as he sits on a garden bench the film cuts to a busy city street; as he walks down the city street he finds himself at the end of a cliff; as he cautiously looks over the end of the cliff, he suddenly stares at a resting lion; as he walks away from the lion and its mate, he stumbles through a hole in the California desert; as he sits on a pile of sand, the film cuts to a lonely rock in the ocean; as he dives into the ocean, the film cuts to a winter landscape and he is instead buried in snow; as he reaches out to lean on a tree, it cuts to the earlier garden where he tumbles to the pavement. Finally, the film cuts to a scene that does not contain Buster at all. The Girl and the Sheik are alone in a large bedroom. The camera tracks in, dispensing with the auditorium and the black borders of the screen and bringing this audience fully into "Hearts and Pearls." And in this world, Buster is no longer a lonely and inept projectionist, but Sherlock Jr., "the world's greatest detective."

Figure 2.3. Buster and the screen (*Sherlock Jr.*).

Carroll has suggested that, in *The General*, the track on which the locomotive runs works metaphorically to "emphasize the rigidity with which single-minded persons maintain their preconceived ideas" and that "Johnnie [Buster], himself, might be thought of as a locomotive."[36] We might extend this idea to *Sherlock Jr.*, which, in this sequence at least, reminds its viewers that the filmstrip is itself a kind of track, as well as that its images function as a kind of machine on this track. As the montage described above suggests, this track moves in just one direction, which is to say automatically and inexorably, just like the locomotive over which Johnnie Gray has only partial control. Keaton's leaps and falls here are in this sense like his acrobatics on the locomotive. Yet in *Sherlock Jr.* this sense of the filmstrip and its images as proceeding automatically comes to reflect upon the experience of the cinema itself, and upon the performer's and even the audience's relationship to these images, such that what the sequence depicts is something like the nature of personhood or subjectivity within the regime of the moving image. With deftness and endurance, Buster must now adjust his movements to the constant movement that is born of its cutting first here and then there.

In this sequence, *Sherlock, Jr.* depicts both a part of the technology behind the moving image (the Projectionist's projector and the screen on which it displays the film) and a couple of the conventions through which Hollywood films construct their meaning (continuity editing and the avoidance of audience address). By presenting a second film image and then depicting a certain relationship (via the character of Buster and his audience) to that film, it offers a particular theorization of the film medium: its re-presentation of a film image provides a particular picture of the ontology of this cinema and its impression of reality. The sequence rests upon the ideas that the Hollywood cinema is naturalist in orientation and that it is dreamlike in the sense of being, in its absorptive dimension, psychically indistinguishable from everyday experience. Bounced around from scene to scene, rejected, swallowed, and regurgitated, Buster diagrams a concept of absorption.

We might also think of this mini-narrative as one that pursues, in turn, three facts about the Hollywood cinema: its projection (Buster falls asleep next to a projector; he watches the film with an audience); its screening (Buster's deepens his encounter with the interior film—his dream image—at the interface of the screen); and its ability to cut between physical spaces (the interior film tosses Buster from location to location). In this movement from projector to screen to the action of montage, the sequence draws attention to the means by which the technological and material basis of the cinema and its powers of artistic convention combine to create a particular impression of reality. That this drawing of attention does not spoil their absorptive power (even as Buster turns to the camera as the interior film fades to black) is a declaration of the power of these technologies and conventions together.

Interestingly, in addition to being a declaration of the absorptive power of a set of technologies and conventions, the interior-film sequence of *Sherlock Jr.* is a declaration of the presence of Buster's desires, and the existence of an audience before him is meant to represent the possibility of their acknowledgment. In this way, the idea of the cinema's ontology as possessing both technological and conventional foundations is connected to a specific declaration of desire. To put this in Cavell's terms, we might think of this desire as participating in the tripartite structure of ontology suggested in my map above. The projection of the interior film—which is isomorphic with Buster's dream—imagines Buster's desire to be open to the minds of others. (His desire is projected before an audience.) Its screening depicts its inaccessibility. (The audience cannot, or does not, enter the interior film.) Its reference to a set of conventions (of montage and audience address) points to the existence of common agreement. (Viewers of *Sherlock* understand its humor only insofar as they understand the conventions to which it draws attention.)

The moving image figures the external world as the world of another mind (that of the camera). On film, as this world is projected before us, we understand this mind as shareable yet distant. The fact of its projection suggests its radical communicability (it comes from behind the audience and is viewed in concert); the fact of its being screened suggests its particular privacy (it is not accessible by the body). Its world may be reached only through the conventions of the medium. These facts held in concert—projection, screening, and convention; communicability, distance, and agreement—reinforce its particular impression of reality. In this way, *Sherlock, Jr.* figures the medium of Hollywood cinema as a place in which the audience inhabits an acknowledging relation between itself and the content of shared fantasy.

What does it mean, then, to call these gestures a form of realism? With all of its "trick" photography and special effects, it is hard to think of *Sherlock Jr.* as any kind of faithful transmission of an antecedent reality. The actors of "Hearts and Pearls" did not actually morph into other persons; Buster did not actually jump through the belly of a peddler; he did not play billiards around an actual bomb, nor are we meant, in any deep sense, to think that these things actually happened. (Keaton did, however, execute the billiards tricks as well as the film's series of motorcycle stunts. The oscillation between these types of meaning, and the understandings of the moving image as fantastic dream, on the one hand, and as evidence, on the other, are characteristic of the particularly varied tonal register of the slapstick comedy.) Instead, the sequence attempts to articulate processes of attunement through a reflection on the medium and media of film.

Apart from a brief account of American slapstick and its relationship to the "fortuitous" that appears in Kracauer's *Theory of Film*, no theory of film realism takes up the physical comedy. While it is not too much of a stretch to claim that many of Keaton's films provide, in ways that would become rare in the decades of studio dominance, pictures of the natural world that bear some relationship to our ordinary perceptions (the exteriors of *The General*, for example, are recognizably the "exteriors" of our own world, whereas the sets of a film such as *The Philadelphia Story* are very much recognizable as sets), *Sherlock Jr.* is in an important sense consonant with the articulation of film realism as it appears in Cavell, and even in Bazin. Unlike theories that focus on the cognitive, ideological, or technological determinations behind film realism, these articulations of realism attempt to articulate the relationship between ontological and ethical reflection that I described both in *The Cameraman*'s interest in material and grammatical automatisms and in *Sherlock Jr.*'s figuration of absorption and desire.

We could say that in Buster's engagement with the interior film, *Sherlock Jr.* is realist in aspiration in the sense that it inhabits an acknowledging relation to the object of its depiction. If the interior-film sequence of *Sherlock Jr.* is a declaration of the presence of Buster's desires, the existence of an audience before him is meant to represent the possibility that other people might acknowledge these desires. Just as I will suggest Charlie Chaplin's *City Lights* (1931) does a few years later, *Sherlock Jr.* understands the screened image as a medium for this acknowledgment. Since I focused before on Buster's absorption into that image, I want to turn now to his reemergence from it, to his reentry into the frame narrative or what we could call the "exterior" world of *Sherlock Jr.*

After saving the girl by riding a car into a body of water, Buster turns that car—a convertible—into a small sailboat. The gesture does not work. Left in the middle of the lake, the couple sinks. Through the action of a dissolve, Buster's swimming becomes a series of involuntary movements on his stool in the projectionist's booth, and he consequently wakes from his dream. What follows is a series of eyeline matches between his place in the window of that booth and the end of "Hearts and Pearls." A first match registers Buster's surprise, the second his disappointment (figured in his turn away from the camera and the screen). In both images, he is framed by the window between the booth and the auditorium below, which we could imagine as a second screen (Figures 2.4 and 2.5).

The art historian Michael Fried has written that the acknowledging action of realism is not a matter of the mere appearance of the camera,

Figures 2.4 and 2.5. Waking up to and turning away from the image of reality.

but of the camera's acknowledgment of "its outsideness to the world."[37] In this scene, we have a doubling of this acknowledgment as well as an accompanying withdrawal. Buster reappears from his thirty minutes of absorption in the movie, and dream, that is "Hearts and Pearls." He finds the world as it was, which is to say in its reality, or separateness. *Sherlock Jr.* itself repeats this withdrawal for us, its audience. Within the frame, Buster is himself framed, and thus acknowledged as having appeared both on and behind a screen. This acknowledgment of his distance from us, and from himself, is then figured again as he turns his back from that screen and from us. These are the limits of the acknowledgment of desire. The camera's distance is the price paid for its image of reality.

Of course, the aspiration toward the acknowledgment of reality is usually reserved for the work of the avant-garde. Five years after the release of *Sherlock Jr.*, Dziga Vertov would make *The Man with the Movie Camera*. Annette Michelson describes *The Man with the Movie Camera* this way:

> It is the manner in which Vertov questions the most immediately powerful and sacred aspect of cinematic experience, disrupting systematically the process of identification and participation, generating at each moment of the film's experience, *a crisis of belief*. In a sense most subtle and complex, he was, Bazin to the contrary, one of those directors "who put their faith in the image"; that faith was, however, accorded to the image seen, recognized as *an image* and the condition of that faith or recognition, the consciousness, the subversion *through* consciousness, of cinematic illusionism.[38]

In distinction from Michelson, we could say that such faith in the "image seen" is part and parcel of what someone such as Bazin had in mind when he put forth his account of film realism. It is a realism that displays not fidelity of the image to the phenomenological world, but fidelity of the image to the world as such. And like Vertov's contemporaneous work, *Sherlock Jr.* itself recognizes the condition of one's faith in the image, or what amounts to one's faith in the world. It puts forth an image of reality.

What, then, of the fact that this acknowledgment comes in the form of comedy? The film returns to the tone of comedy here by staging the reappearance of the girl, and it quickly uses their subsequent recoupling as the material for a gag. It is of course much easier to see the action of acknowledgment in Robert Bresson or Jean Renoir than it is to see it in a four-reel slapstick comedy. Keaton's film hardly seems consistent with philosophical aspiration. (Bresson and Renoir left behind writing that allows us to read their films in this way; Keaton, who claimed to have attended school once and that time for a single day, left a coffee table autobiography.) But rather than search for biographical detail, it may be that our problem is a matter of the tonal variation of comedy and of the instability and unpredictability of that variation. It is also a matter of redrawing our narrow genealogy of modernism to include popular, or vernacular, works such as the slapstick comedy. The conclusion of *Sherlock Jr.* moves from disappointment to love regained and then to a parody of the same. The film closes, typically for Keaton, on an ambivalent image of romance.

This is to say that *Sherlock Jr.* moves from an acknowledgment of the screened image's "outsideness" to a reversal of this fact. The girl appears in the booth and apologizes for having mistaken Buster as a thief. Unsure what to do with her, Buster looks to the film for guidance. Another series of eyeline matches follow, identical to those that marked his disappointment: the romantic lead looks the actress in the eye, Buster looks his girl in hers; the lead takes the actress's hand, Buster takes the hand of his girl; the lead kisses the actress, Buster pecks at his. Buster looks a final time at the screen, which dissolves to a scene of actor and actress surrounded by a bevy of children. Cut to Buster, who raises an eyebrow.

This final gag returns us to the automatism of Buster's gestures: he follows the film's lead in every movement, and then mechanically assumes that the final image of "Hearts and Pearls" means that babies will appear in his own lap. It also casts a skeptical eye on the film's tidy acknowledgment of the camera's distance as well as on any definitive account of the medium. Such skepticism is almost a requirement of its genre itself. In its important moments, the slapstick comedy insists upon the refusal of narrative meaning. It may employ the processes of that meaning, but it does so in service of its own ambivalence. For that reason, we may take seriously both moments, the declaration of the camera's distance, figured as our intimacy, and the final refusal of any such gesture, figured as the very difficulty of maintaining that achievement.

∞

In all of these ways, Keaton's interest both in the camera's automatism and its particular ontology creates an affinity with certain classical film theories, as well as with certain descriptions of the philosophy of photography. But this movement, from automatism to ontology and back again, and Keaton's articulation of the relationship between the automatisms of the technologies of film (both its taking of film and its projection of the same), is not simply an instantiation of a concept or picture of the cinema; it *is* that concept. Buster Keaton has left us a theory of film.

The two discourses with which I began—Keaton's filmic response to the material and psychological rigors of twentieth-century modernity and film theory itself—proceed from the same point of origin, a fundamental ambivalence about the presence (or absence) of the world to thought. In this sense, it is not that Keaton's work is theoretical, or itself constitutes a theory of film, but rather that his films and the larger discourse of film theory both seek to work out the consequences of the emplacement of human beings in this historical moment. Keaton demonstrates that automatism is always and only operational, a function of the way in which we understand technology as a medium for mastery. This is why Buster creates and lives through a series of accidents, moments that open up a new and ambivalent relation to the object world.

If in Cavell's and Fried's work acknowledgment is played "straight," in Keaton's film it is the site of, even a vehicle for, the larger ambivalence with which his performance, and the genre itself, is invested. It gives us an image of the nature of automatism, a model of our own relation to the cinema and to the automatic. The dream-within-a-dream-within-a-dream structure of *Sherlock Jr.* turns this ambivalence into a form that can be grasped. It suggests that one function of the cinema is not to be ambivalent but to embrace ambivalence as a stance toward a mechanical and automated world.

Rather than providing us with the typical occupants of the hermeneutic circle (the movement from theory to text, and most often, conveniently finding in our texts a series of instantiations of the theories that we bring to them), these films are thus images of theory itself, on and through film. In Keaton's work and in particular in its consistency (at least until the dawn of synchronized sound), it is difficult not to discern an *ethos*, a style of being, a specifically filmic mode of existence. It provides us not only with an image of the cinema as one machine among many; it also articulates an image of the project of film theory as both celebration and elegy, an attempt to simultaneously reclaim and mourn the primacy of the human.

3

Redeeming Vision

Charlie Chaplin

> The human body is the best picture of the human soul—not, I feel like adding, primarily because it represents the soul but because it expresses it.
>
> —Stanley Cavell, *The Claim of Reason*

THE FINAL SHOT OF *SHERLOCK JR.* calls into question the acknowledgment of reality upon which that film is built, suggesting that the acknowledgment of reality must always also become an acceptance of the other, a consequence that Keaton depicts, true to comic form, as isolation. Extending John Stuart Mill, we could say that all of this occurs as if "over-seen." Keaton's sense of the medium charts the consequences of the idea of the performer who acts as if he were constantly caught unaware. His performance is intended for us in our privacy. The sense of intimacy of his films is like that of a funny lyric poem—private utterance suddenly imagined as public accident.

It is a critical commonplace that Keaton's style, with its emphasis on the physical world and its interest in the relation of the performer's body to this world, stands in contrast to that of his contemporary Charlie Chaplin, with its memory of the proscenium arch and its commitment to the concept and scale of the human.[1] If Keaton stages his performances as if by accident, it is emphatically *not* the case that we just happen upon the Tramp or that he is most interesting or thrilling from a distance. Chaplin presents his performances as the result of his intention. They are always placed before us as if for our view—that is, as public—and this posture has implications for his account of the medium. In fact, Chaplin's performances continually call into question, and ask their audiences to reflect upon, their relation to the film image, often in the form of the reactions that the Tramp inspires in other people onscreen.

Take *Shoulder Arms* (1917) for example, an early feature in which the stakes of the relation between the Tramp and those around him are given distinct emphasis because they are placed within the context of world war. Here, the Tramp is named simply Doughboy. He is a small soldier stationed at the front during World War I. This soldier, the movie gives us to understand, is ill-equipped for his job, and his inadequacy stems from the fact that he is inwardly resistant to the strictures and rules of life in the army. His resistance is not exactly on the face of it moral but rather almost physiological: he cannot master the parade march; he is less than prodigious with his rifle; he bothers his fellow soldiers with his ignorance of the routines of camp. Doughboy is comic in the Aristotelian sense: he is lower or less than his peers and consequently an object of fun; his actions, as Aristotle would say, lack extension. Importantly, however, it is precisely because he is less confined by the strictures of army life than the other soldiers that he finds the space to be a person, to live with imagination and intelligence. And he accomplishes this, at least in part, by taking, or seeing, the things around him in new and surprising ways. He sees the objects of his world as not *merely* ordinary, but as redemptively so. His intelligence with the world takes the form of imaginative demonstrations that make malleable the objects of war. Doughboy turns common domestic objects into (nonlethal) weapons of war, and he turns the weapons of war toward the tasks of domesticity.

Waiting in his trench, for instance, Doughboy receives a package that contains a round of Limburger cheese and pulls a gas mask over his head to protect his nose. When even the gas mask can't do the trick, he lobs the cheese, grenade-like, out of his trench, where it lands on the face of a neighboring German officer. Or later, having captured a crew of German soldiers and celebrating his victory over a small lunch, Doughboy uses enemy rifle fire to open a bottle of beer and, even more improbably and magically, to light a cigarette. Even the horrible dangers of trench life are shown to respond to Doughboy's imaginative play with ordinary objects. A great rain, for instance, floods his barrack, completely submerging his bunk. Wanting to continue his sleep, he reaches for the horn of a nearby gramophone, which doubles as a snorkel. All of these tasks and performances show the Doughboy to be at home in his world, to be able to claim it for himself, to make it respond to his sentiment and desires. Or as one contemporary reviewer put it, "The bit where he uses a nutmeg grater to scratch his back because of cooties, and the hokum business with Charlie in a camouflaged suit to make him look like a dead tree, were marvelous bits of funmaking."[2]

But *Shoulder Arms* is not only about the imaginative and recuperative intelligence of a single person, but the ways in which other people respond (or fail to respond) to this person's intelligence. The film works to reveal the many varieties of inspired interpretation that are present in the world as well as the interpretive blindness of the persons in its fictional world. In doing so, it employs a hierarchy of intimacy. At its core, a couple (Chaplin and Edna Purviance) sees, we could say, eye to eye. That is, each sees as the other sees without hesitation; each adopts the other's point of view. The film enacts an elaborate ballet around this joining of views, as in Purviance's tending to Chaplin's injured hand while the latter pretends to sleep or a gag that involves moving in and out of a German officer's clothes closet, within which these two people don disguises that, paradoxically, make them more visible to each other. The other American soldiers around Chaplin, while hardly dead to his imaginative play with nutmeg graters and limburger cheeses, only grumblingly put up with his flights of fancy. In the film's final sequence, for instance, Purviance's French maid winningly adopts a turn-of-the-century German moustache—drawn in axel grease—whereas Chaplin's captured comrade has difficulty wearing the costume of a German soldier and suffers mild physical violence at Chaplin's hand. He cannot quite see the moral value of play. And most of the film's German soldiers are resolute in their inability to see through Chaplin's disguises and foolery. They cannot see how persons and objects might be other than they are on their faces, and they are consequently depicted as lacking in imaginative intelligence. In this sense, they refuse what for Chaplin constitutes an ethical, or acknowledging, relation both to other persons and to the wider world of objects in which the persons around them live, one in which inspired play implies a redemptive understanding of the world as such.

This lack of imaginative and ethical intelligence, and Chaplin's redemptive reimagination of the object world, are demonstrated at length in the famous sequence in which Doughboy disguises himself as a dead tree. A small attachment of German soldiers enters the frame where Chaplin stands. (The audience is neither informed about why Chaplin is there nor why he is wearing the suit. Rather, the situation, as happens in many of Chaplin's other films, belongs to the realm of luck or chance.) As the German soldiers set up their camp, one of them begins to cut wood for a fire. This man tours the area and, deciding that the other trees will be too much work to cut down, settles on Chaplin. He knocks his axe against the ground to ready it and spits in his hands. Chaplin pokes him with one of his limbs. Thinking that he's been stuck by a weed, and not what is obviously a man in costume, the man goes at the plant with his axe. Chaplin then hits him powerfully over the head, knocking him out. Soon, the other soldiers catch on, and one of them pursues Doughboy—still dressed as a tree—into a nearby forest. The soldier, who cannot find his man, fires his rifle into the trees and pricks them with his bayonet, but Doughboy, who remains unnoticed, runs off and away.

Of course, part of the humor in the tree sequence derives from the fact that Chaplin does in fact resemble an object onscreen. His funny jog through the clearing on the way to the woods is not that of a person, but that of a (seemingly) running tree. The gag works by turning the real into the hallucinatory, while at the same time asking its viewers, who are put in a position of epistemic sophistication and given the opportunity to exercise moral insight, to see briefly as the German soldier has, to imagine the real possibility that a person may become an object, that he may hold as little value as a tree. The joke, in short, articulates a moment of visual interpretation in which we can *see* multiple ways of perceiving the image before us. It is a wonderful example of the specific condition of spectatorship to which we are invited, the environment of comic distance. Baudelaire once remarked about the tendency to laugh when other people fall. "The man who trips," he said, "would be the last to laugh at his own fall, unless he happened to be a philosopher, one who had acquired, by habit, the power of rapid self-division and thus of witnessing the phenomena of his own ego as a disinterested spectator."³ Like Baudelaire's philosopher, Chaplin here invites us to view our own acts of perception from a place of reflective distance.

Slapstick comedies are full of moments in which one thing (an object, a person, a place, a situation) is taken in a new and surprising way, but Chaplin's work follows this mechanism to distinctly ethical ends. The sense here and elsewhere in Chaplin's work is that the very foundation of human interaction is at stake in ordinary acts of perception. Like most of Chaplin's self-directed films, *Shoulder Arms* is full of moments in which acts of vision are linked directly to ethical judgments, moments in which people, objects, and particular corners of the world are seen in what we could call non-necessary, or unusual, ways. In the universe of Chaplin's films, people who see in ordinary ways and who are hidebound to their usual perceptions are shown to be ethically suspect. Those who allow themselves to see things new, on the other hand, those who are able to imagine different contexts for the ordinary people and objects of the film's world, are shown to display an imaginative intelligence. And it is these people who find meaningful attunement and community with the people around them.

The significance of the way in which all of this is staged for us, the film's audience, is that we are also implicated in these acts of vision and judgment. We can reject Doughboy's way of looking like a tree, for instance, or refuse him the idea that gramophone horns make, in certain circumstances, good snorkels. But these gags attempt to make us understand that the refusal of such agreement has larger consequences for the community of viewership. Chaplin's film understands the act of viewership to be filled with moments of active interpretation, the giving of one's consent to a series of images. And this consent turns out to be identified with our knowledge of others, a knowledge not characterized by the availability or absence of information but by the acceptance or rejection of intimacy. If for Keaton the cinema is the site of an ambivalence about the relation between the ideal and the real, between the self and others, for Chaplin it represents, at least until the dawn of synchronized sound, the promise of intimacy; it is a site in which the performer tests the attunement of himself and his audience, a medium in which the taking and holding of views is always and everywhere an ethical activity.

For Chaplin, the cinema is never simply a matter of seeing, but rather of seeing one thing *as* something else. The objects of Chaplin's world, including the actor himself, are never simply objects; they are always, to paraphrase Heidegger, tools that possess a plastic "towards which." And our relation as viewers toward those objects and toward these images always raises the question of this towards which: How will we, and the characters within the films, respond to the Tramp's imaginative play? Do we see as he sees?

This idea of "seeing as" is one of the principal subjects of Part Two of Wittgenstein's *Philosophical Investigations*. Whereas most film theoretical accounts of aspect perception use Wittgenstein's concept as a means of thinking through the phenomenology of vision, Chaplin's films help us to see that Wittgenstein's concept has to do with the surprising conjunction of perceptual agility, knowledge of the world, and ethical understanding.[4] The philosopher Avner Baz gives us a reading of the rhetorical force and meaning of Wittgenstein's words on this subject, a meaning we might think of as ethical in nature:

> Most of human experience is of what tends to present itself as ordinary and familiar, and so as unremarkable. What we need, then, if this experience is not to be lost on us, not to pass us like nothing, and if we are not to be bored, is the ability to find something about the ordinary and the familiar that makes it worth noting and articulating—we need to be able to find it *new*.[5]

The idea of aspect perception as involving both a sense of newness and an ethical dimension points out the adherence of value judgments within the articulation of perceptual experience, and thereby suggests that the experience of film viewership can be understood as a series of moments in which one's sense of attunement is tested and one's agreement, or knowledge of others, is given or refused. And in just this way, Chaplin's work suggests that the concept's proper use belongs in the realm of value or morality, in the concepts of truthfulness and attunement. In Chaplin's gags, an interest in one's views of things cannot be separated from an interest in the articulation of one's own experience.

Take, for instance, the opening sequence of *The Gold Rush* (1925). The film tells the story of The Lone Prospector, a diminutive and otherworldly man who travels to the Yukon to find his fortune. The story begins with a powerful blizzard, during which The Prospector and another man, Big Jim McKay, stumble upon a cabin in the Yukon wilds. Alone with each other, they wait out the storm, and this waiting provides the impetus for a series of gags around their increasing hunger and desperation.

Of particular prominence is a scene that begins with The Prospector boiling his shoe and eating it for dinner. After witnessing The Prospector pull the patent leather from his boot nails like flesh from a fish and then attempting himself to partake in the little man's meal, a delirious Big Jim mistakes The Prospector for a chicken. Stuck in this vision of The Prospector and crazed with the prospect of a true dinner, Big Jim chases his companion around the property, first with a gun and then with an axe. Interestingly, Chaplin executes this turn in Big Jim's imagination with a dissolve that turns the Tramp to a peculiar, man-sized chicken.

Big Jim, of course, is eventually persuaded that his friend is not who he seems to be—not, that is, a chicken—and he gives up his weapon. Neither man has any compunction, however, about shooting a bear that wanders into their cabin. The bear is food, and he allows the two men to finally quit the cabin, and their hunger, and return to town. A bear is just a bear, but a man can be many things. We see him as that.

The Gold Rush suggests that conditions in which these two characters find themselves have made it impossible for one of them to recognize the other as human—that is, as a being that is not food, not something one eats. That the one sees the other as food is dramatized (and turned into a moment of comedy) by his appearing onscreen in a chicken suit. The ability to see a shoe as food seems to have led to a slippage of categories, a kind of perceptual looseness. For a moment, The Prospector is not simply a man—like the boot, he is potentially something to eat, an image the Tramp unwittingly encourages with his chicken-like movements. For Chaplin, a man may be many things, and he may become these things for all number of reasons (to hide, for instance, or to surprise, to save, to delight). And the behavior of The Prospector in this sense figures intelligence as a kind of perception—a point of view—that is nimble and imaginative.

I think of Chaplin's chicken gag as an attempt to articulate an experience, and consequently, as an attempt to make the world his, hence to redeem it for us. The joke proceeds from the idea that human beings can be strange to one another (nowhere more so than in conditions of hunger and violence), but it uses this sense, in the form of irony, in order to establish a kind of agreement with its audience. *We* know that Chaplin is not a chicken, but Big Jim does not. And later, the women of the story will know that Chaplin is different from the other men in the mining town, but they struggle to articulate the nature and importance of this difference. They are curious about his funny dancing, for instance, and the ways in which he separates himself from the casual violence of the mining town, but they can't fully accept this difference and his material poverty.

In this way, the film demonstrates that declarations of sight such as these gags can be received in multiple ways. To perceive The Prospector as a chicken is not a simple question of seeing him as man *or* chicken—or, to use Wittgenstein's famous example, duck *or* rabbit—but rather a question of a great wealth and range of responses. The chicken gag demonstrates that other people may take up our articulations and affirm our criteria and hence our mutuality, as well as that they can take these occasions as annoyances (or worse, provocations). Stanley Cavell writes, "Suppose we ask: What is my relation to an aspect which has not dawned upon me, is in that sense hidden from me, but which is nevertheless there *to be seen*? What don't I see when everything is in front of my eyes? I find that I want to speak of failing to see a possibility: I do not appreciate some way it might be—not just some way it might appear, but might *be*."[6] For Chaplin, the question of sight is always and everywhere linked to an ethical determination: to see the possibilities inherent in both people and things is to acknowledge them in their separateness. True to this way of thinking, Big Jim is, by the film's conclusion, happy to receive

The Prospector for who he is. (It is less clear how the girl Georgia will take this knowledge. The movie ends with the question of whether she will accept him—before a camera, moreover—just as *City Lights* will six years later.) Part of the pleasure of the chicken gag comes from the fact that Chaplin is in a sense asking us, as his audience, to see *as* he sees, to affirm his perception that a man is like a farm animal, just not so fully that he should be eaten. Gags like this work to articulate experiences of estrangement and identity. They perform acts of humor-by-agreement by using qualities specific to the medium of film, here the cinema's ability to loosely associate the real and the hallucinatory, then claiming these qualities in service of human intimacy (between The Prospector and his friends, between Chaplin and his viewers).

It is significant, in this sense, that the joke is accomplished by means of an earlier revelation, to the audience, namely, that the chicken is in fact Chaplin. Much film theory suggests that the film viewer is sutured into the third-person narration of the fiction film through the action of cutting between views. We are shown a view of things and wonder who sees this view, only to have this question answered in the form of a reverse shot in which the perspective is assigned to the eyes of a character within the story. But this sort of action occurs only tenuously in *The Gold Rush*. While it is clear, in the cabin, that Big Jim does not *see* The Prospector as we do, we are never treated to his literal point of view. Instead, Chaplin lines himself, and more importantly his face, frontally with the camera. In this sense, we might argue that the moment of suture occurs not when we learn to whom the view belongs, but at the moment of the revelation that Chaplin is in fact a chicken. Here, spectator knowledge is not tied to the knowledge of a character within the film's story, but is instead made complete by the action of irony. The gag works because the film's audience has more epistemic knowledge than the scene's two characters. And this knowledge entails a responsibility: do we accept this man for who he is?

Chaplin's play with the chicken, like his later play with his dinner rolls, is subjunctive. It imagines the world, its objects, and its people as amenable to human desire. If in everyday life the normative role for pieces of bread was that of attaching them to forks for the purposes of tabletop dances, his performance would not represent acknowledgment and liberation but a form of being stuck. The gag would simply display the world as it is habitually. What is important in Chaplin's play are not the specific routines before the camera, or even their contexts, but the fact that they work at all—*that* they are funny. Our pleasure and amusement is the index of our shared desire for another world. Successful gags actually reveal a specific activity or experience of vision as a new form of agreement, thus testifying to our capacity for such agreement in the first place. They represent to us the possibility that things could be other than they are now.

The film's audience is thus always implicated in the film's acts of vision and judgment. We can reject the Tramp's lyrical play with his dinner rolls or refuse him the idea that a boot is like a fish. We can refuse, that is, to think of these actions as funny. Like most of Chaplin's work, *The Gold Rush* thus understands the act of film viewership to be filled with moments of active interpretation. And this consent turns out to be identified with our knowledge of others. Big Jim's knowledge of The Prospector may be constrained by his hunger, but his perception takes the form of a kind of blindness. He knows full well that this man is not a chicken, but he can no longer align this knowledge with the world in which he lives. Whereas most philosophical accounts of the problem of other minds take as paradigmatic situations in which one's knowledge is incomplete—the privileged example is the experience of pain: I do not literally feel your headache, hence I cannot know that it exists—*The Gold Rush* provides us with examples in which one's knowledge of other people is constrained and then rejected. After all, Chaplin makes clear overtures to the fact that he is not a chicken.

Instead of thinking about suture as a cognitive process that occurs somewhere below the spectator's awareness, then, we might—in certain instances at least—understand it as the giving of one's consent to a particular visual articulation. In the case of *The Gold Rush*, opportunities for consent take the form of moments of visual flexibility, moments in which our willingness to see in new ways is put to the test and either accepted or rejected. Or as Baz puts it with regard to Wittgenstein, these sorts of moments put "our attunement with other people to the test, which means that it can also provide the occasion for certain moments of intimacy, depending on how far that attunement is found to reach."[7] Unlike Big Jim, upon whom the interpretation of The Prospector as actually being a chicken is forced by the exigencies of his occupation as a miner, we can grant Chaplin his chicken impression—the odd, jerking movements of his head, his subtle high-stepping—or we can refuse to see it. What is at stake here is the measure of our attunement. The film understands such attunement to lie beneath our knowledge of each other and it insists upon the fact that this knowledge is not a matter of simple perceptual knowledge, but rather an entire way of being.

The Gold Rush uses this particular environment in which the stakes (sketched however loosely in the gestures of slapstick) are life and death in order to articulate the ways in which the demonstration or expression of visual perceptions has an ethical cast. Seeing, for Chaplin, takes place at the peculiar conjunction of the perceptual, the psychological, and the ethical; to see something is to endow it with life. In the first part of the *Investigations*, Wittgenstein has this to say about what he calls "dead" expressions: "'Put a ruler against this object; it does not say that the object is so-and-so long. Rather, it is in itself—I am tempted to say—dead, and achieves nothing of what a thought can achieve.'—It is as if we had imagined that the essential thing about a living human being was the outward form. Then we made a lump of wood into that form and were abashed to see the lifeless block, lacking any similarity to a living creature."[8] And just as Wittgenstein directs a therapeutic eye toward the "lifeless" expressions toward which philosophers tend (his intervention here taking the form of parable), Chaplin directs his play with boot leather and dinner rolls toward the blindness of men haunted by hunger as well as that of men and women in movie theaters, asking that they see again and see anew. This is why his films are at heart redemptive: they imagine the world as fundamentally hospitable to human desire.

I have been arguing that a ruling concern of Chaplin's work—something like its vision of the cinema itself—is its declaration that those who are able to imagine different contexts for the ordinary people and objects of the world are shown to display a kind of imaginative and ethical intelligence, and I've argued that this is visible in these films' form and style, most clearly in the way in which they offer a series of performances for our view. At least implicitly, this little chronology, from the late teens to the very heart of the silent era, from *Shoulder Arms* to *The Gold Rush*, suggests that, over the course of his career, Chaplin's films move closer toward the question of the Tramp's relation to others, figured both as his foils onscreen and as ourselves, the audience before this series of views. For this reason and to set these films against those of the Marx Brothers in the next chapter, I want to turn to the features that Chaplin made in the thirties, after the introduction of synchronized sound. Both *City Lights* (1931) and *Modern Times* (1936) retain this earlier interest in "seeing as," in intimacy and attunement, but they do so melancholicly, therefore registering the end of one sense of the medium.[9] At times, they even suggest that the technology and medium of synchronized sound forecloses the sort of seeing that was the defining feature of the Tramp's pantomime and of Chaplin's earlier camera.

In *City Lights*, Chaplin's melancholy about the practice of sound becomes a question about the possible relations between the self and the other; the film calls into question the attunement that was so easily achieved in a film like *Shoulder Arms*, lingering instead upon the potential that the Tramp's play may and will be refused. We could say that *City Lights* foregrounds the question that haunts *The Gold Rush*: Do these people and does this audience accept the Tramp? The film does not simply integrate these gags into its story and its manufacture of pathos but makes our relation to these acts and their interest in attunement into its very subject. If what is always at stake in Chaplin's films is our relation to the Tramp, or more specifically, our acceptance or rejection of a certain style of play or perception, *City Lights* folds this question into its very form. It does not represent the usual settlement between comic play and the forces of narration—the simple stringing of the gag along the slack line of story—but something like an attempt at a sublation of the conflict itself, the realization of an imaginary film in which gag, laughter, narration, and pathos disappear perfectly into the face of the Tramp.

The question of acceptance and acknowledgment is put most forcefully in the film's ending, a sequence that William Rothman has called "one of the profoundest of all meditations on the nature of the film medium."[10] *City Lights* closes with a revelation of the film screen, and it stages this revelation such that the film comes to seem less like a story about wealth and poverty, cruelty and care, than a question that is addressed to us, its viewers. Here, the question that surrounds The Flower Girl—she has regained her sight, but will she have the imagination and the intelligence to see the Tramp for who he is?—jumps metaleptically into the theater. Where and how do we stand in relation not simply to the Tramp but to the screen before us? This makes the end of *City Lights* a kind of companion sequence to Keaton's play on and at the surface of the screen in *Sherlock Jr.* But whereas Keaton asks us to view this moment as if in privacy, Chaplin, with his almost frontal staging and his blunt and even painful use of the close-up, confronts us directly, asking us to declare our point of view.

So, what do we see? It has been almost a year since the Tramp anonymously gifted the blind Flower Girl money for an operation. Doing so has cost him what little freedom he once had. He has just emerged from prison, where he had been wrongly sent for stealing, and his clothes are tattered beyond his usual ability to imbue them with dignity. Miraculously, the Girl has regained her sight and operates a flower shop; the film shows her looking in a mirror, admiring her hair. From these moments until the conclusion of the film, *City Lights* will trade upon the idea of seeing and *seeing*, of the relation between physical sight and the acknowledgment of the other.

After establishing the Girl and the Tramp in alternation—she in her bright flower shop and he in destitution—the film returns us to the fantasy with which it originally began, the Girl's desire to be made whole by a wealthy suitor. Unlike the beginning, however, she now believes this fantasy to have come true, with the important exception that her suitor has not made himself known. Characteristically, *City Lights* understands this knowledge to be related to the faculty of vision: the suitor has fulfilled the Girl's fantasy, but he has not physically or emotionally shown himself to her. As the Girl arranges a large bouquet of chrysanthemums, her back is to a large picture window, through which we see a luxurious automobile appear and park. This too is how the movie began: on the run from the police, the Tramp emerged before her from a car, the sound of its door falsely signifying to the blind girl that he is wealthy. In focus through this same window in the shop, we see a young man in a top hat and tails leave the car and walk to the door. A tall arrangement of flowers obscures the beam between this large window and door such that clear glass, or at any rate a transparent plane, seems to extend from almost the bottom to the top, and from the left to the right, edges of the film frame itself. As Rothman has suggested, the window thus recalls the film screen itself.[11] Importantly, this window-screen also stands between the Girl and the gentleman. She turns and sees him, holding her hand to her heart: could this be the man who saved her from poverty and restored her vision (Figure 3.1.)? In a series of close-ups that Chaplin stages in profile, the man inquires about some flowers and leaves. And in medium shot, the Girl turns toward the camera to confirm her disappointment. If it is him, he does not have the courage to appear as himself.

This movement up to and across the threshold of the store—at the plane of the screen, as it were—establishes a pattern that will be repeated when the Tramp appears in the same location. Before bringing them together, however, the film gives us a scene with the Tramp and the two newspaper boys who have teased him from the film's beginning. So as to further establish the humiliation that he feels after leaving prison, one of the boys pelts him with a pea shooter. The Tramp is too ragged to respond; instead, he bends over to pick up a rose in the gutter of the street, a reiteration of the flower motif with which the movie, and his relationship with the Girl, began. Pitifully, the Tramp's posture reveals a hole in the backside of his pants, and the other boy runs over to pull at his drawers. These too are in tatters, and the boy pulls a handkerchief-sized piece of fabric from the Tramp's clothes. Horribly, as the Tramp snatches back his underwear, the camera tracks right to reframe this exchange and, more importantly, to reveal that all of this has occurred in front of the Girl's window. Recalling her own posture in her first scene, when she sold flowers from a basket on the street, she is seated next to the array of chrysanthemums.

Figure 3.1. Fantasy at the threshold of the screen (*City Lights*).

The tracking movement makes it clear that the Girl has witnessed the whole exchange with the boys, and what is worse, that she is laughing. Her laughter is casual, but it is not exactly mean-spirited: its affable character is reinforced by her general air of happiness and by her returning to the arrangement of flowers before her. As such, it brings to mind our own laughter before the Tramp, with its admixture of aggression, empathy, and ambivalence. Importantly, this little routine with the pea shooter and the rag, the clarity with which the *mise-en-scene* figures the Tramp as an *object* of sight, and the respective positions of the Tramp and the Girl on either side of the transparent frame of the shop window establish the scene as calling to mind the positions of film performance and viewership, and more importantly, the fact of their separation at the plane of the film screen. In retrospect, we can see that the film has given us, in just a few minutes, a rich account of this relation, on the one hand as allowing for and even producing a kind of fantasy and desire (the wealthy man appears on this screen and then briefly crosses its threshold, only to recede again) and on the other hand as establishing an environment of distance and objectification (the Girl's laughter is licensed by the fact that the screen is also a wall that divides them).

The flower still in his hand, the Tramp recognizes the Girl and the fact that she has regained her sight, hence that she can, for the first time in the film, see him (Figure 3.2). The pathos here derives not merely from the fact that he must appear to her as humiliated, but that he must relinquish his control of her perception, a control that the film earlier staged through his stealing a car and through some play with her home Victrola. Because she not only sees him for the first time, but does so through the screen of the window, *she* now exerts control.

The question whether she has the ability or the willingness to see and acknowledge him is first answered in the negative. As the Tramp's shock turns to an inviting and vulnerable smile, the Girl's surprise turns to a more patronizing laughter. She turns away from the Tramp to her assistant, and a title card gives us her speech: "I've made a conquest!" As the petals fall from the rose that the Tramp had retrieved from the gutter, she picks up a fresh rose and offers it to him. (Her lips move as she does this, the absence of a title card suggesting that he cannot hear

Figure 3.2. Sight and screen (*City Lights*).

her, hence that she is separated from him by a screen that admits only silence.) In his surprise and pleasure, he fails to respond, and the Girl takes this lack of response in the worst possible way, as shyly imploring that what he needs is not a flower but money. She turns again to her assistant, who brings her a coin, which she then holds up next to the rose in a final articulation of the film's central theme of the incompatibility of wealth and beauty.

Still made dumb by his pleasure at seeing her whole, the Tramp continues to stare, so she stands up and comes to the shop door, that is, to the threshold of the screen, just as her imagined suitor had done minutes before. Now there are two fantasies at stake: the Tramp's fantasy (that she will see him for who he is, that he will finally be acknowledged) and hers (that her suitor is indeed out there, somewhere, a fantasy that will soon be transformed, because of the discrepancy between the Tramp's actions and his appearance, into the question of her ability to come to terms with the relationship between reality and desire). Still misunderstanding him, she offers him first the coin, which he does not accept, and then the rose, which he takes (thus siding, as he has throughout the film, with the power of beauty and not that of wealth). Wishing him to also have the coin, the Girl steps finally across the threshold to place it in his hand. Without having made the decision to do so, she has left the screen behind and will now be confronted with the knowledge of her desire. Fascinatingly, the film suggests that it is the street side of the shop window, which is to say, Chaplin's side, the side of performance, that is allied with the real, hence that to see fully, completely, and with imagination, one must accept, confront, and enact one's desires. Performance is here imagined as a medium, or screen, between the real and the imaginary. The film then cuts to a medium close-up of the two figures, the Tramp's back to the camera and the Girl frontal to us. She places the coin in his hand.

Her initial and patronizing pleasure at this exchange is immediately interrupted by the force of recognition: she looks into the Tramp's eyes and understands who he is. Yet the film is careful to stress that this *anagnorisis*, both literal and virtual, occurs not (or not merely) through her faculty of vision but through her familiarity with the feel of the Tramp's hand. The film cuts to a close-up of her hands over his, and then of one hand touching his arm and finally his lapel. She puts her hand now not to her heart (the locus of her fantasy) but to her head (the locus of her knowledge). "You?" a title card reads. The Tramp nods, and the camera cuts again to her in medium close-up, her hand now moving from her head to her heart, as if to suggest her understanding of the relation of these two modes of relating, of the contact between fantasy and recognition.[12]

The Tramp points to his eyes, his hand still clasping the flower in a further gesture of his ability, or desire, to marry vision and beauty, perception and imagination. Two title cards are interspersed with close-ups of these figures: "You can see now?" "Yes, I can see now." The alternation ends with the Girl, in the same medium close-up, holding the Tramp's hand in her own and bringing it to her heart, and then, in the final shot of the film, with the Tramp, in tighter framing, the flower still in his hand and his fingers picking at his teeth as he waits, unbearably, for her response. She has acknowledged him for who he is, but what will she do with this knowledge?

The film, of course, does not answer this question. Part of the tension and ambivalence with which this scene is invested is that these two cannot become a couple. If the Tramp were to actually find love, his power over us, his audience, would vanish; his persona would cease to have the mimetic power that it possesses when it is not part of our world but rather an expression of its poverty. That this beggar is somehow better than us, that he can realize a world that responds to his desires and to our own, is a fundamental source of our fascination with him. We could say that the Tramp's poverty is always an inverse image of our own, and we enter his films at the chiasmus formed by these two experiences. His vulnerability and disappointment here at the end of *City Lights* is a condition of the fact that if the Tramp and the Flower Girl were actually to couple, his audience would be left with a feeling of despair. His imaginative play (with another boxer's rabbit's foot, with a statue pompously dedicated to "peace and prosperity") would no longer be an expression of hope—for a better, more imaginative human community, and for the sufficient acknowledgment of our desires—but would instead become a kind of acquiescence. His claim of the power to see things new must always signal a restlessness with things as they stand. Or as Rothman wonderfully puts it, the moment imagines "the overcoming of all the barriers that human beings have created to ward off the knowledge that human happiness rests in human hands."[13] This is why the ending of *City Lights*, like that of *The Gold Rush* several years earlier, has both a raw emotional power and a sense of tautology. The former actually derives from the latter: the Tramp *cannot* be with this woman, yet these moments, and the possibility of just this couple, acknowledge our hope that such a union of hope and reality is possible.

City Lights is, in this sense, a eulogy for the silent cinema. If with the release of this film Chaplin could claim that "because the silent or non-dialogue picture has been temporarily pushed aside in the hysteria attending the introduction of speech by no means indicates that it is extinct or that the motion picture screen has seen the last of it," by the mid-thirties, with the release of *Modern Times*, the question had become how he would integrate synchronized sound and dialogue into his pantomime.[14] With the introduction of sound, one important sense of the screen, its imagination of a porous relation between self and other, between fact and fantasy, was, for Chaplin at least, to disappear.

Hence, *Modern Times* figures the cinema entirely differently than does *City Lights*, understanding it as a realm in which the possibility of attunement within and without the film frame is not called into question but has instead been foreclosed upon and, consequently, within which a different sort of attunement between star and audience must be constructed, one in which the star stands in more obvious separation from the images onscreen. Chaplin declares all of this not at the end but at the beginning of *Modern Times*, where he announces a wholly different relation between silence and sound, or more specifically, a different relation between sound and the sort of perception that appears in these earlier films. *Modern Times* mourns the possibility of attunement and "seeing as" that characterizes the earlier features.

In one sense, *Modern Times* might be said to return us to Buster Keaton. The film responds self-consciously to the issues of automation and dehumanization that I argued are central to Keaton's work. Interestingly, *Modern Times* was recognized by contemporary audiences as replying to these concerns, but these audiences did not take these themes terribly seriously. In the *New York Times*, for instance, Frank Nugent called the "foreword" to *Modern Times* "dangerously meaningful": "'Modern Times,' Nugent says, quoting from the movie's first title card, "'is a story of industry, of individual enterprise—humanity crusading in the pursuit of happiness.' Verily, a strange prelude to an antic." And he goes on to suggest that the film manages to get its social comment out of its system in the opening sequence: "Sociological concept? Maybe. But a rousing, rib-tickling, gag-be-strewn jest for all that and in the best Chaplin manner."[15] In a similar rhetorical gesture that is common among early reviews of the film, an anonymous writer in *Film Daily* opens his review by acknowledging the presence of social comment but quickly moving past this to confirm Chaplin's "great talent"—confirming, in short, that concerned audiences will still find the old Chaplin alongside the social comment in which they may be less interested: "Charlie Chaplin—you will remember him, no doubt—last night returned to basic fundamentals in story construction, coupling with it an ironic poke or two at the System, as constituted today, and combined with that his great talent in his first screen appearance since 'City Lights.'"[16] Like many early reviewers, these writers took into account the film's status as social satire, but quickly worked to reassure audiences that they need not peer too deeply into such comment. Indeed, the issue was really that early audiences couldn't avoid bringing up the question of satire because its production had raised controversy on exactly these grounds. The highest reaches of the Soviet film industry, in the form of the director of Soyuzkino, Boris Shumyatsky, had publicly praised the film.

There are all sorts of reasons for the ambivalence of these early reviews, from a worry that this film star (and a comedian at that) might move away from the universalist and apparently apolitical aspirations of his earlier films to the sense that the film addressed these concerns in an almost polemical fashion. But what the earlier material on Keaton brings out here is that the satire of *Modern Times*, with its explicit interest in factory labor and automation and its concern with the fate of the human in this environment, may very well have struck its original audiences as belated. Frank Nugent and the writers of *Film Daily* may not have read Thorstein Veblen's *The Theory of Business Enterprise*, which had put these issues in clear form more than thirty years earlier, but they would have encountered this discourse around automation for years if not decades by the time of the film's release. In short, it is perhaps in retrospect, and as part of an imaginary past, that the film seems to have the satirical force that many critics of our time assign to it.

Yet it is also the case that the peculiar temporality and even anachronism of *Modern Times* is central to the film's rehearsal of these questions, especially with regard to its account of the medium of film and the apparently automated nature of synchronized sound. For the Chaplin of *Modern Times*, sound film introduces the sense of the cinema as surveillance, in part because of a shift in temporality that synchronized sound seemed to occasion. The opening credits of *Modern Times* play over a clock face, which, in distinction to *City Lights* (the credits of which play as a series of title cards that apostrophize a specifically silent cinema), announces that the images to follow are not simply to be understood in relation to a particular and constraining sense of time but that a sense of regulated time may be internal to a cinema that speaks. In *Modern Times*, time is present in way that is incompatible with the revelation and acknowledgment of fantasy that is the heart of *City Lights*. Everywhere ambivalent about its relation to sound, the film sets this first image of a clock against a title card ("'Modern Times.' A story of industry, of individual enterprise—humanity crusading in the pursuit of happiness") that declares that we are also to read this film as a kind of allegory. This sense of allegory is further reinforced by what seems initially to be the first image of the diegesis—a herd of running sheep—but which instead turns out to be a non-diegetic insert (and homage to Chaplin's friend

Sergei Eisenstein) that the movie consequently pairs with an image of a mass of people leaving a subway tunnel. A series of shots then imply that these people, none of whom will figure as characters in the film, are employees of a factory that also employs the Tramp.

The film subsequently picks up the image of the screen that closed *City Lights*, but this screen is now radically transformed. The screen is no longer a site around which to experience, negotiate, and acknowledge desire, as it had been at the Girl's shop window, but is rather a tool of surveillance, a space defined by the absence or secrecy of desire. On this screen, we see the president of the Electro Steel Corporation. Because his machines have disburdened him of the need to work, he fidgets with a jigsaw puzzle, the pieces of which recall the gear motif of the film as a whole. After picking up and quickly setting down a newspaper, this man uses a device on his desk to flip through a series of images of his factory. And while this device may be a kind of cinema—literally, a series of moving images—it is perhaps best described as a closed circuit television: he uses a series of knobs on a box at his desk to move between channels, the images of which are then displayed on a screen behind him. Importantly, these images are understood to be simultaneous, so that what we have is not the sense of an imaginary past that characterized (and continues to characterize) most narrative cinema, but rather a time experienced as entirely and only present, a time familiar to early television (and indeed to Internet video).

The president's screen, it turns out, functions two ways: his images of the factory floor give way to an image of the factory that belongs to the wider frame of the film itself and within which the president himself appears on a large screen set within one of his giant machines. True to the ambivalence of the opening credits, this image is first accompanied by non-diegetic orchestral music (its sprightly quality making this look and sound like a silent film) and then by the president's voice, which barks orders at his foreman ("Section 5, speed her up, four one!"). (This voice is not exactly disembodied—his image appears on the screen—but Chaplin voices his skepticism here of a voice that can be so thoroughly separated from its body.) The first instance of the human voice synchronized with a body in the entirety of Chaplin's work is thus figured both as the antithesis of the comic (the president is not a clown; he is not even straight man) and as allied with a constraining, even cruel, sense of labor and time.

In response to these orders, the foreman moves a lever that speeds up the conveyor belts upon which the workers labor. A pan of the factory floor (accompanied by non-diegetic music that calls to mind silence as well as by the sound of the president's voice) introduces us to the Tramp, who is at work with two wrenches on a conveyor belt. His job is to tighten bolts on a series of widgets, a task that he first performs with startling aptitude and then ineptly when he stops to scratch his armpit. This failure occasions a series of gags in which the other men on the conveyor belt, constrained by their own need to tighten the bolts, fight with the Tramp as he seeks to keep up. The sequence not only establishes one of the ruling concerns of the film—the Tramp's fraught relationship to the time of the factory and indeed to the time of sound film itself—but, recalling the philosopher Henri Bergson, the fact that the automatic is in a sense internal to the comic itself, that the comic might always be invested with ambivalence because it relies upon the image of a lack of plasticity. Indeed, as some Ford Motor Company educational and industrial films of the era made plain, the conveyor belt is itself another way of imagining the nature of the film strip.[17] In this sense, the conveyor belt here sets up a ruling question for the film, one that it in a sense fails to answer: Can this automatic technology be used to human, or humane, ends?

The president again barks an order, through his screen, to speed up the conveyor belt, and the film cuts to Chaplin on the line. An anonymous, disembodied voice says, "Relief man passing," and another worker comes to take Chaplin's place. Chaplin leaves the line with a series of jolts and tics that signal the fact that he has internalized the movements of his work. He then marches to the time clock (calling back to the opening image of the film and its announcement that this movie is about the senses of time that it represents), punches out, and walks into a bathroom to enjoy a cigarette. Curiously, the bathroom is also the site of a large screen, which is situated on its far wall (Figure 3.3). As Chaplin, his body returned to the relaxed, natural movements of a human being, leans against a sink, an image of the president appears on this screen. His face and body, which are greatly magnified by the size of the screen, swivel toward Chaplin (suggesting that Chaplin's cigarette break has somehow interrupted *him*). Looking directly at the Tramp, he yells, "Hey! Quit stalling, get back to work! Go on!" Again, we have here something like the obverse image of the sense of the screen's relation to desire and knowledge at the end of *City Lights*, the former sense of a porous and enabling boundary having been replaced not simply by a sense of surveillance but of privacy interrupted, of not a screen but a wall between fantasy and its acknowledgment.

After some further business at the line, the film cuts back to the president's office. A secretary ushers in three salesmen and a large machine. They are announced by a non-diegetic trumpet call, a mocking gesture that calls back to the beginning of *City Lights* and its aural account of the pomposity of its city leaders. In a further instance of this continual and

Figure 3.3. The screen as surveillance and wall (*Modern Times*).

ambivalent relay of diegetic and non-diegetic sound, the chief salesman (mysteriously dressed in black coattails) sets down a record player, cranks it, and stands back. We then hear the disembodied voice of the record, to which the salesmen synchronize their pantomimic demonstration of the machine:

> Good morning, my friends. This record comes to you through the Sales Talk Transcription Company, Incorporated; your speaker, the Mechanical Salesman. May I take the pleasure of introducing Mr. J. Willicombe Billows, the inventor of the Billows Feeding Machine, a practical device that automatically feeds your men while at work. Don't stop for lunch; be ahead of your competitor. The Billows Feeding Machine will eliminate the lunch hour, increase your production, and decrease your overhead. Allow us to point out some of the features of this wonderful machine. Its beautiful aerodynamic streamlined body, its smoothness of action made silent by our porous, electromagnetic ball bearings. Let us acquaint you with our automaton soup plate. Its compressed air blower,

no breath necessary, no energy required to cool the soup. Notice the revolving plate with the automatic food pusher. Observe our countershaft, double-knee action corn-feeder with its synchro-mesh transition, which enables you to shift from high to low gear by the mere tip of the tongue. Then there is the hydro-compressed, sterilized mouth wiper. Its factors of control ensure against spots on the shirt front. These are but a few of the delightful features of the Billows Feeding Machine. Let us demonstrate with one of your workers, for actions speak louder than words. Remember, if you wish to keep ahead of your competitor, you cannot afford to ignore the importance of the Billows Feeding Machine.

The satire here is obvious enough; indeed, the record player's lecture seems to bleed into the style of the narration as a story foisted upon, or sold to, us, rather than told. Considered as a response to, or as an image of, synchronized sound, however, the scene continues to imagine a world in which sound, and above all the human voice, has been thoroughly instrumentalized, a world in which people speak to each other only to command and to sell and even then by means of a kind of nonsense. What is more, this is a world in which people are no longer connected to, hence no longer responsible for, their voices, the only dialogue, to this point, having been relayed through intervening media, first the president's two-way television and then Mr. Billow's Victrola. Finally, all of this is treated to a further inversion as the salesmen themselves perform a devaluation of pantomime. The movie explicitly marks their pitch as a performance, but they do this performance not for playful, comical, or ethical effect but merely in service of profit.

The worker on whom the Billows Feeding Machine will be demonstrated is, of course, the Tramp. After a title card ("Lunch time"), we are given one of the best-remembered scenes in the film, Chaplin struggling to eat at the hand of this malfunctioning machine. The sequence begins with a shot of the conveyor belt as it slows down and then stops. As Chaplin leaves the line, he cannot help but continue the tightening movements for which he is paid, and in another and much darker iteration of the willful, imaginative activities of perception that defined the earlier films, he involuntarily tries to tighten the buttons of a secretary's dress. Unlike the routine with the dinner rolls in *The Gold Rush* or the play with the rabbit's foot in *City Lights*, we're not asked here to see *with* the Tramp, but to see how he might come to see things this way. He has lost the shamanic quality that allowed him to lead us to see things new; he has instead become an object of pity.

The salesmen eventually whisk Chaplin into the feeding machine and turn it on by means of a series of levers that recall the levers that the foreman had earlier used at the president's command to speed up the conveyor belts. The machine then goes through each of the functions that the recording had described earlier in the president's office, from the automaton soup plate to the sterilized mouth wiper. And like the conveyor belt, this machine too speeds up past the capacity of its "worker" to respond, although the speed is, this time, an accident, caused by an electrical malfunction.

On the one hand, to see this scene in light of the sort of perception that defines films like *Shoulder Arms* and *The Gold Rush* is to see a world in which objects are *less than* plastic; these machines cannot respond to the imagination because they have been so thoroughly defined. Snorkels and dinner rolls are simple enough to be marvels; a conveyor belt just is what it is. Like the pantomime with the record player and the tightening of the woman's buttons, the feeding gag works as a kind of terrible inversion of the values of the comic. If the great Russian critic Mikhail Bakhtin, for example, could imagine the carnivalesque as defined by gross and exaggerated activities of the body, from exuberant sexual display to ravenous eating ("the lowering of all that is high, spiritual, ideal, abstract . . . a transfer to the material level, to the sphere of earth and body"), exuberance is now turned against the figure of the Tramp, who must indeed eat ravenously but at the hands of a mechanism that is anything but a liberation from the constraints of the world of work and order.[19] He is forced, even, to eat two of its "nuts," and in the scene that follows, an even larger machine will itself swallow him.

Yet there is another sense in which Chaplin plays all of this *for* an audience, or rather two—the president and the salesmen, on the one hand, who position themselves almost self-consciously for a show (performance perhaps become demonstration, gags become literal gagging), and those of us in the theater, on the other, to whom twice Chaplin turns and addresses directly with his eyes, first when the chief salesman pushes the Tramp's face into position for the machine and second after his initial surprise with the mouth wiper. The staging thus accentuates the fact that we know that these gags are performed for us, even if we're unaware of the fact that Chaplin himself controlled these mechanisms over the course of the scene by means of his own series of levers beneath the surface of the machine.

Regardless, all of this is in an important sense not funny. The scene and its gags are defined by a pessimism that is foreign to the earlier films, a despair that derives from the nature of the Tramp's will here, or rather, his lack of it. Like Keaton, the Tramp never exactly stages his aggressive relationship to the world as one that might actually be successful: when he kicks Jack Cameron (the "ladies man") in the pants in *The Gold Rush*, for instance, his aggression is real but we know that he can't help himself. And he knows that he will, on some level, receive punishment for this gesture. A defining feature of this comic structure is the combination of the gesture's oppositional character with the fact that it will not be taken seriously within the world of the story. This is the very nature of comedic license. But the opening scenes of *Modern Times* drastically revise this structure, where—at least as far as the diegetic world is concerned—the Tramp's behavior has a more purely involuntary character, one that stresses the degree to which he is acted upon. (The Tramp administers a kick in the pants knowing how it will be received; here a machine administers a gag to him.) The feeding machine is legible as a kind of torture, and it will lead, in the scenes that follow, to a "nervous breakdown" and the Tramp's consequent hospitalization, humor having become medicalized.

This is why a confusion of temporal registers may be central to the movie's relationship to its stated title, the "modern" in "times." Chaplin's film understands the modern as necessarily an experience of time as asynchronous, as a jumble of plural and irreconcilable times. The movie is an almost Benjaminian attempt to think through the relation between the cinema and apperception, the factory's conveyor belt standing in ambivalent relation to and identified with the film strip.[20] "Modernism defines itself as modern not because of its being in the present," as Bernhard Stricker has argued about *The World Viewed*, "but because of a particular relation to time in which presence, i.e., being related to one's time and to the past, has become a task, something to be achieved, instead of a natural part of our condition."[21] Rather than think of the film as merely anachronistic (a word that much better suits *City Lights*), we might think of it as Chaplin's anticipation or realization of a specifically modern*ist* cinema, a cinema that registers the experience and effects of a specifically asynchronous time. This too helps to explain the curious reaction to Chaplin's film as both a betrayal of an earlier universalism (now legible as a kind of nostalgia for silence) *and* as evidence that what we have here is "classic" Chaplin—the same old figure, the same old comedy. *Modern Times* is in point of fact neither: it represents Chaplin's last attempt to make film modern.

Chaplin may have felt threatened by the expectation of synchronized sound dialogue, but he ended *Modern Times* by staging a kind of settlement with sound technology, singing nonsense before a nightclub audience. Yet the presence of these other technologies—of radios, record players, and a television—signals a sense of the cinema as definitively plural, one in which the purity that licensed the confrontation with and acknowledgment of desire in *City Lights* must be surrendered to a new regime, one in which the ontology of film shifts radically in response to the presence of the human voice. For this reason, I want now to think about how the Marx Brothers—performers whose stage work did not begin in pantomime but with a distinct style of verbal repartee—worked with synchronized sound to form their own account of the possibilities of film sound.

4

Bodies of Silence, Bodies of Sound

The Marx Brothers

As CHAPLIN'S MELANCHOLY indicates, the arrival of sound fundamentally altered the nature and possibilities of the cinema. Most immediately, the American film industry's adoption of synchronized sound caused important changes in production practices and film style. The necessity of silencing loud arc lamps and noisy cameras resulted in more static camerawork during the transitional years of the late twenties. Boomless, omnidirectional microphones necessitated awkward cutting patterns around filmed dialogue, and the studios often used multiple cameras to film single scenes, a practice that attempted to reproduce some of the more rapid cutting that had characterized the late silent feature, but which now gives some of these movies the look of network sitcoms.

It's interesting to look at the average shot lengths (ASLs) of films by Buster Keaton and the Marx Brothers because they demonstrate the difficulty of adapting new sound technologies to silent film style. Whereas the ASL of Keaton's *The Cameraman* (1928) is six seconds, the ASL of the Marx Brothers' first feature, *The Cocoanuts* (1929), is 17.9, about three times slower than a movie that feels, to twenty-first-century eyes, a bit slack.[1] This difference has not only technological origins but generic ones. As Keaton's career at MGM clearly suggests, the environment of early sound cinema privileged comedians, such as the Marx Brothers and

Jimmy Durante, who were still working on the stage and whose theatrical productions were easily adapted for the talking screen. Indeed, the frontal staging of *The Cocoanuts*, which was filmed in Paramount's studio in Queens, appears to have been borrowed wholesale from its original Broadway production.

David Bordwell has insisted that these stylistic changes are less dramatic than they first seem. He makes his case by comparing Ernst Lubitsch's 1924 feature *The Marriage Circle* with the filmmaker's 1932 sound remake of that film, *One Hour with You*. These two films, Bordwell says, display "differences of stylistic devices (voice, shot length, cutting rhythm, camera mobility) but fundamental similarity of the systems (coherence of causality, space, and time)." The greatest stylistic difference between the two eras, he argues, is the sound cinema's eventual substitution of the moving camera for the faster cutting of the silent era.[2]

But while Bordwell's idea of functional equivalence—of systems not individual devices—may be appropriate for thinking about stylistic change in an industry ruled by an oligopoly that was concerned to innovate its technology and maintain stylistic similarity while at the same time keeping down its production costs, it distracts critical attention from some of the surprising, textually specific aspects of these films, such as their self-conscious interest in technologies of sound recording and amplification and their curiosity about the nature of film sound. Hollywood may have possessed a group style, but on top of this style, particular films display a remarkable awareness about themselves and their conventional and material bases.

Importantly for thinking about the Marx Brothers, the story of the industrial process of synchronization is also the story of competing and convergent representational technologies. In the late twenties, competing manufacturers were struggling to define film sound as the provenance of one of three preexisting mediums: the telephone, the radio, and the phonograph. Both through their own prior experiences with these technologies and through the advertisements of their manufacturers, the public had come to think of film sound not as an entirely new technology but as derivative from previous innovations in electronics. For this reason, as Donald Crafton has argued, "what was at stake for the corporations that controlled the technology was to convince consumers that sound belonged to a particular manufacturing group and that the group enjoyed a 'natural' claim to exploit sound."[3] Who was the father of film sound—AT&T and the Bell Labs, RCA, or Vitaphone?

Western Electric, the AT&T subsidiary that developed the technology that eventually came to dominate the industry, promoted the idea that film sound was fundamentally telephonic. On a billboard for John

Barrymore's *Don Juan* (1926), for instance, the grandiloquent phrase "WARNER BROS. by arrangement with Western Electric Co. and Bell Telephone Laboratories presents" precedes the film's title. At the same time, the Radio Corporation of America (RCA), which then enjoyed a government-sanctioned monopoly on the radio industry and would later come to dominate broadcast television, proudly announced that film sound was the progeny of a radio father. RKO's famous "Titan" advertisement of 1929 demonstrates this clearly: a shirtless giant holds a film camera in his right hand while his left points to a block of text that reads, "RADIO . . . fulfillment of daring dreams . . . colossus of modern art and science . . . *now enters the motion picture industry!*" Finally, Vitaphone's sound-on-disc technology suggested a comparison between film sound and phonography. A Vitaphone advertisement in an exhibitors' trade magazine announced—somewhat less dramatically than RKO's Titan—that "the high character of Warner Bros. Singing, Talking Technicolor Productions demand the utmost in Sound Recording and Reproduction. Vitaphone Discs supply just that."[4] And as some of these advertisements suggest, each technology was understood as different in character. Telephonic sound had been designed with the primary goal of making the human voice intelligible; radio was a broadcast medium that sent sounds across large distances; and the phonograph sought fidelity to its original source.

In advertising, in trade magazines, and on its screens, the industry of the transitional era repeatedly asked "What is film sound?" and producers and technicians struggled to settle upon an industry-wide conceptual model for answering that question. One issue was both ubiquitous and fraught: Should film sound behave like the camera? That is, like radio and to some degree the phonograph, should it deliver sound in perceptual fidelity to the visually integrated onscreen "world" of the film? Or should it, like the telephone, stress intelligibility over fidelity and seek to deliver narratively salient information to its audiences about the objects and persons—the sources of film sound—that these films conjoined to film space? As Rick Altman and others have documented, this conversation took place throughout the late 1920s, when most influential sound engineers argued for parity between image scale and sound scale. Most technicians believed that the amplitude of an actor's voice, for example, should vary with his distance from the camera. (Some engineers even went as far as to develop an arithmetical system by which this amplitude could be calculated in relation to the size of its source onscreen.) By the late 1930s, however, this debate had subsided, and the industry settled into a practice by which the soundtrack (and in particular, the human voice) stays more or less constant in amplitude while the image scale changes. It had become clear to sound engineers that their soundtracks were praised not for their spatial realism (the province of radio sound in particular) but for their clarity, and in particular, for their ability to produce clarity of dialogue (the strength of telephonic sound), in large part because this dialogue was the privileged vehicle for narrative information.[5] In other words, film sound came to be understood as the sound of the picture, not the sound of the things that these pictures represented.

Just as Chaplin's comedy of the late twenties and early thirties was taken up with the question of film sound, the Marx Brothers' Paramount films (*The Cocoanuts* [1929], *Animal Crackers* [1930], *Monkey Business* [1931], *Horse Feathers* [1932], and *Duck Soup* [1933]) are full of gags that refer directly to, and explore, this context of technological and industrial change. They openly and sometimes bluntly play with sound's paternity and the question of the relation between sound, image, and reality. The self-reference that is present in the Paramount films is, to be sure, never as total as it is in Keaton's *Sherlock Jr.* (1924) and Chaplin's *Modern Times* (1936), both of which have an ontological quality from beginning to end. But this is not especially surprising if one keeps in mind that, unlike Keaton and Chaplin, the Marx Brothers did not direct or produce their own films; it becomes clear that they evidence less a coherent account of the medium than a chain of situations in which humor produces opportunities for certain interests and anxieties to surface. We can therefore read their gags as thinking through ramifications of the technological and aesthetic change of synchronized sound. The films the Marx Brothers made between 1929 and 1933 display and can be understood as thinking through the studio-era cinema's attempt to absorb preexisting technologies of sound as well as the conventions of realism these technologies brought with them. In this sense, they realize an ontology of film sound.

The Marx Brothers' gags often take up preexisting sound technologies individually. A prominent gag sequence from *Monkey Business*, for example, figures film sound as distinctly phonographic. Having made an ocean crossing as stowaways without passports, the ship's steward refuses to let the brothers disembark. When Zeppo gleefully informs his brothers that he has stolen Maurice Chevalier's passport, they proceed to work through a scene in which, confronted by a dour customs officer, each of the brothers attempts to impersonate Chevalier in order to gain passage. ("You've got to sing like Chevalier to get off this boat," Zeppo says, offering his Chevalier impression. "That's dandy," Groucho says in response, "If you sing like that, they'll throw us all off the boat.") Wearing Chevalier's characteristic straw boater and jutting their chins to mimic his cartoon-like physiognomy, first Zeppo, then Chico, and then Groucho come forward with the stolen passport. Each time, the officer expresses skepticism that the man in question is Chevalier, and each time the brother attempts to convince him by singing Chevalier's trademark "You Brought a New Kind of Love to Me" (recently performed in Chevalier's 1930 film *The Big Pond*). Of course, none of them can plausibly, let alone perfectly, reproduce the distinctive qualities of Chevalier's voice. In fact, each impression is successively worse, beginning with Zeppo's pleasant sing-song and then progressing through Chico's burlesque Italian and what is, in Groucho's voice and gestures, an obvious parody of the original.

Finally, Harpo comes forward. This is supposed to be the show-stopper: How will this mute clown mimic any singer, let alone Chevalier? Before this can be answered, however, Harpo intervenes with a series of visual puns. The increasingly frustrated officer asks him for his passport; Harpo hands him a piece of pasteboard. The officer asks again; Harpo hands him a washboard. Having run out of props, Harpo then gives over the passport. Faced once more with the officer's skepticism, Harpo commences to sing a poorly lip-synced version of Chevalier's song. His moving lips are accompanied by a recorded version of Chevalier singing that is, by virtue of its scratchy quality and poor tonal range, distinctively marked as a recording. It is of course incommensurable with Chevalier's actual, living voice, and is therefore legible both as a recorded simulation of his voice and as a direct indication of how this voice would sound through its "natural" reproduction on film. When the recording slows down, distorting Chevalier's voice into a wordless mess, Harpo turns around to reveal a phonograph strapped to his back, which he then rapidly cranks, thereby restoring Chevalier's voice to its apparently proper speed and tone. When the officer throws him out of the line, Harpo first stamps the officer's bald head and then sets about destroying the neatly stacked papers, forms, and stamps that grace the customs table.

The use of the phonograph and its song make a clear comparison between film sound and the phonograph disc.[6] It imagines film sound as phonographic. More specifically, the gag realizes the perceptual fidelity model then associated with phonographic sound—the idea that the speed and continuity of a voice in song, for instance, should seem natural to the physical movements of the body from which it is supposed to emanate. At the same time, however, Harpo seems to burlesque this model, the evidence for the supposed power of the phonograph being not a singing Don Juan but himself mute, who only gives the appearance of singing a song associated with another film and another actor. Understood in this sense, Harpo's body becomes a middle term. The mute clown imagines himself as a living speaker through which a distinctly phonographic film sound might run. The gag is something like film sound imagined in the form of *mise-en-abyme*. Because the fidelity of this ventriloquized voice, not to mention the synchronization, is aggressively lacking, and because it references not reality as such but rather another film and another actor, it works to figure film sound itself as unmoored, malleable, and unnatural. Film sound was (and is) just these, of course, but here we can see Harpo working against the conventions for recording and reproduction that seek to bury this fact.

The Chevalier gag also displays an interesting relationship between the four Marx Brothers and the film's larger musical accompaniment. As each sings his passage of the Chevalier song, he is spontaneously accompanied by an invisible orchestra, whose reverb-less sound identifies it as existing not in this diegetic space but in the film's background. That is, this music does not function like classical accompaniment, which in addition to being "invisible" is definitively tied to the practices of continuity and narration.[7] Unlike traditional accompaniment, in other words, its presence is declared, not hidden.

Here, the music's direct address to the viewer (the orchestra appears as if miraculously each time one of the brothers sings but is otherwise nonexistent) gives it a form that is reminiscent of such accompaniments in the film musical, where obviously non-diegetic music sometimes breaks into the diegesis. (To pick one of Chevalier's movies, Rouben Mamoulian's *Love Me Tonight* [1932] opens with a series of rhythmic sound effects produced within the world of the film, but two minutes later non-diegetic orchestral music begins to accompany these sound effects and the people singing onscreen.) But the fact that none of the performers sings the entire song from beginning to end, as well as the fact that the singing is tied to the production not of sentiment but laughter, gives the brothers' use of recorded sound a distinct character. Here, the musical accompaniment has a characteristic that is typical of slapstick more generally; instead of producing continuity, developing the film's narrative, or helping to foreground the characters' participation in song, the singing follows the internal logic of the gag. It is a "gag orchestra" backing "gag singers." And if this gag in turn possesses its own formal structure (built, in part, by the soundtrack itself, with its repetition of Chevalier's song), this structure turns out to be related to but oblique to the larger narrative of the film. It is one way in which the film manages a narratively salient event—the brothers' disembarkation—but what separates it from other genres is the fact that the presence of the music itself declares this fact. The foregrounded music joins with the gag to comment upon the fact that what we are seeing and hearing is of course produced. And it helps to create humor by standing outside of the world of the film's story, here represented by the uniformed figure of the ship's angry officer, who marks the diegetic world—in distinction from the Marx Brothers themselves—as flat and without affect.

All of which is to say, *Monkey Business* burlesques the idea of technological progress. We could read the instability of the action of burlesque as a reflection of a general industry insecurity that attended the adoption of sound, but instability also seems to attend the particular self-awareness of the comedy at work here. Its self-awareness is an unsteady one, often at war with the dramatic meaning upon which it is parasitic; these gags walk a thin line, relying upon a cycle in which the diegetic world is produced and then disrupted, over and over again. Irony is in this sense the driving mode of Marx Brothers films and the basis of their self-reference. The anarchic action of burlesque, rather than the ordering relation of narrative, shapes the mood in which these films reflect upon themselves and their medium. In this sense, the Marx Brothers are paradoxical figures, birthed in the "progressive" moment of synchronized film sound—these recorded voices niftily lip-synched—yet forever clowning in its margins.

∽

If Keaton's work defines the medium as the moving, projected, photographic image, the advent of synchronized sound made this definition obsolete. As I have argued, Chaplin had a melancholic reaction to this turn of events: *City Lights* and *Modern Times* eulogize a specifically silent cinema in which pantomime was capable of producing a sense of attunement between the performer and his audience. As sound cinema's industrial history makes clear, the presence of these new technologies had the effect of foregrounding the material bases of the medium. Audiences did not immediately perceive film sound as natural and beyond comment; rather, advertising, filmmaking, and audience expectation worked together to declare the newness and interest of synchronized sound. And of course, the new presence of sound drew attention to the fact that the cinema's reality effect was not natural to it but rather the result of a skillful use of a set of aesthetic conventions. In this sense, the early sound cinema made plain the fact that the material foundation of cinema had always been intermedial: a changing arrangement of moving photographs, more or less ordered sound, and theatrical spaces that varied tremendously in nature.

Perhaps unsurprisingly, the Paramount comedies continuously foreground and play with this intermedial basis. A second scene from *Monkey Business*, for instance, drops the phonograph analogy entirely and compares film sound to the radio. The Brothers have successfully disembarked; Zeppo is fighting with the mobster Alky Briggs (Harry Woods) in a hay pile on the floor of a barn. While Harpo and Chico improvise a cashless faro wheel in one corner of this pastoral, premodern space, Groucho oscillates between avoiding the fight and performing a running commentary on it. The commentary, at first done sporadically, as if improvised, eventually takes the form of a radio broadcast. He sits in the seat of an old buggy and talks into a carriage lamp that is covered with spider webs, which functions as an improvised microphone:

> Well, here we are again at the ringside and, folks, it looks like a great battle. Now the boys are locked in the center of the ring. Oh, baby, what a grudge fight!
>
> *[Sounds of punching. GROUCHO leaps up and down in the buggy.]*
>
> Zowie! Zowie! Zowie! That makes three zowies, and a man gets a base on balls.
>
> *[Dust showers down on him from the canopy of the buggy.]*
>
> Ending of the first inning, no runs, no errors, but plenty of hits. Whee![8]

Groucho's commentary (like most of his monologues) is digressive and marked as playful upkeying, a moment when a new frame is introduced into the existing discourse. Effectively, it gives us *the image* of someone producing narration, Groucho's words here turning an actual tussle into a boxing match and his "zowies" parroting the sound of the punches offscreen. And all of this moves back and forth between the representation of sound (both narration and sound effect) and an action of self-reference that comments upon this replication. It is this last effect, for instance, that licenses Groucho's sudden discursive jump from boxing match to baseball game, then back again. His final line, for example, uses the action of a pun ("plenty of hits") in order to turn the monologue back to the boxing match. Thrown back onto itself, we could say, the commentary implodes. What is more, despite the fact that Groucho looks at the fight below (he looks offscreen right to deliver the punchlines of his jokes), the cutting does not suggest suture (the viewer seeing what Groucho sees) but something like a parody of the coverage of live sporting events. The action is therefore understood to be occurring not as the result of his perception, but as concurrent with his commentary.

The effect of all of this is to call attention to the structure of the sentences themselves, such that the monologue does not so much comment on the action as comment upon commenting. It's interesting to consider all of this in light of the industry itself. The studio Hollywood film coalesced around the rigor of the shooting script and its taut dramatic constraints, but this gag is marked by its rich excess, words for words' sake. And like the buggy in which Groucho jumps up and down, his words go nowhere. Onscreen, they are transmissions without a receiver; beyond the screen, the audience receives them as a kind of purposive purposelessness.

Just as with the earlier Chevalier gag, the idea here is the incommensurability of sound and image, the ways in which there simply can be no perfect or natural synchronization. In Groucho's monologue, the conventions of spatial realism that characterized contemporary radio come up against the convention of narrative intelligibility that the studio cinema inherited from the theater. The scene is perfectly representative of the medium close-up sound that was (and continues to be) normative Hollywood practice. Zeppo and Alky Briggs fight across the floor of the barn, yet the amplitude of the accompanying sound does not alter with camera placement, while the film mixes Groucho's voice with the sequence rather in the way of a radio announcer. It imagines him as "offscreen" or separate from the event itself while also simultaneous or "live," and his closeness to the fake, onscreen microphone is more or less identical to his position toward the actual microphone that transmits his voice to the film's audience. Here, a realism of voice (Groucho's dialogue is undistorted) works alongside an interest in narrative intelligibility (the audience has no difficulty understanding this voice and its narrative placement), yet this intelligibility is predicated on its being in one sense exterior to the action onscreen. Indeed, we might see and interpret the fight between Zeppo and this mobster *without* any play-by-play commentary at all, so that Groucho is, in another sense, talking to himself. We seem to overhear this much like some radio broadcasting.

It is notable, that, just as in the Chevalier gag, Groucho's monologue takes place inside a machine of transport, here not the ship but the jalopy. *Monkey Business* implicitly compares representational technologies to vehicles, analogizing the conflict and convergence of representational technologies with those of machines of transport. This is not unique to the Marx Brothers or even to screen comedy: *The First Auto* (1927), for instance, an early Warner Bros. Vitaphone feature, compared the change from silent to sound cinema to the transition from the horse-drawn carriage to the automobile. Regardless, the interesting presence of vehicles links *Monkey Business*'s representational technologies to the idea of movement, a movement that is in turn related to the idea that media express and transfer—that is, *move*—human knowledge. In *The First Auto*, and in industry discourse more generally, the fantasy is that of a perfect vehicle, of cars and communications technologies that know no distance, of metaphors whose tenors are indistinguishable from their vehicles. We could also think of Groucho's gag as an inversion of the high seriousness of a film such as *Intolerance* (1916), within which vehicular and communicative technologies combine to dramatize a grand teleology of human history.[9] Unlike *Intolerance* or *The First Auto*, however, Groucho's fight monologue is plain in its sense of the impossibility of this fantasy—the fact that it is fantasy. But the boxing match Groucho produces is also a metaphor, both for the "real" fight happening below and for the succession of sound technologies that his "broadcast" burlesques: the broadcast is this metaphor's vehicle, this succession of technologies its tenor. And like the horse-drawn vehicle out of which this comic speech is delivered, the vehicle of Groucho's play-by-play actually breaks down against the reality that it attempts to describe. It is in this sense that the ironic action at work in *Monkey Business* allows the film to reflect upon its material basis.

If the phonographic model understood the challenge of film sound as the maintenance of fidelity to an original source and radio sound understood it as the production of spatial realism, the telephonic model was oriented toward questions of clarity and intelligibility. In this sense, it was the most obvious model for a narrative cinema in which spoken dialogue would play a central role. Here again, the Marx Brothers use this model as an occasion not simply for comedy but to articulate the basis for a cinema that speaks. A very short gag from *The Cocoanuts* stages a comparison between film and telephonic sound in order to call into question the ontological stability of Hollywood film sound. Early in that film, Harpo walks up to the empty front desk of a grand hotel. The concierge's phone rings. Not knowing how to answer (Harpo is no telephone expert) he picks up the whole device and hears nothing. He then takes a small, surreptitious bite from the transmitter and chews it. Happy with this experience, he takes a larger bite, which he then washes down with ink from an inkwell.

Part of the joke here is that even if he knew how to properly answer the telephone, the mute Harpo would not be able to talk into the transmitter. As the other films that the Marx Brothers made for Paramount make clear, reflection about the nature of film sound often expresses itself around Harpo's silence. It is also notable that—just as Harpo's Chevalier routine in *Monkey Business* was accompanied, before and after, by his destruction of the written word in the form of customs forms and fountain pens—this gag is preceded by his having ripped up the hotel's mail and then polished it off with a libation of ink. *The Cocoanuts* in this sense invokes a Rabelaisian atmosphere of festivity and engorgement, a gleefully destructive sense of experience, or what Bakhtin, in reference to carnival, called "the negation of the entire order of life."[10] If for both Keaton and Chaplin the acknowledgment of the medium of cinema provides an opportunity for the attunement of performer and audience (albeit in quite different ways), the fact that the objects of Harpo's destruction are technologies of signification makes his movements into gestures of what we might call "negative acknowledgment." Indeed, one of the fascinating aspects of this scene and its gag is that there is very little sound at all; the microphone runs, picking up the sound of the phone hitting the desk, for instance, but it is otherwise emptied of both diegetic and non-diegetic noise. In this sense, the gag does not so much suggest that film sound is somehow equivalent to its telephonic counterpart, but figures the eating of a telephone as the negation of the possibility of synchronization itself. Seen against the other gags, Harpo's gag does not really acknowledge the nature and possibility of film sound as telephonic but seeks attunement with the audience by means of a declaration of the limitations of this model. Just as for Bakhtin the negations of carnival were in structure "closely linked to the affirmation of that which is born anew,"[11] Harpo's function here is to open up the creative potential of new representational technologies, to suggest the vastness of their possibility in ways that the studio cinema would increasingly decide to shun.

It is important to remember that Harpo is mute but not silent. Here, his muteness and his consumption of the telephone, paired with the liberal use of sound effects that in other parts of the film accompany the props that he takes from his outsize coat, suggest an auditory world that is distinct from and potentially more varied than the medium close-up dialogue that characterizes the "straight" actors in the film. By abstracting Harpo from what is otherwise a film musical, *The Cocoanuts* points to the potential for a sound cinema that does not always *speak*, a cinema in which sound is not marshalled for dialogue and song but for the imagination of a living world. After all, for Harpo, the telephone is not even an acoustic technology; it is rather one more object from which sound might be made. The gag imagines the phone as occupying the same plane of existence as Harpo's body in his odd and grandiloquent coat, as merely one more object in a world of objects. We could say that if the Chevalier phonograph burlesques the synchronization of voice to the moving image, the hotel telephone represents the physical comedy's resistance to the naturalized surfaces of synchronized sound and its insistence upon the sense in which the human body is whole and fixed.

∼

Like the gags in *Monkey Business*, *The Cocoanuts* uses this joke to raise the figure of a technology whose conventions the broader studio system wished to absorb. And like those other gags, this moment of quotation becomes an occasion for humor. Interestingly, however, *The Cocoanuts* does not borrow the authority of the telephone, but rather negates it, seeking in the process to interest its audience in possibilities of sound that were cut off and unexplored, like the decentering of film dialogue and an interest in the aural life of the object world. Of course, if Groucho's "play-by-play" burlesques the style of radio address, his voice continues to be amplified and broadcast, in a form similar to that of the radio, through Paramount's audio technology. Groucho's joke is parasitic upon this earlier form. Harpo, on the other hand, merely takes up the telephone and eats it. Importantly, this negative acknowledgment is figured through the relationship between a technology of sound and its accompanying onscreen body. Harpo literally consumes this technology, making his body the middle term between his performance and the production of meaning. As I will later suggest is the case with Jerry Lewis, in this performance the human body helps to signify a relationship to the medium that is somewhere between intentional and involuntary.

Early in the debate over sound scale, one of RCA's technicians, John L. Cass, worried about the use of a uniform sound scale, which would lead, he thought, to the formation of an unnatural spectatorial body. In an inversion of the fear of some critics of early and transitional cinema who were concerned that audiences would recoil from onscreen close-ups of heads separated from their bodies, Cass wondered whether audiences might be disturbed by the otherworldly powers of the cinema's ear, an ability to hear both whispers and screams at the same amplitude. The sound that results from a soundtrack that is oriented toward intelligibility above all, Cass wrote, "may not be said to represent any given point of audition, but is the sound which would be heard by a man with five or six very long ears, said ears extending in various directions."[12] As if to counteract Cass's picture of the monstrous, multi-eared spectator, a proper and uniformly scaled soundtrack would become the anchor that kept his body in place while the spectator's eyes flew around a widely varied image space. Cass's comments obliquely point out that, with the help of narrative absorption, constant and intelligible sound actually sanctions the classical cinema's voyeuristic changes in view by producing an underlying sense of continuity. (Seen in this light, it is no coincidence that the early sound cinema saw the creation of a new kind of censorship in the form of the Production Code. The superaddition of sound may actually have called forth a desire to contain an excess of meaning.) The soundtracks to the Marx Brothers' Paramount films are by no means marvels of experimentation, but gags like the ones that I have been describing have the effect of referring to the flatness that characterized Hollywood sound practices, most of which were tied to the desire to produce a sense of invisible narration.

These soundtracks do not simply license changes in point of view by providing aural cover for disturbances in the image, they work to absorb the spectator into the film's diegesis, and it is the diegesis that does the real work of providing cover for the visual discontinuity that characterizes almost all film practice. In this sense, Altman writes, "The referent of Hollywood sound is not the pro-filmic scene at all, but a narrative constructed as it were 'behind' that scene, a narrative that authorizes and engenders the scene, and of which the scene itself is only a signifier."[13] Or, as he goes on to argue about point-of-audition sound in particular (i.e., sound that the film marks as being heard from a particular place within the diegetic world and which would therefore seem to be a case where spatial realism trumps narrative intelligibility), this sound "always has the effect of luring this listener into the diegesis not at the point of enunciation of the sound but at the point of its audition."[14] That is to say, far from simply connoting a sense of spatial realism, point-of-audition sound interpellates the spectator by placing him directly into the narrative and providing him with the sensation that he controls the sound-image relationship. Because the spectator hears the sound as if he were himself within the diegesis, the spectator is not addressed by the actors, but rather seems to overhear them.

Again, all of this is dramatically complicated by the Marx Brothers, whose relationship to studio-era narrative and its carefully synchronized soundtrack is hardly paradigmatic. Altman's model for narrative-dominant point-of-audition sound does hold true for many moments in the Marx Brothers' films. Early in *Duck Soup*, for instance, a large diplomatic party waits for the arrival of Rufus T. Firefly (Groucho). After he is announced, the party sings the end of the Freedonian national anthem, pausing in silence at its end so that Groucho may enter in full pomp. After several versions of this song, the film cuts to Groucho lying in a large bed, where the line of the anthem reemerges muffled and at lower amplitude, thus suggesting a spatial relation between the two rooms. While the absorption into the film's narrative here may not be as powerful as the absorption at work in films the principle interest of which is a story (and not, say, a series of gags), this particular construction of image and sound does provide a deeper sense of the diegetic world as extending beyond the boundaries that are visible onscreen and thus into what seems to be an extensive and realized diegetic space.

But these films are also full of examples in which the actual aural construction of narrative space is considerably less classical in nature than this example from *Duck Soup*. In the debutante ball sequence of *Monkey Business*, for instance, Groucho talks with the gangster Joe Helton, his putative employer:

> HELTON: Say, you're a funny kind of duck, but I like you. You stuck by me, and I'll stick by you.
>
> *[GROUCHO claps him on the shoulder, clasps his hand and addresses him in a Texan drawl.]*
>
> GROUCHO: Sheriff, I ain't much on flowery sentiments, but there's somethin' I jes' got to tell yuh. . . . Shucks, man, I'd be nuthin' but a pizenous varmint and not fitten to touch the hem of yo' pants if I didn't tell you you've treated me squar, mighty squar, and I ain't fergettin' it.
>
> *[With bowed legs, he walks into the drawing room, past a couple standing in the doorway, the MAN wearing a cowboy outfit. Then he comes back towards HELTON, grabbing the MAN's ten-gallon hat as he passes.]*
>
> Sheriff, I ain't fergettin'.
>
> *[He goes off in the foreground with his legs bowed, wearing the hat. Sound of a horse neighing.]*
>
> Whoa theah, Bessie, whoa theah.
>
> *[Hoofbeats. HELTON and his guests burst out laughing.]*[15]

The gag here begins with Groucho's transposition of Helton's gangster idiom (which itself references a contemporaneous cycle of gangster films) into mock-Western patois (a kind of slant reference to that genre). The irony at work here, like the *mise-en-abyme* of Chevalier, does not really, as Bordwell suggests, "encourage us to read filmic space as story space" nor does it contribute to what Altman calls "a narrative that authorizes and engenders the scene." Rather, it suggests that viewers read filmic space and narrative as somehow referring beyond themselves to *other* film spaces and narratives. And like Groucho's bit as a radio announcer, the western joke is self-referential down to its conclusion, the laughter of the party guests within the scene. Here, Helton's gangster and the extras at the party direct their laughter at Groucho's performance, thus aligning their response with our own. At the same time, however, we understand Helton's laughter as in an important sense inadequate: he gets the joke, we could say, but he doesn't understand the extent to which he is also part of its target.

Furthermore, although it begins with the same medium close-up sound that Altman identifies as typical of the era, the construction of sound space here is of particular interest because it ends with a sound effect that is entirely unmotivated by the film's diegesis: a series of phantom hoofbeats that accompany Groucho's offscreen departure. After Groucho leaves the frame, he continues to speak, first by making the sound of a neighing horse and then by speaking to this imaginary horse ("Whoa theah, Bessie, whoa theah"). The soundtrack then lowers the amplitude of his voice, creating an instance of point-of-audition (we hear him speak as Helton and his guests do) that extends our sense of filmic space. Yet directly following this rather patient, classical construction, the soundtrack adds a series of hoofbeats that are not produced by a visible object. The effect is of a phantom sound creating a phantom space. There is no horse and no self-sufficient, diegetic world within which that horse exists. It is as if the excess of this verbal joke—the two mock accents, from Helton and Groucho—has bled through the surface of the film's soundtrack and penetrated the aural and spatial construction that would contain them. A bit of humorous dialogue actually begins to motivate the film's form. And while we could read the hoofbeats as a kind of parasitism, a confounding of an aural expectation in which mimicry of an imagined animal becomes the "real" thing, the aural figure of the hoofbeats also references the constructed nature of the film's soundtrack. The phantom sounds connote not an actual offscreen horse but rather the cinema's ability to conjure such an animal. This is not the presentation of an animal, but rather the image of the presentation of an animal.

Like Harpo's consumption of the hotel telephone, this humor runs through the middle term of the human body. If the absorption of new technologies of sound representation caused the cinema to redefine itself, the western gag makes clear that the addition of sound altered the nature of the screened human body. In the western gag, an offscreen body and its offscreen voice stumble upon themselves to create a disembodied sound. The accompanying laughter is the result of a *punctum* not of sentiment but of humor. We had expected the continued alignment of Groucho's voice and body, even as we imagined them offscreen. This joke occurs offscreen almost by necessity, where the classical alignment of voice and body finds room to loosen into the spectral and nonreferential. At stake here and elsewhere in these films is the Hollywood cinema's structuration of voice and body and the relationship of this structuration to that cinema's strategies of formal and ideological containment. Many of the Marx Brothers' gags work by selectively mangling the relationship between the synchronized voice and its classical body. If Groucho and Chico give body to the aural excess that accompanied sound synchronization (in particular, to the particularity of accented speech), Harpo figures the negation of synchronization itself. Through this dialectic of excess and negation, the performers form a limiting case for the impact of classical, synchronized sound on the screened body.

Like the repeated references to the contest between sound technologies, the split between voice and body that is evident in the western gag has an industrial history. The studios initially understood the actor's voice as a separate and detachable commodity, in keeping with the early sense that sound films were simply silent films with the (often only partial) addition of synchronized sound. Economic and technological factors contributed to a colloquial sense of the star's fragmented persona, a screened image separable from her broadcast voice. Gradually, the industry would come to unite body and voice in the actor's specificity—her individual "presence"—and this specificity would in turn license the sense that voice and body, separated in the recording process, reconstituted in postproduction, and then unified in exhibition, cohered naturally onscreen.

Industry practice in the transitional era provides a sense of the instability of this combination. Just as sound engineers initially advocated for perceptual fidelity and then settled upon a system that favored intelligibility (with selective inclusions of the fidelity model such as point-of-audition sound), the industry of the transitional era went through several phases in thinking about the sonic aspects of the actor's voice. Crafton dubs these phases the quality, naturalistic, and hybrid models of spoken dialogue. The initial, quality phase assumed that the actor's voice should be "modeled to an ideal vocal standard derived from the legitimate stage."[16] Soon after this, producers shifted to the idea that the quality voice was stilted and artificial, preferring instead the naturalistic tones of specific voices. And finally, the industry settled upon a hybrid model whereby "vocal style had to be intelligible and intelligent, fit the character and dramatic situation, and, most important, convey a sense of illusionistic 'presence.' "[17] That is, vocal style—like sound scale and many other formal qualities of the studio cinema—served a twofold goal: it had to serve the interests of narrative while at the same time serving as a marker of realism in the Aristotelian and naturalist senses of the term. Each of these goals depended upon the voice's proper synchronization with onscreen bodies.

The instability of the attempt to combine voice and body while preserving a sense of stylistic uniformity is especially evident in the early sound comedy, whose origins lay not in the proper stage but in the more accented environs of vaudeville. Henry Jenkins suggests that early sound comedies display a tension within the studio system as that system attempted to domesticate the tradition of stage vaudeville. These comedies, he writes, "cannot be fully explained through reference either to classical Hollywood norms or the vaudeville aesthetic but represent some overlap or interplay between the two formal systems."[18] Early sound comedies, in this account, are one more instance of attempts by the classical paradigm to assert itself in the face of the era's wild stylistic and technological diversity, which constantly threatened to bare the machine.

Yet the idea of "overlap or interplay" does not get at the parodic edge of a film like *Animal Crackers*. In that film, Groucho parodies the diction of Eugene O'Neill's *Strange Interlude*, Margaret Dumont mocks the Anglicized accent of the proper stage, and Chico's burlesque-Italian discovers a fellow denizen of the Lower East Side in the seemingly posh Roscoe W. Chandler and his masked accent. Between the ridiculousness of the stage and the revelation of an actor's "real" voice, *Animal Crackers* repeatedly sends up competing ideas about the proper nature of the onscreen voice. That is, the action of parody takes the conventions of a competing formal system and turns them into the material of laughter. In each of these examples, the film celebrates the epistemic sophistication of the audience, which recognizes this formal competition. But the film's burlesque of vocal strategies finds its most interesting expression in the relationship between these voices and their screened bodies. *Animal Crackers* ends, after all, in prostrate, bodiless silence, Harpo having knocked an entire party unconscious with an ecstatic dispersal of pesticide.

In these sorts of ways, many sound slapstick comedies play with and rearticulate the coherence that producers sought in the imbrication of image and sound. In this they reflect upon the material heterogeneity of the medium. In these films, laughter is often a mark of excesses internal to the medium and its consequent inability to achieve the perfect replication of its ideological ends. While not necessarily liberating, this laughter often functions as a mark of rupture. In the Marx Brothers' work, it is the mute Harpo that most embodies the problems inherent in the unity of voice and body. He whistles, he slaps his knees, he takes big falls that other characters do not. Many of the sounds he makes have the sound of sound effects: they are the commenting noises familiar from the cartoon. In this way, Harpo challenges the ontology of the sound cinema as that ontology has been put through the sieve of synchronized sound.

Harpo's challenge to this order can be described as a contest between classical and "grotesque" bodies, a contest that is here played out not strictly within the body, but in the body's refusal or acceptance of linguistic exchange. The classical canon, Bakhtin wrote, presents an entirely finished, completed, strictly limited body, which is shown from the outside as something individual. That which protrudes, bulges, sprouts, or branches off (when a body transgresses its limits and a new one begins) is eliminated, hidden, or moderated. All orifices of the body are closed. The basis of the image is the individual, strictly limited mass, the impenetrable façade. The opaque surface and the body's "valleys" acquire an essential meaning as the border of a closed individuality that does not merge with other bodies and with the world. All attributes of the unfinished world are carefully removed, as well as all the signs of its inner life.[19]

The idea here is that rather than sound itself imposing limits on the screened body, then, it is the spoken word—in particular, the regions of the spoken word that are most directly connected to sense-making—that structure and contain the body. The body is understood merely as the visible evidence of a larger, coherent subject. In the classical picture, language is an instrument through which an already formed subject expresses himself, and language and the material world have no say in this constitution. These comedies instead shake the Etch-a-Sketch: here, the screened subject in the form of the Brothers is only tenuously classical or Cartesian, and in the case of Harpo, he is studiously neither. Harpo personifies the festive and grotesque aspects of these comedies. Never uttering a word, never entering into the social contract inherent in verbal expressions, frequently negating the dialogue of his co-stars, Harpo maintains his grotesquerie by virtue of his silence.[20]

Duck Soup provides a salient example of the grotesque body and its slanted relationship to synchronized sound. Pinky (Harpo) has been hired to spy on Firefly (Groucho) by a diplomat from a neighboring state. After some business during which Pinky conducts a phone conversation by using a series of horns, Firefly takes notice of him and begins to ask a series of questions. Harpo's answers take the figure of various tattoos on his body:

FIREFLY: Say, who are you, anyway?

[PINKY *pulls up his coat sleeve, and we see . . .* PINKY'S *face tattooed on his arm. . . .*]

I don't go in much for modern art. Have you got anything by one of the old masters?

[PINKY *pulls up his other sleeve; oriental music is heard. Close-up of a girl tattooed on his arm. She does a belly dance in time to the music as* PINKY *flexes his muscles.*]

Not bad! . . . You don't happen to have her telephone number?

[PINKY *drops his collection of horns and pulls up his shirt.* FIREFLY *copies the number off* PINKY's *side* . . .]

Say, you could be a big help to me. Where do you live?

[PINKY *starts to pull open his shirt. A closer shot of the two of them as* PINKY *displays a picture of a dog kennel tattooed on his chest.* FIREFLY *leans forward to look.*]

Well, it's not much of a place, but it's home.

[PINKY *beckons him closer, and he leans forward.*]

Meow!

[*A dog's head appears at the kennel door, seen in close-up, and barks loudly. Resume on* PINKY *and* FIREFLY, *who leap back in alarm.*][21]

From its odd, literal tattoos that recast symbolic exchange as a series of deictic references to its series of sound effects that are motivated not by the requirements of narrative but by the instigations of the gag to its parodic reference to high modernist painting, this sequence displays an abundance of nonclassical tropes. I want to focus, however, on the odd, double-exposed image of Harpo and the dog (Figure 4.1 on page 98). With its refusal to signify the diegetic world behind the transparent plane of the screen, it constitutes a marked break with the classical image. And the odd, layered image does not quite identify him with the dog (although his gestures indicate that he lives in its doghouse) as much as it figures his body as permeable, uncontained, fecund—in a word, grotesque.

According to Bakhtin, the grotesque body "is looking for that which protrudes from the body, all that seeks to go out beyond the body's confines. Special attention is given to the shoots and branches, to all that prolongs the body and links it to other bodies or to the world outside."[22] Similarly, Harpo's body (and to a lesser extent, the bodies of Chico and Groucho) is an alternate figure for the body onscreen, one

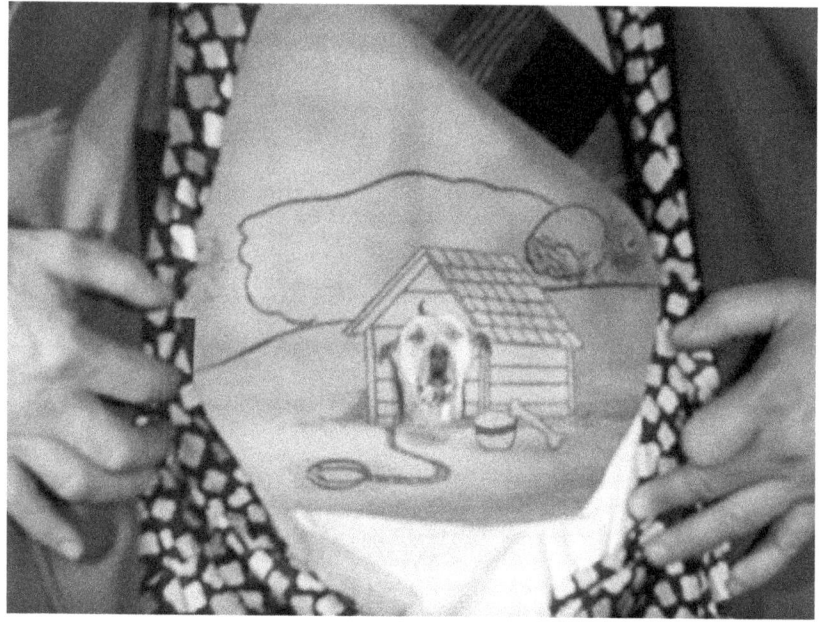

Figure 4.1. The grotesque body (*Duck Soup*).

that we are more accustomed to viewing in cartoons. Most importantly, this peculiar, doubled image is unimaginable on the body of a character that speaks. It belongs to the one character whose refuses to enter into the social contract of linguistic exchange, thereby preserving a place at the margins of representation. These jokes work by moving between the literality of Harpo's visions and the "proliferations" of Groucho's speech, between the lack and the excess at work in synchronized sound.[23]

Monkey Business and *Duck Soup* are limit cases for Bordwell's model of the sound era as defined both by its attachment to the devices of narrative and by its configuration of a classical, impermeable body. Those films do possess (somewhat) coherent narratives and most of the bodies within them conform to classical, Cartesian strictures. Yet their individual gags—not their narratives—provide the underlying justification for much of their sound practice, and some of their bodies resist classicization and put forth instead a fragmented, almost antihuman account of the body. As Jenkins notes, these films are evidence of the classical paradigm at work to absorb a countertradition of stage vaudeville. Yet at the same time, they often take the resistance to such absorption as their subject. Harpo's half-animal body gathers its force from the resolutely classical bodies around him. (This idea is made apparent in the tall blondes that he chases from frame to frame.) Groucho's accented speech whips itself into its frenzies of excess by virtue of the proper stage accents that surround him. These forces of classicization and resistance form the two poles upon which the Marx Brothers' films turn.

This bipolarity of the early sound cinema reveals what Miriam Hansen has called "the two faces of American cinema: the classical norm . . . and the seemingly nonclassical, or less classical, undercurrent of genres that thrive on something other than, or at the very least, oblique to the classical norm."[24] Just as early Soviet films, says Hansen, "urge us to reconsider the relationship between classical cinema and modernism, a relationship that within cinema studies has been thought of as an opposition, as one of fundamentally incompatible registers," these comedies suggest the fissures within the classical model itself.[25] The fissures lie not simply in our theoretical models of that cinema, but in the medium's very self-definition. The modernity of these comedies lies in their contestation of classical structures of narration and its containment of the monstrous, post-Cartesian body. Harpo's grotesque body and Groucho's excessive speech are examples of a plurality, a heterogeneity, and a series of negations in the middle of the Hollywood cinema.

Given the success of early sound comedies like *Monkey Business*, we could say that the classical cinema was never fully classical—least of all in its transition to sound. Instead, these comedies show the medium both reflecting upon and working to define itself in a moment of formal and technological instability. In these actions, they reveal the heterogeneity of the medium, its plural material bases. If the exemplar text for a classical cinema is one in which this instability has disappeared into the seams of narration and formalization, these comedies point out a disunity at the heart of the system itself. Like his nibbling the telephone in *The Cocoanuts*, Harpo's odd tattoos, with their queer literalization of the film image, figure the very negation of technologies of reference, the impossibility of their fantasies of transfer and expression.

5

Hollywood, Television, and the Case of Ernie Kovacs

THE COMEDY OF SELF-REFERENCE took on a decidedly different tone in the years between the establishment of aesthetic and technological norms for the sound film and the expansion of the television market, a period that coincided with the height of the studios' economic power. The system of production, the technological bases, and the stylistic conventions of Hollywood cinema largely stabilized after the transition to synchronized sound and would remain consistent until the slow dissolution of the studio system, the adoption of widescreen and new color processes, and the spread of commercial television. This environment of relative stability, combined with an absence of powerful performer-directors, seems to have been less fertile ground for comic self-reference, which, like the operational aesthetic with which it shares a history, is legible as a response to the newness of different technologies and mediums; most of the films under consideration in the earlier chapters are sites at which this newness and aesthetic potential is negotiated between the industry, individual artists, and audiences. No longer ruled by an instinct of curiosity about a new medium or technology, the comedy of self-reference of these years is on the whole more knowing and even aggressive about its relationship to both the formal conventions and to the institution of Hollywood itself.

Thomas Schatz has characterized the forties as a kind of paradox for the film industry: Hollywood was in the very middle of its "golden age," producing many of the films that now represent, in public memory, the cherished object of Hollywood itself, while it was at the same time working against the forces that would eventually send the industry into decline. In the early part of the decade, producers were hobbled by declining European markets for their product, government interference in the form of antitrust action and anticommunist fighting, and a series of protracted labor battles. The war changed all of this and moved the industry out of its post-Depression doldrums: a new ideological consensus made the broadly interventionist and sometimes progressive messages of much of its output acceptable to the country as a whole; antitrust action temporarily disappeared while the government set about propping up the industry and engaging it, both formally and informally, to produce films for the war effort; and huge influxes of capital into the war industries gave workers the disposable income to see movies on a more reliable basis.[1] The years 1940 and 1941 would mark the industry's highest outputs of feature films (both previously and thereafter), while studio profits reached $119.9 million in 1946, a tenfold increase over 1940. Attendance also peaked in the early postwar years—before the widespread availability of television—when the industry averaged 90 million admissions a year in a country of 140 million people.[2]

Studio-produced physical comedies of the era reflect this economic stability and the corresponding absence of technological and stylistic change either by more insistently breaking with aesthetic norms or by articulating an ambivalent relationship to Hollywood as an institution. Ole Olsen and Chic Johnson's *Hellzapoppin'* (1941), with its intense and repeated focus on the fact and nature of film, is an example of the former strategy. The film is organized entirely around a series of self-referential gags and distanciation jokes. Indeed, *Hellzapoppin'* opens on a theater marquee and then a projection booth, where Shemp Howard (formerly and latterly of the Three Stooges) rather haphazardly threads the movie that we're about to see through the projector. It is apparently a Hollywood musical, but the grand staircase on which its chorus sings shortly flattens, sending its dancers into a fiery hell, over which the credits roll (and which themselves end with a sign that reads ". . . any similarity between HELLZAPOPPIN' and a motion picture is purely coincidental"). Over the film's theme, dozens of actors dressed as devils do the work of making this nether-Hollywood run, roasting actresses on spits, for instance, and subjecting actors marked as movie performers to torture (a man in coat and tails, for instance, is stuffed into a 55-gallon drum marked "Canned Guy"). Olsen and Johnson soon appear out of a taxicab ("That's the first taxi driver that ever went straight where I told him to"). Unsatisfied with the punishment they have enacted on their driver, they address Shemp Howard in the projection booth, telling him to rewind the film, and we are given the previous minute played backward (Figure 5.1). They then run off the set into a gaggle of camera equipment and the man who seems to be directing the movie. He gives them a script, which he identifies as "a picture about a picture about *Hellzapoppin'*." And this launches an interior film that, like these first ten minutes, is a veritable catalogue of self-referential gags, from further scenes in Shemp's projection booth to still photographs that move and talk to a series of gags that utilize writing on the surface of the screen.

With its repeated and transparent address to its film audience, *Hellzapoppin'* is legible as a filmed staging of Olsen and Johnson's successful Broadway play of the same name, a play that owed its structure and mode of address to the tradition of vaudeville. *Hellzapoppin'* is, in this sense, considerably less classical than even a film like *Sherlock Jr.*, which, despite its unusual form and obvious interest in the medium of cinema, seeks to contain this reference within the bounds of its narrative. Despite the fact that *Hellzapoppin'* is itself structured around these gags, however, the film has a much more knowing and aggressive tone toward its medium. One senses that it is the very familiarity and ubiquity of the feature-length Hollywood film that calls forth *Hellzapoppin*'s great

Figure 5.1. Olsen and Johnson in the projection booth (*Hellzapoppin'*, 1941).

volume of distantiation gags, as if the comedy of self-reference can no longer license the thought that was produced in simpler and more elegant form in Keaton's work. That is, the fact that the film throws up so many of these jokes and gags suggests an underlying anxiety that none of them will land, perhaps because audiences were now so familiar with the technological and conventional bases that the movie lampoons. (It is also no accident that the film was produced at Universal, a studio whose commercial strategy relied upon the production of B-features and which therefore had something of a slant relationship to the aesthetic norms of the pictures produced by the majors.)

A somewhat less aggressive form of self-reference appears in the Bob Hope and Bing Crosby "road" pictures of the era. These movies also feature a distinctly presentational mode of address, one that is licensed by the fact that Hope and Crosby are themselves playing vaudevillians, something that the movies play for irony. In *Road to Utopia* (Walker, 1945), for instance, this address is supplemented by the fact that the humorist Robert Benchley plays a narrator who interrupts the film—from an apparent "tear" in the celluloid or screen itself—in order to comment upon the movie's flaws. In a scene that recalls the opening of Jerry Lewis's *The Bellboy* (1960) fifteen years later, Benchley addresses the audience at the outset of the film, explaining that, "For one reason or another, the motion picture which you're about to see is not very clear in spots. As a matter of fact, it was made in order to demonstrate how to make a motion picture and at the same time win an Academy Award." (The film was indeed nominated, for Melvin Frank and Norman Panama's screenplay.) The film also includes a scene in which Hope and Crosby ride a dog sled across an Alaskan prairie, only to see the Paramount logo appear on the mountain before them. ("Get a load of that bread and butter!" Hope says.) While considerably less aggressive than the jokes in *Hellzapoppin'*, these jokes work to license the film's deviation from narrative norms and to encourage audiences to adopt a position of distanced pleasure from the story and spectacle while at the same time flattering them by acknowledging their awareness that Hollywood product is "hokum." It is this latter idea that marks their difference from the self-referential turns in the silent and early sound eras. (A similar movement from curiosity to sophistication occurs in television comedy, where the direct address of *Your Show of Shows* becomes the show-within-a-show form of, say, *The Mary Tyler Moore Show*, which itself then resurfaces in the knowing comedy of *30 Rock*. Interestingly, given this little history, one of the primary subjects of *30 Rock* is the lead character's anxiety about her status as an author.)

The question of the nature and basis of film sound, the locus of much of the Marx Brothers' Paramount comedies, continues to surface in the war era, if now belatedly. The Three Stooges' Columbia-produced short *Micro-Phonies* (Bernds, 1945), for instance, relies for much of its humor upon the fuzzy ontological status of recorded sound, and on the action of lip-sync in particular. Entering a radio studio where the Stooges are involved in a bit of play with a record player, an influential woman mistakes Curly for a talented soprano. He goes on to perform at the woman's "musical party" that evening, where he reprises this role for a crowd in formal wear and where he lip-syncs over the voice of the actual soprano. In addition to the evident absurdity of Curly in drag, the success of these gags depends not upon the premise that the recorded voice approaches or can even stand in for live sound (as it had in advertisements for recording and broadcast technologies for many decades), but upon sound done in *mise-en-abyme* as well as upon the film's reliance upon the power of *synchresis*, like the torn fabric that the movie lays over Moe pulling Larry's hair or the slide whistles that accompany each slip and fall. Notably, *Micro-Phonies* opens on an image of the station's call letters and a set of see-sawing, subhuman vocalizations that we soon learn come from Larry and Curly as they work with a wrench, thereby asserting their oppositional relation to clarity of sound and dialogue. In this sense, The Three Stooges take the carnivalesque body and style of Harpo Marx (and other, earlier comedians) and more fully transpose this aesthetic into the environment of the sound film.

In keeping with the knowing tone of *Hellzapoppin'* and the Hope-Crosby films, many of the shorts made at Warner Bros.' "Termite Terrace" in the forties and early fifties, from *Hollywood Steps Out* (Avery, 1941) to *Swooner Crooner* (Tashlin, 1944), lampoon industry personalities and stars and, through a particularly aggressive and distinct form of grotesquerie, work to articulate some of the ontological difference of the animated cartoon. (This seems to have been due in part to the influence and genius of Tex Avery, who served as a director in Leon Schlesinger's unit and who was a key influence on Frank Tashlin's and Jerry Lewis's film work of the late fifties and early sixties.) The animators at Termite Terrace actively caricatured and parodied the industry in the forms of individual stars and the star system, the particular publicity of the movie industry, and to a lesser extent, the formal features of Hollywood film. In Donald Crafton's fascinating account of these films, this caricature is highly ambivalent—an aggressive gesture toward the system as a whole as well as a sublimation of these feelings into the realm of the aesthetic, a feature that sometimes joins these cartoons to Keaton's account of the medium.[3]

Bacall to Arms (Clampett, 1946), for instance, is structured around a representation of the filmgoing experience itself, and it stresses the grotesque possibilities and freedoms of the animated short, with particular emphasis on the representation of sexual desire and violence. The short opens on a theater marquee that reads "Next Week: Ann Sheridan in Selected Shorts" (Sheridan was then a contract player for Warner Bros.) and takes us inside a theater, where an audience of anthropomorphized animals watches first a newsreel that depicts a man's attempt to use the wartime technology of radar for the "peaceful" means of alerting his family to the presence of his mother-in-law and then what stands in for a feature film. This "film" is composed of a series of short caricatures of Humphrey Bogart and Lauren Bacall ("Bogey Go Cart" and "Laurie Be Cool") that burlesque Bogart's trademark casual aggression and Bacall's suggestive speech and movements. What is more, the interior film repeatedly breaches the surface of its screen, first in a joke about the MGM lion (the screen quickly rotates to reveal that the roar of this lion comes from the fact that his tail is on fire), then in a comment that the Bogart caricature addresses to a man in the audience ("Hey fat boy, this is the beginning of the feature—if you want to see how it ends, sit down!"), and finally in a series of gags that recall *Uncle Josh at the Moving Picture Show* (Porter, 1902) and other yokel-at-the-movies early shorts within which a suave-looking wolf becomes more and more overheated by the words and gestures of Bacall. His antics become so exaggerated, in fact, that the Bogart caricature reaches out of the frame and shoots him in the theater (an action that oddly leaves Bogart in blackface). The film is in this sense far more aggressive in its parody and self-reference than the earlier films under consideration here, an aspect that it shares with *Hellzapoppin'*.

Viewed against the medium of live-action cinema, the animated cartoon reestablishes the presence of the human hand, as if in opposition to its (and the world's) mechanization. This is why so much animation angrily, if also impotently, returns constantly to images of mechanization—here in the form of our automatic registration of a performer's caricature, as if to point out how easily the persons of Bacall and Bogart, even the moviegoing experience itself, can be reduced, thus both attacking and reveling in our automatic relation to them. In one sense, this is the problem that Tashlin (who himself worked in Termite Terrace) later takes up in his work with Lewis, in a series of movies that frequently raise the issue of the Idiot's relation to the animated image. (I can't conjure a funnier still image from a movie than Lewis posing for Dorothy Malone, in *Artists and Models* [1955], as she sketches a cartoon mouse.)

The period of relative stability that surrounded the war came to a quick end at the end of the decade. The fifties and early sixties saw a substantial alteration in production processes as the studio system came under assault from the widespread expansion of television, a corresponding decline in movie attendance, the divestiture of the studios' exhibition arms as a result of the Paramount decree, and larger changes in the demographics of film viewership. These basic economic effects were also attended by the activities of the House Un-American Activities Committee and the difficulties studios faced in responding to rapidly changing social mores, which were occurring as the children of the Baby Boom grew into adolescence. As a result of these circumstances, Hollywood-wide production dwindled to a total of just 143 films in 1963, down from the figure of 379 in 1941.[4] To put matters in terms of attendance, by 1960, the peak of film admissions than had been achieved in 1946 had been cut by more than half.[5]

Changes in admissions were accompanied by changes within the studio production structure. By the mid-fifties, the major studios were no longer overseeing individual films from the first phases of preproduction through their consequent production and distribution. Largely as a result of the 1948 Paramount decree, they became distributors of films that were produced by a network of independent producers to whom they also rented space and equipment. Janet Staiger has called this new process of production "the package-unit system" (thereby distinguishing it from the "producer-unit" system that preceded it) because the process centered around not a producer and his "unit" within a studio but around individual "packages" of talent created for individual films.[6] "Rather than an individual company containing the source of the labor and materials," she writes,

> the entire industry became the pool for these. A producer organized a film project: he or she secured financing and combined the necessary laborers (whose roles had been previously defined by the standardized production structure and subdivision of work categories) and the means of production (the narrative "property," the equipment, and the physical sites of production).[7]

This meant that even though the same people worked on films that continued to bear the labels of the same studios that only ten years previously would have controlled every part of their production and release, the studios now simply financed and distributed films, which were in reality organized by independent producers, talent agents, and big-name creative talent.

As the next chapter will describe, these changes in the structure of production are sometimes directly addressed in Lewis's work. Lewis's *The Patsy* (1964), for example, uses the nature of the package-unit system, and the ways in which the new system shifted power toward a small number of successful actors and actresses, as the basis for its plot and the motivation for its gags. Lewis directed, co-wrote, and starred in the film, which begins with the death, in a plane crash, of the famous comic "Wally Brandford." More concerned with their careers than with the death of their employer, Brandford's team of handlers decides to find and groom a new talent to take his place. As they form this plan, Lewis appears as the inept Stanley (a reprise of his role in *The Bellboy*), and the managers, for reasons that remain mysterious to say the least, are immediately sold on his star power. As is the case in many of his self-directed films, the story of *The Patsy* involves Lewis coming into his own as a star and claiming his authorial power.

In addition to these changes, Hollywood's actual technologies of representation had changed, in large part as a series of attempts to differentiate film products from their televised counterparts by means of color and widescreen processes. In 1950, color films represented 15 percent of Hollywood's total output; by 1955, a full 50 percent of all films were produced in color.[8] It is perhaps no coincidence that these statistics are roughly correlated with the spread of television—in 1950, 9 percent of American homes had a television; by 1955, the figure was 65 percent.[9] The studios' proprietary widescreen technologies ranged in sophistication from Paramount's VistaVision, which ran 35mm film stock horizontally through the camera in order to produce a wider aspect ratio, to various short-lived multiple-projection and anamorphic processes (e.g., Cinerama and CinemaScope) that attempted to produce a total and immersive spectatorial experience. (Although his invention was invisible to spectators, Lewis himself contributed to this period of technological change by creating the video assist, a closed circuit video system that allowed directors to view takes immediately after their completion, thus creating another layer of authorial agency.) We could say that the economic environment of the fifties and early sixties created an atmosphere in which the formal declaration of cinematic specificity became something of a financial necessity.

In certain film comedies of the era, these senses of differentiation and specificity are the sources of parody. Tashlin's *The Girl Can't Help It* (1956) and *Will Success Spoil Rock Hunter?* (1957), for instance, begin with humorous acknowledgments of their CinemaScope technology. *The Girl Can't Help It* opens on the Twentieth-Century Fox logo in black and white and within the Academy aspect ratio. Tom Ewell then appears surrounded by various instruments of a band: he addresses the audience directly, actually pushing the film's vertical frames to the right and left, like sliding doors, thus dramatizing the wide CinemaScope ratio. Afterward, he announces the film's "gorgeous, life-like color by DeLuxe," thus initiating an onscreen transition from grayscale to the garish blues and reds that define the film's color palette. For its part, *Will Success Spoil Rock Hunter?* opens in color with Tony Randall seated a drum set to the far left side of the studio's logo; he appears to play the music that typically accompanies Fox's large pyramidal form surrounded by searchlights. The little prologue goes on to include a series of mock advertisements, thus reflecting upon (and undermining) the use of the technology as a means of product differentiation, as well as pointing out that moviegoers are spared noisy commercials. Throughout the fifties, television is everywhere the subtext of film comedy.

For that reason, I want to linger over the question of television comedy in the form of Ernie Kovacs's work. Kovacs's work gives us a chance to see the comedy of self-reference in another medium (as well as during the years in which this medium became commercially viable) and because it will help to reveal something about Lewis's anxiety about the televisual. In the fifties, television was largely understood as a medium for live performance, one that was broadcast and not exhibited, and hence staked out an entirely different temporality than that of the cinema. As Lyn Spigel has argued, "television at its most ideal promised to bring to audiences not merely an illusion of reality as in the cinema, but a sense of 'being there,' a kind of *hyperrealism*."[10] Television shared (and indeed continues to share) something with the live stage, but it generated a wholly different kind of reception, a situation in which people understood themselves as an audience that was simultaneously public and private. Television offered viewers a new and distinct form of publicity insofar as it did not require them to leave their homes and sit in a theater with strangers but at the same time, through the experience of broadcasting, connected them invisibly but palpably to a larger communications infrastructure. As the settings of so many sitcoms suggest, this experience was inextricable from the nature of suburbia itself, the dawn of which spelled the end of the great urban cinemas and with which what we could call the private publicity of television enjoyed a symbiotic relationship.

In his early book on television, Raymond Williams argued that radio and television had a fundamentally different technological history, and therefore a fundamentally different formal character, than previous tools of mass communication. "Radio and television," he wrote, "were *systems primarily designed for transmission and reception as abstract processes, with little or no definition of preceding content.*"[11] That is, the mediums of radio and television came into existence first as technologies of communication and then as bearers of specific messages. Regardless of the historical inaccuracies this account carries (particularly in its implication that the content of the cinema was somehow foreordained), Williams's point is of major interest in thinking about comedies of the era: radio and television were conceived at a historical moment during which it was possible to imagine the various *processes* of mass communication before imagining actual instances of that communication. That is, if the cinema eventually came into historical being as a mode of mass communication, this was not something that its various creators had in mind during the process of its invention. Cinema, we could say, matured as a medium of mass communication. Radio and television, on the other hand, had the goal of that communication as the reason for their very being.

For Williams, this historical fact is significant because it means that the medium of television is characterized by "two apparently paradoxical yet deeply connected tendencies of modern urban industrial living: on the one hand mobility, on the other hand the more apparently self-sufficient family home."[12] This meant that, despite evident similarities of both form and content, television created greatly different publics than the cinema. This is borne out in the economic shock that the film industry bore during the spread of television ownership. The fifties saw not only a great boom in the country's general population but also a massive transfer of the middle-class population to suburban areas around the urban communities that had sustained the great downtown, first-run movie theaters and the filmgoing culture that they propagated. In tandem with a domestic political situation dominated by the concerns of the Cold War, this population transfer resulted in new censorship regimes inside and outside federal and local governments. Television was uniquely suited to this situation because, according to Williams, it "served an at-once mobile and home-centred way of living"—it constituted "a form of *mobile privatization*."[13] Transmission of its content may have been centralized, but its reception was thoroughly private.

For Williams, the formal character of television proceeds from its distinct combination of centralized transmission and decentralized reception. These economic and technological circumstances led to a "new kind of communication phenomenon," what he characterized as an aesthetic of "flow."[14] The flow of television separates it from earlier forms of mass media that traded in discrete, self-contained objects. This is evident, for instance, in the distinction between the serial and the series. A serial—take, for example, a novel like Dickens's *Our Mutual Friend*—is composed of a dramatized action divided into discrete sections that together form a whole. A series, on the other hand—any television situation comedy, or network police procedurals like the *CSI* franchise—is composed not in terms of dramatic continuity but in the continuity of characters and of the ways, or styles, in which they relate. The crucial difference here is the means by which the two forms generate continuity. As Williams put it, on television "the apparently disjointed 'sequence' of items is in effect guided by a remarkably consistent set of cultural relationships: a flow of consumable reports and products, in which the elements of speed, variety and miscellaneity can be seen as organizing: the real bearers of value."[15] That is, it is not that the televisual has no interest in structures of narration (if anything, the historical record points to the contrary), but that its structures of narration fall beneath the more totalizing organizational principles of "speed, variety and miscellaneity."

In the environment of early television, the comedy of self-reference took on a distinct cast, often working with just these principles. Television spurred new interest in and demand for vaudeville performers, whose acts were understood as well-suited to the medium of television as well as having been tested before live audiences, of which the television audience was a kind of distinct, if also huge, subspecies. This environment led to the broadcast of many variety-themed shows, which stressed direct address to their audiences (both in the studio and in suburban living rooms) and which often sought to articulate the ontological boundaries and possibilities of television as a distinct medium. As Spigel has noted, situation comedies of the early fifties moved freely between "legitimate," narrative-dominant sequences and more broadly presentational comedic address—the soon-to-be vestigial influence of the variety show—thereby offering opportunities for commenting upon themselves and their medium. She understands this action as both distancing viewers from the program and bringing them into more intimate relation with its performers, a technique that is familiar from silent film comedy:

> The self-reflexive strategies of early television worked in two, seemingly opposite, directions. On the one hand, self-reflexivity provided viewers with critical distance from everyday life—the ability to laugh at the stagy artifice of domesticity. On the other hand, it encouraged viewers to feel closer to the scene of action, as if they had an intimate connection to the scene. By acknowledging its own artifice and theatricality, the family comedy encouraged viewers to feel as if they had been let in on a joke, while at the same time allowing them to take that joke seriously.[16]

This can be seen, for instance, in the form of *The George Burns and Gracie Allen Show* when Burns moves between the set of the home to a stage in which he addresses his television audience, or in individual episodes of *I Love Lucy*, like one in which Lucille Ball goes behind her television set in order to stage a mock-commercial ("Lucy Does a TV Commercial," 1952).[17]

Ernie Kovacs forged a distinct place for himself within this environment. Unlike successful TV comedians like Burns, Kovacs, who was a generation younger, had not toured on the vaudeville circuit. Raised in an immigrant Hungarian family in Trenton, New Jersey, Kovacs was an amateur actor who eventually found his way into radio. At WTTM in Philadelphia, he developed a series of broadly comedic programs, including a quiz show (*The Kudra College of Knowledge*) that served to sell the wares of a local furrier and a weekday morning show (*Coffee with Kovacs*) that featured popular music, news, and disc jockey ad lib. Kovacs gained a reputation for radio acts that lay somewhere between gags and stunts; these acts often emphasized the distinct nature of both radio technology and the environment of radio's production and reception. Kovacs once stayed up for an entire week, for instance, in order to broadcast continuously from the New Jersey State Fair or took his listeners through a series of weekly flying lessons that involved strapping radio equipment into a small plane. A gag that is perhaps apocryphal actually mimics a device familiar from the early cinema, giving it a live twist: Kovacs supposedly took his microphone to the Trenton railyard and lay down on the tracks in order to capture what it felt like to be run over by a train.[18]

Fascinated by the new technology of television, Kovacs found a position as a booth announcer at WPTZ, the Philadelphia NBC affiliate, and this led to his first television programs, beginning with a local cooking show and a hybrid quiz and fashion program. Quickly thereafter, Kovacs developed his own morning shows (*3 to Get Ready*, *Time for Ernie*, and *Ernie in Kovacsland*), where he steadily built a reputation, locally and then nationally. The programs were low-budget, early-morning affairs that formed the template for the work that he later did in New York on the major networks and for which he is now remembered. The various programs on which he appeared throughout his career are too numerous to name here, but they include morning shows, extended stints as a replacement on late night programs, and a series of half-hour specials, like the now famous "no dialogue" show, which, aside from an announcement of the conceit, Kovacs performed entirely in pantomime. (Notably, this show, which occurred just after the Martin and Lewis act broke up, actually followed Lewis's first major television solo performance.) Kovacs's work was stitched together by his penchant for churning out vast volumes of material; a surreal, almost literary sensibility; and a gift for a manic (if also sociable) form of improvisation, the latter of which he maintained even in his recorded work. Notably, Kovacs also wrote a semiautobiographical and critically successful novel (*Zoomar*) about a high-minded television executive, and acted in several, now mostly forgotten, Hollywood films. Nevertheless, and perhaps because of the relative "difficulty" of his work, Kovacs never achieved the fame of Burns, Milton Berle, or Steve Allen. His self-produced shows have a defiant, anomalous, and television-specific form. They possess no narrative dimension whatsoever and are legible as broadcast ancestors of the variety stage, at the same time trading upon Kovacs's ability to perform comfortably within the flow of television. He is the broadcast ancestor of many comic YouTube personalities.

The mixture of Kovacs's highly referential sensibility, his unique inheritance of the variety stage, and public curiosity about the new medium of television led to rigorously self-referential comedy. At times, Kovacs's self-reference shares a posture and a style with movies such as *Hellzapoppin'* and *Road to Utopia*, as when, in an August 1951 episode of *Ernie in Kovacsland*, Kovacs does a straight monologue from Euripides's *Helen* only to interrupt himself to discourse on the nature of the play and then to communicate with the man in charge of his sound effects. And like *Hellzapoppin'* (or even *Sherlock Jr.*, to which Kovacs's work has sometimes been compared), Kovacs repeatedly took the camera past the edges of his sets or allowed one camera to show his audiences the form (and operator) of the other.[19]

Nevertheless, Kovacs's shows earn their spontaneity, an apparent sense of intimacy with their audience, and an interest in the specificity of television that is simply not present in film comedy of the time. It is the fact and nature of broadcasting, in combination with the possibilities of televised sound, that is articulated and emphasized in Kovacs's work and which extends from his morning shows of the early 1950s to the ABC Specials of 1961, which aired just before his untimely death. This interest does not take the knowing form of self-consciousness familiar from parody within an established medium but instead has some of the curiosity and philosophical impulse that is apparent in certain silent film comedies. Indeed, despite the familiarity of its device, an important aspect of the Euripides gag is that its spontaneity and the intimacy of its address are in an important sense medium-specific. Viewers knew that Kovacs's act—or perhaps more accurately, his "presence"—was being broadcast live (and, as he often admitted, without much rehearsal), hence that it possessed a peculiar sort of being. His performances were both present *and* distant, private *and* public. Kovacs took advantage of the distinct nature of this presence to play upon his relationship with his audience and to highlight the broadcast nature of the medium. Contrary to the image of television viewers as passive consumers (and in keeping with the commercial imperative to gauge viewership by means of volume of mail), for instance, Kovacs once invited his audience to mail in "artistic" pictures of their television sets ("snepshots") picking up a broadcast of *The Ernie Kovacs Show*—a kind of DIY surrealism.[20]

This intimacy was not established by simply playing with the possibilities of the new medium but often worked by drawing viewers' attention to the medium itself. A March 1951 episode of *It's Time for Ernie*, for instance, begins with Kovacs giving a short tutorial on how to tune a TV set. Around his neck, Kovacs wears a piece of plywood at the bottom of which is a series of dials. After an exchange with his cameraman, who has dollied in a bit too close ("Don't bump the desk please with these cheap cameras"), he explains that two of the knobs control the horizontal and vertical orientations of the image (i.e., the horizontal and vertical holds). He then twists these knobs and then contorts his lips to suggest that they are being pulled toward the frames of the imaginary set. In both cases, he mimes as if the contortion is causing him pain ("That's too far! That's too far! The other way!"). Here, the joke does not simply acknowledge the fact that viewers are "receiving" Kovacs and his performance through a particular technology, but stresses their own ability to play with the televised image as well as the distinct ontology of the performer within broadcast television, a situation that the gag figures as being "stuck" within it. The joke couldn't be further from one that might be staged on film, where the relative passivity of reception and the distinct pastness of the image call for an entirely different approach to gagging.

Like much early and more formalized theory of television, Kovacs's work displays an interest in liveness, but some of the more memorable work was indeed taped, even if it preserves images of liveness—like Bobby Lauher's blooper reel fall during his entrance as Tonto to Kovacs's German Lone Ranger, "Das Einsam Aufseher." A better word than live for this material is *broadcast*, a form of transmission that is utterly different from that of the cinema. A taped special such as *Kovacs on Music*, for instance, is not enunciated in the "this-happened-once" tense of film but rather in the "this-is-now" tense of television. We could say that cinema is, in this sense, fundamentally about the past (occurrences or history) whereas television, for Kovacs, is about the present (events or experience). And as Williams later described, broadcasting takes the form of flow: even if something is recorded, or replayed (as in the case of movies on television), it is always in an important sense instantaneous, interruptive, one element within a larger stream of transmission. (To be sure, movies are empirically part of a larger environment of production. But one does not experience them this way in a theater; television, on the other hand, always refers back to its own flow.) The concept of the blackout gag (a fragmentary, isolated gag without any surrounding narrative or even spatial context) is almost perfectly suited for this context; indeed, the blackout gag, by the way in which it announces itself as fragmentary and discrete, calls back to the larger flow in which it is situated. This means that the core difference between film and television comedy cannot be wholly captured by the polarity narrative/nonnarrative. Instead, we have, in a filmmaker like Lewis, a series of gags structured by environment or spatial context and, in a television comic like Kovacs, a series of blackout gags and sketches that reference the variety program. The former can of course accommodate itself to narrative (however weakly), whereas the latter insinuates itself (first at the level of the gag, then of the sketch or segment, then that of the program itself) into the flow of the medium by means of a more purely accretive structure.

What we might call Kovacs's theory of television is particularly well elaborated in the eight half-hour specials that Kovacs made for Dutch Masters cigars in 1961 and early 1962 and which are the final programs that he produced and wrote before his death. They are notable for having been produced under relative leisure: unlike most of Kovacs's earlier programs, which were cheap, live, and highly improvisational, the individual specials were well funded, planned and recorded over the course of an entire month.[21] This leisure was the result of the more lax production environment of early television and, more particularly, Kovacs's advantageous relationship with Dutch Masters, whose cigars he smoked on air and for whom he made a series of commercials. As Diana Rico has described it, Kovacs, usually dismissive if not outright hostile to executives of all stripes, was persuaded to speak with Dutch Masters after he noticed the vice president of its parent company carrying around several volumes of Berthold Brecht.[22] (As I will describe below, Brecht would become a major presence in the specials.) The specials aired on ABC and sometimes augmented, at one-month intervals, the series *Silents Please*, a silent film showcase that Kovacs hosted from the library of his Beverly Hills home.[23] The ABC specials are the work toward which all of Kovacs's earlier output marched, from the morning shows of a decade earlier that played with the broadcast ontology and production environments of network television to the programs on which he pioneered his distinct form of televised comedy. They imagine and achieve a particular sort of intimacy, one that is a relation between the performer, his audience, and the revelation of the medium and its conventions.

With the exception of the sixth episode, which reprises the "no dialogue" Eugene episode of 1957, the specials follow a single, highly distinct form that moves between a series of blackout gags, Silly Symphony-like set pieces that synchronize music to images linked less by narrative than association (and parody), and commercials for Dutch Masters cigars. Rico notes that "the basic structure of the specials was a refinement of the loose format [Kovacs] had devised for the 1959 *Kovacs on Music*. With eight or ten related blackouts popping up throughout the half hour, viewers would get a mixed bag of two or three longer sketches, some unrelated blackouts, and one or two lengthy 'sound-to-sight' pieces, the highlights of the show."[24] But this description suggests that the form of the specials is almost haphazard, which is certainly not the case. They are rigorous in their adherence to a recognizable form. The episodes (again excepting the sixth) are remarkably consistent in form, a fact that indicates that Kovacs understood both the set of specials as a coherent series (or unit) and that this particular form provided for the unification of the individual shows while at the same time giving room for the exploration of a series of themes.

We can be a bit more specific by taking one episode as typical of the rest. Episode Seven, which aired on December 12, 1961, has six major segments:

1. Professor Rensselaer Ewing and his miniature motorcycle [~3.5 minutes]

2. A series of blackout gags overlaid with "Die Morität von Mackie Messer" and intercut with an oscilloscope registration of the song [~3.5 minutes]

3. A Dutch Masters sponsorship announcement and commercial [~1 minute]

(*) Brief appearance of Rensselaer Ewing and his miniature motorcycle

4. A history of the Hollywood western (really, a series of blackout gags unified around this conceit) [~8 minutes]

(*) Brief appearance of Rensselaer Ewing and his miniature motorcycle

5. "The Story of a Drop of Water" (sight-to-sound piece) [~8 minutes]

6. Credits (rolled over Rensselaer Ewing and his miniature motorcycle) [~2.5 minutes]

In this case, as in each of the other specials, a single gag (Rensselaer Ewing and his miniature motorcycle) opens the show and is then repeated with variations throughout the episode. Around these variations-on-a-gag are first placed a series of unrelated blackout gags. After this, the show cuts to Kovacs in the production booth, announcing his Dutch Masters sponsorship, followed by a commercial for the cigars (created by and starring Kovacs and indistinguishable in tone and style from the rest of the show). Then, after returning briefly to the Ewing gag, the show stages its two set pieces: a parodic history of the Hollywood western and a "sight-to-sound" piece ("The Story of a Drop of Water"). All of this builds toward a kind of absurd climax or variation on the vaudeville showstopper, a credit sequence in which the character Rensselaer Ewing chases his motorcycle through an increasingly unlikely set of locales, like the Arctic and outer space.

The segmentation helps in this sense to point out a central problem for variety comedy: How does one generate nonnarrative continuity that manages to both facilitate humor and provide audiences with a sense of form? Kovacs solves this problem in a way that would be inherited later by Monty Python and other performers: a structuring gag calls back to our sense of the show as a whole (it serves a telescoping function, reminding us that we are seeing a single program) while the two series of blackout gags are stitched together, in the first case, by music ("Die Morität" and the oscilloscope) and, in the second, by voiceover (Kovacs narrating the history of the western). All of this is of course framed by the persona of Kovacs himself, whose performance is something like the show's dominant.

There are several interesting features to this form, not the least of which is that it allowed Kovacs to riff on a series of themes through the long march of the blackout gags. As I will detail below, the blackout gags frequently have to do with the relation between the comedian, violent acts, and his audience (in part because violent actions have a kind of finality that is well suited to the form of the blackout gag). A typical gag in segment 2, for instance, involves Bobby Lauher dressed as a stage magician: the magician's act involves shooting a vase with a pistol, but as he and his assistant come forward to take a bow, we see that he has instead shot her. Moreover, the blackout gags and their themes sometimes overlapped from episode to episode, as when Joe Mikolas, having shot Bobby Lauher during a track meet in episode four, shoots him again—through a television set no less—at the outset of episode five. As the duration of each segment indicates, Kovacs's form also left space for longer sketches, which could be plugged in more or less at will. These spaces could accommodate two separate sight-to-sound pieces (as in episode four, which depicts kitchen implements and foods dancing to calypso as well as people dressing to a piece of classical music); they also allowed Kovacs to organize a series of more closely related gags or short sketches into a more coherent whole (as in the history of the Hollywood western, above, or episode eight's survey of "the contemporary artisan," which includes short sketches with Tension Brett, a kind of fey modernist poet, and Miklo Schmolnar, a frustrated Hungarian sculptor). The form of the specials is therefore both rigid insofar as it guarantees each episode a sense of wholeness (as well as a relation to the other episodes) and elastic insofar as it accommodates (even represents a sense of) improvisation.

Many of these gags are fascinating examples of *mise-en-abyme*, from a camera operator who is shot in the eye by a gunman's bullet (in the aforementioned history of the western) to Kovacs's frequent appearances in the broadcast booth, where he sometimes speaks, on camera, with his actual crew. Instead of cataloguing these jokes, however, I want to pause on the first series of blackout gags and Kovacs's use of "Die Morität von Mackie Messer." Again excepting episode six, every one of the specials synchronizes its blackout gags to this song and intercuts them with an image of the song itself—the soundtrack run through an oscilloscope (see Figure 5.2).[25]

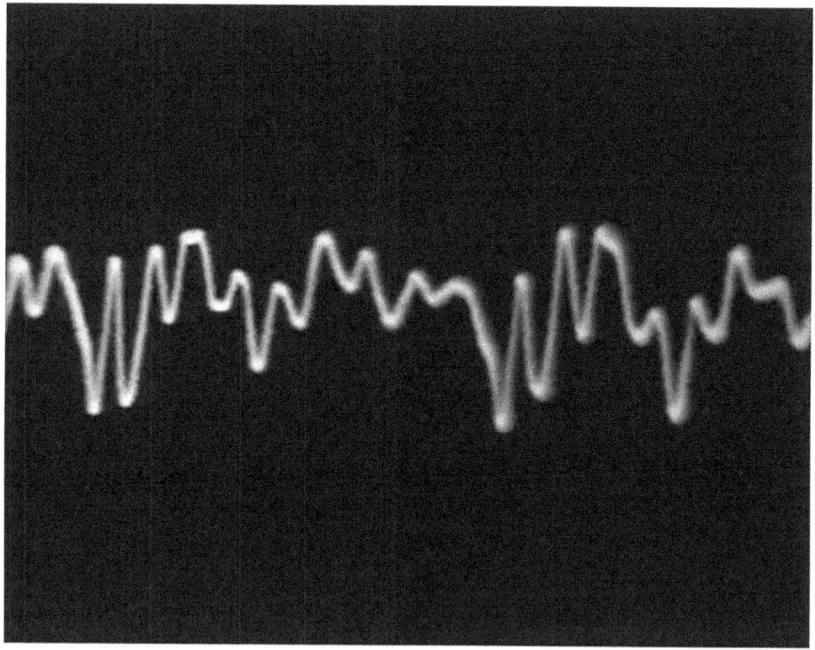

Figure 5.2. "Die Morität von Mackie Messer" as 'seen' through an oscilloscope (*The Ernie Kovacs Show*, September 21, 1961).

Whereas Bruce Ferguson has suggested that the pantomime Eugene episode "acts like a manifesto of the Kovacs aesthetic—a concentration or privileging of *visuality* in the medium—effected paradoxically and necessarily by a careful attention to the role of *sound*," this device, and indeed a careful reading of the shows themselves, suggest that all of the specials (including the distinct Eugene episode) demonstrate an overarching concern with the synchronization of sight and sound.[26] (Ferguson similarly refers to sound effects that are "used sporadically and effectively to underscore many of the motions and gestures of the actors and of the props," but these effects are hardly sporadic: they are instead the very heart of the sketches, which rely for their humor upon the varied and surprising ways in which sound can be meaningfully synchronized to image.) On the one hand, then, Kovacs's work here calls back to the Marx Brothers' earlier experiments with sound—a distinct interest in the intermediality and synaesthesia of recorded images and sound and the carnivalesque ways in which these sounds can be tied to images of the human body—but Kovacs lays on top of all of this an interest in video as well as an emphasis on the broadcast nature of television and the specific publicity that the medium affords. This is in some sense evident in the miniature motorcycle gag, which while trading upon our sense of the "presence" of sound also stages the professor and his invention as part of a larger televised event, but it is clearer in Kovacs's frequent use of the matte, as when a hula hoop is shown to have sawed in half the body of a young woman.

In addition to emphasizing the broadcast flow of television in the form of Kovacs's distinct brand of variety, then, the ABC specials articulate an understanding of television as, to extend Michel Chion, broadcast synchresis.[27] They emphasize the nature and fact of the broadcast image (and only secondarily the fact that it is screened) just as they understand this image to be fundamentally *audio*-visual—even as creating a distinct environment for the reception of images that are at the same time sounds. While it is tempting to think of Kovacs's work as televised vaudeville, as in fact many people (including performers and producers) thought of most television comedy at the time (the idea had enough currency to spawn a portmanteau—"vaudeo"), Kovacs's work constantly references and explores the possibilities of television, so much so that both his tapings and live shows frequently failed to attract full studio audiences because the gags did not play to the audience (whether imagined as real or as metonymic for viewers at home) but in fact needed to be seen on monitors in order to be appreciated. More to the point, the ABC specials repeatedly reference the specific temporality of television as broadcast (a temporality that is related to, but not isomorphic with the sense of its being live) while at the same time they explore a distinct set of sound-image relations. It is this interest in and articulation of specificity that prompted Robert Rosen to call Kovacs "commercial television's first (some would say only) video artist."[28] If the title is appropriate, it is because Kovacs might be said to have discovered these possibilities of the medium.

Of course, "Die Morität von Mackie Messer" takes us back to Brecht, who (with Kurt Weill) composed the song in order to introduce the protagonist Macheath of *The Threepenny Opera*. Brecht and Weill imagined the song as a traditional murder ballad with barrel organ accompaniment, but set it within an opera that progressively combined light opera and jazz. The song details the exploits of Mackie Messer (a series of crimes that include murder, rape, and arson) while at the same time taking Mackie Messer's audience to task for its interest in and indeed complicity with these crimes. Brecht himself understood Mackie Messer as a kind of "gangster capitalist" and imagined the opera therefore as confronting its bourgeois audiences with their own complicity with the broader economic and political forces of its time.[29] As the original refrain goes: "And some are in the dark,/ And others are in the light./ But one only sees those in the light;/ Those in the dark one doesn't see."

Needless to say, and despite its apparent popularity in Weimar Germany, this is not the version of the song that would later thrill American audiences. In 1954, the American composer Marc Blitzstein translated and adapted the song for a successful off-Broadway production of *The Threepenny Opera* in New York. His jazzier, partly sanitized version of the song became the basis first for Louis Armstrong's recording of "Mack the Knife" (1955) and then the Bobby Darin (1959) and Ella Fitzgerald covers (1960). (As Sharon Guthrie points out, each of these versions of the song contains its own oppositional gesture, from Armstrong's implicit setting of the song in New Orleans and hence its contextualization in Black American experience [Brecht himself liked Armstrong's version] to Fitzgerald's improvised version that highlights the politics of gender difference.[30]) Kovacs's ABC Specials occurred just after the grand success of Darin's cover (itself launched on *The Ed Sullivan Show*), which helps to contextualize Kovacs's use of a German-language version that preserves the melody of the original.[31] In a simple sense, the fact that Kovacs employs a hurdy-gurdy, German-language version of the song at a time when Darin's and Fitzgerald's recordings were making the Top 40 marks it as an oppositional gesture, a claim that is further evidenced by the story about the vice president of Consolidated Cigars.

More importantly, however, the slow, dirge-like quality of the German-language version suits both the form and the tone of Kovacs's specials, which, in addition to having a flair of the exotic in the guise of the Hungarian Kovacs (an appearance Kovacs sometimes played for laughs), at times possesses an almost accusatory, if also ambivalent relationship to its audiences, whose laughter is both cajoled and called into question by the song. In this sense, Kovacs does not use the song to merely accompany the gags, as if to string them together in continuity, but instead works in a relationship of reciprocity, where the song can be used to reveal something about the gag. (This is no surprise if we keep in mind the fact that the set piece of each special was its sound-to-sight sketch, a genre that—as Kovacs's notes make plain—considered the question of synchronization in great depth.[32]) Moreover, the specials imagine each blackout gag as coequal to one stanza of the song (sometimes two), with the intervening image of the oscilloscope being used to end the stanza (and hence the gag) and introduce a new one (the following gag). And the specials do not typically play "Die Morität" from beginning to end, but instead double back to particular stanzas (most often the first two, which, in the context of *The Threepenny Opera*, introduce the character of Mackie Messer). Alongside the simplicity and repetitive quality of the melody, this gives the song a more recursive and iterative nature, much like the form of the specials themselves. In this sense, it is not simply that the song functions to comment upon the gags and the larger show, but that the form of the show is, by virtue of the editing of the song, made to alter the form of the song.

This helps us to see the ABC specials as a *series*, both in the obvious way in which, say, *The Lone Ranger* was a series (to pick a show that is parodied in Kovacs's work) and in the way that certain paintings or drawings form a series, where the idea of series is meant to indicate, or articulate, a set of variations on a theme or concept. "Die Morität," we could say, is metonymic of the ABC specials as a whole. While the simple, repeating melody and verse structure of "Die Morität" is in itself iterative like a series, Kovacs's serial use of "Die Morität" is reinforced by his repetition of particular images and situations, both within individual episodes (e.g., Renssalaer Ewing or a recurring situation involving a villain from stage melodrama and a hapless female victim) and across all eight of the specials, where, for instance, the oscilloscope registration of "Die Morität" recurs in variation across the series itself, as when, in the final episode, we see Kovacs himself reach down into the oscilloscope pattern, eventually turning it into a stream of milk (Figure 5.3 on page 122). Importantly, a series need not have a clear beginning and end, even if, by virtue of production the shows have air dates that literally indicate them. (A series of paintings may be hung sequentially on a gallery wall, but this does not suggest that we are to read them in storylike succession.) A series is instead a meaningful, iterative totality, to be understood

Figure 5.3. Turning the oscilloscope to milk (*The Ernie Kovacs Show*, January 23, 1962).

according to the principle not of pure sequence but of repetition. This further indicates the distance between Kovacs's television work and the form of film and television narrative. Unlike the film comedies under consideration here, which articulate narrative closure (even if they typically ironize this closure), Kovacs's specials, like the vast majority of his TV work (and, as I will suggest below, like some of Lewis's movies), instead spin certain images and themes as if centrifugally, leading not to closure but to a sense of the image as simultaneous, somehow both whole and fragmented.

Most notably, the reciprocal relationship between "Die Morität" and the gags adds to the ambivalence of the latter, as when a stanza about the rape of a young widow ("*Und die minderjaehrige Witwe / deren Namen jeder Weiss / wachte auf und war geschaendet— / Mackie, welches war dein Preis?*") is heard over a gag in which Kovacs uses a woman's mouth as a tee for a golf ball and which, after panning up to Kovacs's torso, culminates in his hitting her in the head with his driver. Like various Kovacs gags in which a magician accidentally murders his attractive assistant, this one is openly and disturbingly misogynist, as the humor trades on the fact that the woman has the looks of a model. But the aural reference to Mackie Messer, and the context of the original *Threepenny Opera*, encourage careful viewers to read the gag as the audience having allowed or even encouraged Kovacs to do this. The gag is in this sense ambivalent because while it is clear that this synchronization of song and gag is not legible as a critique of this violence, neither is it simple pleasure, uninhibited by critical reflection. The synchronization is a doubling back, an image (in the broadest sense) that both encourages laughter and interrogates its cause. This action is different than the laughter of Baudelaire's philosopher, then, insofar as it is not a release from the entanglements of everyday life and feeling, but something closer to the opposite—an acknowledgment of this very entanglement, a sense that our lives and desires are in conflict with one another. (All of this of course raises the issue of the relationship between Kovacs's use of the song and its original appearance in *The Threepenny Opera* as well as the modernist potential of Kovacs's comedy more generally. The next chapter addresses the question of the modernist potential of this comedy in the context of Lewis's work, but suffice it to say, the story here is not the similarity of various forms—variety comedy and the modernist search for forms unencumbered by realist narrative—but the movement between them. In the case of Kovacs, a commercial comedian picks up a gesture from Brecht and Kovacs's work then later inspires people who understand themselves as video artists.)[33]

There is one further aspect of interest here and that is way in which the oscilloscope itself both references the technological basis of television and, more importantly, imagines the medium as a kind of monitoring. An oscilloscope is an electronic device for measuring the voltage of an input (or series of inputs), and its invention and evolution is tied closely to that of television itself. Just after he invented the cathode ray tube in 1897, Karl Ferdinand Braun produced the first cathode ray tube scanning device, the cathode ray oscilloscope, a screen that represented inputted electrons as light. It is this device that anticipates television as we know it (even if the cathode ray tube has now been replaced by digital technologies). And while television producers used film for many years to tape shows or to create "kinescopes" of existing material for rebroadcast, it is this technology that establishes the electronic nature of the medium in distinction to the more obviously mechanical (and chemical) basis of film.

All of this suggests a crucial difference between film and television images. Whereas the former are legible as a record of the past (even when it represents something taken to be current, as in a newsreel), the latter are more like a monitoring of the present (even when they are presented with a delay, as in a taped program). The cathode ray oscilloscope provides us with a clear image of this: it is a more or less meaningful representation of an electronic signal (a "current"). In the case of broadcast television, this representation consists of an image that is iconic; in the case of hospital equipment, this representation is more obviously that of data. In both cases, however, the oscilloscope acts as a monitor, and hence contains an entirely different relation to its objects. They are measured and watched for signs of change or interest, rather than captured and viewed for delayed gratification.

The oscilloscope registration of "Die Morität" is therefore a kind of key to the ABC specials. It both helps to provide form to the blackout gag sequences (acting as a kind of refrain, to extend the musical metaphor) and suggests how we are to take the gags, even the episodes, themselves. In *The World Viewed*, Cavell writes that, "in live television what is present to us while happening is not the world, but an event standing out from the world. Its point is not to reveal, but to cover (as with a gun), to keep something on view."[34] This is comparable to the idea of television as flow, where the thing that "stands out," "is covered," or "kept on view" is recognizable as temporarily removed or isolated from that flow. The idea of flow moreover emphasizes the idea of broadcast transmission, for which the state of being live may be paradigmatic but upon which it does not depend. Indeed, the medium of television itself encourages an understanding of our experience as that of a flow out of which we isolate certain details (or objects or situations); it is not a viewing as if unseen (a "furtive feast," as Christian Metz said of the cinema[35]), but a process of monitoring and selection. The ABC specials stress the iterative basis of this selection; they understand the action of monitoring as the isolation of individual themes and effects. The oscilloscope registration of "Die Morität" is therefore an image of this action of selection: it monitors the sequence of the song, the nature of the song's relation to these gags, and finally, the transmission of the television signal into the home, television as the ability to broadcast a synaesthetic image of the senses themselves.

6

Nouvelles Blagues

Jerry Lewis

If the Marx Brothers' Paramount films worked to articulate an account of the place of the body, even of the human, amid the synchronization of sound and image, and Ernie Kovacs's work explored the possibilities of television as broadcast synchresis, the films of Jerry Lewis were formed in the cinema's confrontation not with itself but with the medium of television and against the backdrop of the demise of the studio system itself. The appearance of television caused a crisis in the studio cinema's sense of itself, both in the nature of its production processes and in its form and style. In images of television, the comedy of self-reference reveals these events as a crisis, a kind of splitting. Lewis's *The Ladies Man* (1961) and *The Patsy* (1964), for instance, no longer use images of self-reference to investigate themes of absorption and mutuality, as occurs in both Keaton and Chaplin; they do not form acknowledgments of negation, as I suggested they do in the Marx Brothers; and they do not, as in the case of Kovacs, constitute the playful exploration and reorganization of the synaesthetic possibilities of a new medium. Lewis's work instead diagrams the anxieties that attended the cinema in its contact with television.

Fascinatingly, however, the anxieties that accompany these films' exploration of the medium are also attended by worries over absorption and mutuality. Lewis's work is everywhere characterized by the anxiety of its author, an anxiety whose object is the authorial status of the finished work as well as its star's ability to connect with his audience.¹ Indeed, the liveness of television can be seen to haunt Lewis's film work of the early sixties, which reaches for the apparent intimacy and spontaneity of the televisual but is always restrained by the pastness of the film image. In this sense, Lewis's films constitute a particular picture of the breakdown of the studio-era cinema and its self-sufficiency. They allow us to complete this sketch of the ontology of studio-era cinema by drawing a picture of its devolution. In looking at Lewis, I want to pay attention to two sets of Lewis's films: most importantly, the self-directed features that he created between 1960 and 1965, and, more tangentially, one of the films of the late fifties and early sixties that he made with Frank Tashlin.

Lewis's work appears in the twilight of the studio system, and the marks of this history are visible everywhere in these films—from their parodic interest in the medium of television to the flat, garish tones that call attention to the surface of the screen to their self-conscious, *auteurist* aspirations. If, as Paul Monaco has argued, the year 1960 marked the birth of a new "cinema of sensation,"² Lewis's self-directed work seems both to look forward into a resurgence of sensationalism and to stare backward into the maw of the studio-era film. "The themes, décors, traditions, myths and techniques of the American Cinema reoccur again and again in Lewis's films," the editors of *Cahiers du Cinema* wrote in a special 1967–68 issue dedicated to Lewis. "His work constitutes at one and the same time an extension and a critique of these 'mythologies.'"³ Lewis's films, like the infinite plasticity of their star, are ambivalent records both of a time past and of a future that never quite materialized.

∽

In contrast to Keaton's and Chaplin's understanding of and indeed hopes for the cinema, and unlike Kovacs's similarly forward-looking relationship to television and video, Lewis's films offer a serious acknowledgment of the plural, dis-unified nature of the cinema as it stood at the end of the studio era. This is especially apparent in Lewis's early work with Frank Tashlin, which not only served to orient Lewis's later style as director and producer of his own films but from which originates a distinct interest in the cinema as one element of a larger communications and economic infrastructure, a world saturated by the presence of other media and toward which the comic performance of impotence seemed one of only a handful of possible responses. In order to articulate this vision of a manically plural, proto-electronic cinema, Tashlin and Lewis framed the cinema in terms of a relation both to a broader world of consumption and commodification and to that of high modernism.

The Paramount-produced *Artists and Models* (1955), for instance, opens by situating itself in relation to the creation and exhibition of modern art. After the opening credits (which are accompanied by a jaunty song about art from medieval Italy to Greenwich Village: "And there's modern art for you to see / that makes you wonder what the heck it's meant to be"), the film provides us with a view of a giant billboard in midtown Manhattan (Figure 6.1). Rick Todd (Dean Martin) is at work painting an ad for a brand called "Trim Maid Cigarettes," which depicts the disembodied, open-mouthed face of a pretty woman, while Eugene Fullstack (Lewis) sits in a small room behind it, manically reading a series of comic books (Figure 6.2 on page 128). Martin and Lewis converse through a hole in the billboard, which corresponds to the space of the woman's mouth. The hole is intended to serve as the chimney for a smoke machine, which is to provide a literal, or material, dimension to the image of the glamorous, brand-defining woman whose face dominates the surface of the ad.

The scene and its gags turn around a situation in which the billboard is to be tested: the owner of the billboard and the head of Trim Maid have come to view the finished painting and to witness a demonstration of the smoke machine, which will provide a unified, multidimensional, multisensory image of the brand. But when Lewis turns on the machine, its billows suck his precious stack of "Bat Lady" comic books into the mechanism. Recognizing that Lewis is incapable of operating the machine, Martin works out a plan: he'll manage the machine while Lewis fastens

Figure 6.1. Rick Todd (Dean Martin) and the Trim Maid (*Artists and Models*).

Figure 6.2. Eugene Fullstack (Jerry Lewis) and his "Bat Lady" comic books (*Artists and Models*).

the chute to the woman's mouth from the outside of the ad. But when Martin turns on the machine in proper order, it spits not smoke but the torn pages of Lewis's comic books (Figure 6.3). In his frustration, Lewis

Figure 6.3. The Trim Maid spits the pages of Eugene's comic books (*Artists and Models*).

manages to kick several cans of paint onto the billboard's owner, the man from Trim Maid, and a passing policeman (Figure 6.4).

This final image and, to a certain extent, the mechanisms by which Lewis has spilled this paint, refer explicitly to the popular discourse that then surrounded Abstract Expressionist painting, and to the work of Jackson Pollock in particular. It may seem surprising to find an image of high modernist abstraction in a Martin and Lewis vehicle, but *Artists and Models* comes into better focus if one thinks of it less as a Hal Wallis-produced comedy than as a two-hour pastiche of middlebrow culture of the 1950s, with repeated references to comic book culture (and to Fredric Wertham and his *Seduction of the Innocent* in particular), to the mushrooming domain of commercial advertising, and to popular images of the country's nuclear weapons apparatus.

Images of Pollock featured prominently in this cultural landscape, from profiles in *Time* ("Jack the Dripper") and *LIFE* ("Is he the greatest living painter in the United States?") to the floor of the House of Representatives, where Congressman George Dundero of Michigan argued that such painting "aims to destroy by the creation of brainstorms."[4] (Eventually, even Norman Rockwell and *Lost in Space* would repurpose Pollock to their own ends.) Two instances seem particularly apposite to Tashlin's representation: Lewis's playful smattering of paint recalls the famous 1949 *LIFE* magazine spread that depicted Pollock clothed in a paint-splattered smock, astride one of his large works; the image even

Figure 6.4. Accidental abstraction (*Artists and Models*).

more closely resembles Hans Namuth's frequently reproduced photographs of Pollock at work in his studio. By 1955, Abstract Expressionism, and Pollock's practice in particular, had been popularized as part of a larger importation and reinterpretation of the concept of modern art in the United States, a practice of creation and exhibition that was linked to the maintenance of a postwar (and Cold War) *pax Americana*. In this context, Pollock's work was lionized as a privileged example of American modernity and as evidence of the freedoms enjoyed under American capitalism, while at the same time a middle-class public, whose aesthetic sensibility tended toward various forms of homegrown realism, struggled to see the value or importance of abstract painting. The parody in *Artists and Models* plays on this dynamic: Lewis, the so-called Witless Genius, creates this "masterpiece" by accident.[5]

What we have here then is another image, even another reading, of Pollock and his work—not Harold Rosenberg's Pollock, or Clement Greenberg's, or even Norman Rockwell's, but Frank Tashlin's Pollock. We might of course read Tashlin's sequence as the kitsch debasement of Pollock's painting, the repurposing of high culture as fuel for the engine of pop cynicism. As Greenberg had put the issue a few years earlier, kitsch uses "for raw material the debased and academicized simulacra of genuine culture"; it "pretends to demand nothing of its customers except their money—not even their time."[6] In a certain sense, *Artists and Models* does just what Greenberg describes: in substituting Lewis for Pollock, it flatters the cynicism of its adolescent (or adult-adolescent) viewers and provides a simulacrum of "genuine culture" in the easy-to-digest form of a joke.

But Tashlin's film does not simply lampoon, in the form of Jackson-Pollock-as-Jerry-Lewis, the popularized present of modernist painting—that of Abstract Expressionism and its aftermath—but rather articulates an alternative vision of modernism. That is, Tashlin is not interested in Pollock himself, but rather in how a representation of Pollock might be used to articulate a stance toward the modernity of the mid-century United States. *Artists and Models* articulates a "Tashlinesque" modernism; it is concerned with the issues of specificity, intention, and commodification that so exercised these artists and their theorists in the articulation of modernism itself.[7]

To bring Tashlin's Pollock into better view, we might set this figure alongside another Pollock, one to which it stands in bright contrast—that of Greenberg. Tashlin and Greenberg were contemporaries, and in retrospect their careers can be seen to have run in parallel. Both were born and raised in New York in the first decades of the twentieth century, Tashlin in Weehawken, New Jersey, and then in Queens; Greenberg in Brooklyn. They were in this sense not exactly marginal but suborbital figures. Like the outer boroughs in which they were raised, they were, as young men, separated by geography, ethnicity, and education from the epicenter of high cultural production. Tashlin began his work life as a tradesman in the animation studios. He took a job at Fleischer in 1929 at the fresh age of sixteen, worked his way up through the ranks from inker to animator at Van Beuren, and then made his way to Warner Bros. and the Hollywood studio system. Like Tashlin, Greenberg possessed artistic ambition, although he expressed this ambition in a different manner. The young aesthete first styled himself a poet, coming to art criticism after having, in his own eyes at least, failed in that endeavor. His first essays were published in the late thirties and forties, largely at *Partisan Review*.

In an important sense, the defining distinction between the two men, and hence between their visions of the modern, is geographical: Tashlin left New York for Los Angeles in 1933; with the exception of his disastrous (and brief) military service, Greenberg spent the rest of his life in New York. As Greenberg was toiling away at his government clerkship and writing for *Partisan Review*, Tashlin was serving as an animator and production manager in various Hollywood studios, from Warner Bros. to Columbia. (These endeavors included, notably for the self-reflexive quality of Tashlin's later film work, a stint with the great animator Tex Avery.) Both men's careers changed greatly after World War II. After a break with his first editors, Greenberg went on to become a kind of seer of the American art market, largely through his defense, in the pages of *The Nation*, of abstract painting. Tashlin, who created cartoons for the war effort, would become a feature filmmaker, directing a series of physical comedies the most memorable of which are his many films with Jerry Lewis and two comedies that star Jayne Mansfield. This is the modernism of New York and the fledgling MoMA, on the one hand, and that of Los Angeles and the ironic pitch of the culture industry, on the other.

Tashlin's Pollock is one image within *Artists and Models*' rather densely populated landscape of mass media representations; Greenberg's Pollock came, for a time, to stand in for Greenberg's sense of modernism itself. The art historian Caroline Jones has argued that Greenberg "encountered Pollock's paintings, and made them modern for himself and others by weaving them into what he took to be the texture of modernity."[8] But if Greenberg achieved a kind of modernist exemplarity defined by what Jones calls a "bureaucratization of the senses," Tashlin brings us into contact with a different modernity, not the cool ocularity and distance that Greenberg sought to impose upon the paintings about which he wrote but the frenzied, synaesthetic, pop aesthetic of Hollywood, a modernity that is particularly well realized in both animation and slapstick comedy. Like Greenberg's pedagogical interest in abstraction, the sensibility of Tashlin's films—with their colorful images of the culture of consumption—provided the public with an aesthetic experience of larger material, social, and psychological changes. But if Greenberg's modernity was distanced, single-sensory, and hygienic, the modernity of Tashlin's work lies in its embodiedness, its synaesthesia, its contagiousness. The modernity of both men's work is concerned with the nature and effects of mass consumption, but whereas Greenberg attempts to transmute the power of this consumption into the ocular control of the single viewer, Tashlin's films embrace this culture to the point of absurdity, the contagion of laughter spreading across viewers in a crowd.

These two lives, Tashlin's and Greenberg's, are in this sense instantiations of a problematic, that of the split—theoretical, practical, even geographical—between so-called high culture and mass culture, or what we might think of as two forms or manifestations of the modern, the avant-garde and the vernacular. Tashlin's work was emphatically "kitsch," to use Greenberg's word, formally aligned with cartoons and advertisements (a fact about which *Artists and Models* itself has something to say). Greenberg's chosen painters (Kandinsky, Hans Hofmann, Pollock), on the other hand, produced work that was first consumed by a small number of elite viewers and then recast for popular consumption in the pages of *LIFE*. To paraphrase Greenberg: a movie by Tashlin and a painting by Pollock—is there a "perspective of culture [that] is large enough to enable us to situate them in an enlightening relation?"[9]

Greenberg intended "Avant-Garde and Kitsch" as an answer to this question. "One and the same civilization," he wrote, "produces simultaneously two such different things as a poem by T. S. Eliot and a Tin Pan Alley song, or a painting by Braque and a *Saturday Evening Post* cover."[10] Greenberg's picture of this cultural totality, of course, is determinedly pessimistic and reductive: the relationship between avant-garde and kitsch, his essay rehearses, is that of host and parasite. Kitsch poems, films, and paintings, in Greenberg's account, are the processed foods of the culture industry; they provide the form of experience without at the same time providing its nutriment. In response to such parasitism, Greenberg argues, "living" culture has entrenched itself in the form of an avant-garde, and he suggests that the formal recalcitrance of the works of the avant-garde has been formed in reaction to the encroachments of a cheap, surrounding mass culture. These works, according to Greenberg, refuse the easy, premasticated forms of kitsch in favor of strategies of resistance, difficulty, and intellection. Famously, this action results in an overarching drive toward medium-specificity that Greenberg spent his career sussing out in modernist painting and which became a consistent theme of his writing, from early essays such as "Avant-Garde and Kitsch" through later work like "Modernist Sculpture, Its Pictorial Past" and his eventual championing of "post-painterly abstraction" in the work of artists such as Kenneth Noland and Morris Louis.

Somewhat surprisingly, *Artists and Models* begins by framing the same problem, that of medium-specificity and the conflict between "avant-garde and kitsch," although it reaches a dramatically different set of conclusions. That is to say, the opening sequence of Tashlin's film might be understood as an alternative, self-conscious, Hollywood modernism, one that contains its own theorization of medium-specificity. From its beginning, *Artists and Models* announces that it is not simply a kitsch product or artifact but is concerned with the ways in which kitsch itself is presented and viewed, from its interest in the look and reception of advertisements to Lewis's peculiar and rabid internalization of the horror comics to its parodic interest in live television. These ideas are particularly well focalized through the figure of the billboard, from its status as urban distraction to its close relationship to much mid-century painting.

These two modernisms arose in tandem, one almost calling for the other. The same year that *Artists and Models* was released, Greenberg published the essay "'American-Type' Painting," his articulation and defense of Abstract Expressionism and of Pollock in particular. The essay contains a reiteration of Greenberg's grand theory of modernist painting ("It seems to be a law of modernism . . . that the conventions not essential to the viability of a medium be discarded as soon as they are recognized"[11]), as well as a familiar gesture toward the reasons for the purifying drive toward specificity. ("Conventions are overhauled, not for revolutionary effect, but in order to maintain the irreplaceability and renew the vitality of art in the face of a society bent in principle on rationalizing everything."[12]) The idea here, as it was in "Avant-Garde and Kitsch," is that the specificity of modernist painting is a result of the tradition's desire to maintain and renew its autonomy as part of a defensive reaction to the "rationalizations" of mass culture.

The opening sequence of *Artists and Models* amounts to a strange inversion of these ideas as they might pertain to the Hollywood cinema. The bright, artificial colors that Lewis unleashes from the height of the billboard, for instance, refuse the muted tones of the abstract works about which Greenberg was writing, aligning themselves both formally and diegetically with the color of advertisements. The joke with the paint cans is a way of harnessing the exuberance of this most "rationalized" or instrumentalized form of aesthetic expression while at the same time turning this exuberance against the means of its instrumentalization, here represented, as it often is in physical comedy, by figures of authority. Lewis's final "painting," if it can be called that, is in this sense a figure for the studio cinema of the fifties itself: widescreen, composed somehow of both depth and an overweening superficiality, aglow in garish Technicolor.

Artists and Models also self-consciously refuses the quality of flatness that is essential to Greenberg's account of modernist painting. In the advertisement with which the film begins, this refusal occurs not in service of a projected or constructed third dimension, as it would in, say, painting of the Renaissance (the space around the woman's face does not suggest an environment or a scene), but in service of an "actual" third dimension, which is made manifest both by the presence of smoke and by the tiny room behind the image (and inside the woman's mouth), a room that suggests a kind of filmic subconscious and that is (more or less) large enough to hold Lewis and his spastic imagination. (The room is also a kind of projection booth, its mouth an aperture that will spit out images from another medium in a kind of burlesque montage.) If modernist painting, in Greenberg's account, works to pare itself toward a flatness made essential by the canvas support, popular film, in the Tashlinian imagination, is the site of a vast plurality; it does not simply refuse flatness as much as serve as the container of an infinite depth. (The scene articulates the sense that, onscreen, objects both flat and round have interiors.) In Tashlin's hands, this is not the mimicked depth of premodern painting but a constructed depth that takes on the quality of absurdity insofar as we see that it may be infinitely repeated.

Indeed, the fact that this refusal of flatness does not result in its notional opposite is of significance to the understanding of the declaration of specificity at work here. Through the mechanisms both of irony and of Lewis's plasmatic body, Tashlin's film has the effect of declaring an emptiness in Hollywood film practice (the fact that film space is not contained, that it is infinitely repeatable) and of confronting the viewer at the plane of the film screen by means of a denial of her desire for absorption.

A final and I think very interesting twist to this idea is that this specificity is declared by means of an *accident*, rather than by means of a declaration, a refusal, or, as is the case in other of Tashlin's films (and especially those starring Lewis), the experience or performance of infantile regression. It is Lewis's uncontrollable, plasmatic body that knocks over the paint cans that create this painting, not, one wants to say, his self. Tashlin's film appears to claim that something can become an art object or artifact despite the fact that it was created by accident (or by means of a peculiar form of comedic and bodily anti-intentionality). This aligns it, at least in part, with a much older tradition that understands the photograph and then the film as constitutively automatic in character, or as built by means of a series of automatisms. If Pollock's work has sometimes been understood in the context of an automatism of gesture inherited from the Surrealist tradition, Lewis and Tashlin's exercise reveals a different aspect of the same automatism, both its accidental quality and its repressed relationship to social and aesthetic failure.

This represents a fascinating inversion of the sense of intentionality that is implied in Greenberg's account of modernist painting, one that has affinities with the sense of intention that would characterize much of the Pop Art that would follow. Using the example of Pollock, we could say that it is constitutive of the meaning of his work that Pollock attended to his canvases and that this attention is visible on and within his finished paintings (e.g., his "drips" are demonstrably the marks of a hand and brush, not those of a machine. Indeed, they are in this sense similar to automatic writing: they divulge an automatism that one feels had previously been embedded or hidden within a human being). Similarly, the sense of intention in Greenberg's account is tied to a larger historical movement within painting that is working to ensure the autonomy of the medium itself. In Lewis's gesture, as in the VistaVision frame, different senses of intention and automatism are revealed: this painting is an accident, yet it is visible as a painting nonetheless (however "bad").

In all of these ways, the specificity that is at work in Lewis's painting-film is heterogeneous and discontinuous. That is, the specificity that the film articulates is related not to a movement of purification—the discarding of unnecessary conventions—but to a movement of amalgamation—the absorption of new conventions and automatisms and a parody of the same. The cinema, this sequence declares, is definitively plural and intermedial. This movement is neither critical nor negating, in Greenberg's sense, nor is it parasitic and recuperative (in the way that Greenberg might have imagined). Tashlin's film merely, and quite interestingly, uses the action of parody, and the relationship between the cinema and another medium, to declare the material and conventional bases of the cinema and to situate filmic practice within the larger dynamic of high modernism and mass culture. If Greenberg intended his Pollock to be a force of renewal and vitality, Tashlin's Pollock—in the person of Jerry Lewis—is something like the obverse image of this: a man who resists the "rationalization" of everything not through a heroic expansion of energy but through an internalization of social norms that is so complete as to render them absurd.

∽

After his break with Dean Martin, a similar disarticulation of the cinema often arises in Lewis's films with a corresponding acknowledgment of the properties of television. In the Tashlin-directed *The Disorderly Orderly* (1964), for instance, Lewis plays Jerome Littlefield, the eponymous orderly of a California sanitarium. In an early gag, Jerome is called to fix the television set of one of the sanitarium's many wealthy female patients. The set is full of static, and as he unscrews the unit's screen from the set that is bolted to the wall, the machine unleashes a ferocious storm of white snow. The joke trades on a pun—television static is sometimes called "snow"—but it also serves as an image of the formal and economic chaos unleashed by a medium that had bitten into a large portion of the Hollywood audience.[13] Interestingly, this comedic business around the television set takes part in the less-than-realist aesthetic of the animated cartoon (the "snow" has no realistic motivation; the incident causes the patient to be consumed by her hospital bed), just as it has no place within the film's larger narrative. In comparison to Miriam Hansen's sense of the disarticulation of the classical body in *Artists and Models*, Tashlin and Lewis's gag goes a step further here to disarticulate studio-era film form more generally.[14] The body, in this sense, is metonymic for the more abstract issue of form, a kind of obstruction to the cause-and-effect structure of traditional forms of narration.

The concepts that Raymond Williams attributed to television—its "speed, variety, and miscellaneity"—help to draw out some of the more interesting aspects of Lewis's self-directed films, many of which take on the episodic, even distracted, nature of television. Gags unfold and then end and there is a clear pause before the next scene or gag, for instance, as if to suggest a space for commercials. These values come into better light if one begins by understanding Lewis's self-directed films as constructed not out of traditional structures of narration but of a series of sequences that are related by a principle of general association. That is, these films work not in Donald Crafton's sense of the gag as "a calculated rupture, designed to keep the two elements [of narrative and slapstick] antagonistically apart," but as entirely different ways of constructing continuity, not as radically nonnarrative as Kovacs's work but highly inventive in relationship to studio-era norms.[15] In Crafton's theory, early slapstick represents a spectacular assault on the forces of narrativization, but Lewis's films do not so much assault these forces as forgo them for other compositional structures. Instead of depending upon narrative conventions for continuity, the principle of association in Lewis's work achieves continuity by means of space, time, and a peculiar foregrounding of authorial anxiety.

Chris Fujiwara has suggested that "a typical trajectory in Lewis's cinema is a running to and fro, a starting-off in one direction only to turn back confusedly," and he goes on to compare this movement to what "Maurice Blanchot calls 'a dis-cursus—a broken, interrupted course that . . . imposes the idea of the fragment as a form of coherence.'"[16] In Lewis's work, this discursivity takes the form of everything from short acts of pantomime to the structure of individual sequences, even to the composition of entire films. But by structuring themselves around the composition and ordering of discurses, these films take up a stance of critical reflection: the very presence and prominence of the fragment within them suggests the insufficiency of the imagined whole. If the archetypal classical film takes the form of a chain in which one dramatic unit links to the unit that preceded it as well as to the unit that follows, thus moving the spectator from a beginning to an end (which is itself modeled on the beginning that preceded it but is only significant insofar as it achieves an iteration of difference), Lewis's comedies sometimes take the form of a nautilus shell, a structure in which an accretion of instances of a single pattern creates a new and circular whole. Partly as a consequence of this structure, their endings are only superficially differentiated from their beginnings. If in Kovacs's work, the momentum that is legible at the beginnings and endings of individual programs is centrifugal, even poetic, the final moments in Lewis's self-directed films tend instead to bare the structure or frame of the film as a whole and to call into question the classical achievement of difference.

These principles of association and discursus are particularly clear in two films of 1961, *The Ladies Man* and *The Errand Boy*, the former achieving continuity around its construction of space, the latter around an interest in time. In *The Ladies Man*, Lewis plays Herbert H. Heebert, a recent graduate of Milltown Junior College who, we are given to understand in the film's prologue, is terrified of women. He travels to Los Angeles to find work and accidentally takes work as a houseboy in an immense rooming house for single ladies. The vast majority of the film (nearly ninety minutes of its ninety-five-minute runtime) takes place within this house, the set for which was enormous: at four stories, 25,000 square feet, and sixty rooms, it took up two Paramount soundstages.[17] Promotional materials called it "Hollywood's biggest, most elaborate, most expensive stage set of all time." If Lewis's memory can be trusted, the set itself cost $975,000 and took eight months to build, while the production employed a specially built forty-five-foot crane, which was referred to as "Jerry's Toy."[18] (While the film possesses a rudimentary narrative (Herbert's goal is to overcome his fear of women), it is this set and the opportunities that it affords Lewis for clowning (and not a larger story) that gives *The Ladies Man* its particular formal structure.

Fujiwara has suggested the more specialized term *block* for the almost self-contained units that comprise Lewis's films, and the term is useful in distinction to the words *sequence* and *segment*, which rest more comfortably within more narrative-oriented paradigms of Hollywood cinema. The Lewisian block, Fujiwara says, consists of "a collision of bodies and the space-time that contains them, a set of poses or actions ('hanging there and groping there') that are present with each other but that remain apart instead of complementing or embracing each other."[19] For Fujiwara, this constellation of "bodies and space-time" provides Lewis's films with a unique form of continuity: "Because it is only a single unit, without hierarchies, the block frees the isolatedness of the gestures or actions it contains and lets them exist for themselves, without subordinating them to a narrative logic."[20] That is, the block forms a whole in and of itself, without reference to a larger whole created by narrative. To be sure, it is not that Lewis's films have *no* narrative logic in the strong way of, say, Luis Bunuel's *L'Age d'Or* (1930). Lewis's films appear to rely on simple plot devices such as the accidental discovery of a bellboy's talent and his consequent attempt to conform to his handlers' wishes (*The Patsy*) or a young girl's struggle to identify a caretaker among her loony relations (*The Family Jewels* [1965]). It is the case, however, that within these stories narrative action remains subordinate to the block structure of continuity. In this sense, the term *block* refers to units of film that form discrete wholes as the result of spatial continuity, unity of gag (which, in Lewis's case, is almost always isomorphic with spatial continuity), and unified duration.

What do these individual blocks look like in practice and, more vexingly, how do Lewis's films stack them together to form continuous wholes? The blocks of *The Ladies Man* are contained and unified first by the space of the boardinghouse (that is, through spatial continuity) and secondarily through the psychology of Herbert H. Heebert. The lexical nature of these principles is evident in an early block that sets the stage for all of the gagging that will follow by providing an image of the house as a whole. Lewis has taken a job as the houseboy the previous night, largely as the result of meeting the house's less-than-alluring housemaid (Kathleen Freeman). Waiting to take a tour of the house, he has felt reassured that his fear of romantic attachment will not be put to the test. A new block then commences with an image of Lewis asleep in an inverted fetal position, accompanied by the sound of a single trombone. The film cuts to an image of pretty blonde woman in her pajamas, playing this trombone in bed, and the next three and a half minutes consist of a choreographed display of the fifty or sixty women who live in the boarding house and their march from the building's bedrooms to a dining room downstairs (Figure 6.5).

Figure 6.5. The space of continuity (*The Ladies Man*).

The joke, of course, is that the female-fearing Herbert has wandered into a house whose every room contains three or four beautiful women and thus the assurance of his total breakdown. The scene seems to provide the set-up for dramatic conflict (however humorous), a pretext for Herbert's confrontation of his fears. More than the introduction of dramatic conflict, however, the block works as a means of introducing the principle of spatial continuity that will come to structure the film as a whole. And although we are given, in this scene, to admire the space of the set for its sheer size and the way it is capable of containing so many actors, the moment is not simply one of spectacular excess but an image of the order of the whole film. By walking through the house—out of its individual rooms, through each of its corridors, and down its many stairs—the women form a pedagogical image, one that prepares viewers for the film's distinct strategy of continuity by means of space.

That the concepts of space and gag take precedence over ordinary story causality in Lewis's self-directed work is made plain in Lewis's 1971 book for aspiring filmmakers. Lewis describes a hypothetical session with a screenwriter. "We might have The Kid playing the role of a bank teller," he says:

> We examine the possibilities. For openers, he gets locked in the vault. After that, someone passes him counterfeit money. He is nuts about a chick who comes in every Monday at

exactly two o'clock to make a deposit. So there's a chance for the love interest. The necessary menacing factor might be the bank guard. He's been there forty years. He hates any kid, let alone The Kid. Before the session is over between the straight writer and the comedy creator, there are eleven things to do with the bank teller without ever having to leave the bank.[21]

As the final sentence makes clear, it is the need for gags ("things to do") and a single space within which to play these gags ("without ever having to leave the bank") that define Lewis's process of script construction. But this process also manages to absorb the traditional narrative considerations of heterosexual romance and dramatic conflict ("a chance for the love interest," "the necessary menacing factor") into an overarching pattern of gagging and spatial continuity. If the passage suggests the potential for cooperation between "the straight writer and the comedy creator" (the names of which imply an important categorical difference), the chapter as a whole makes clear the "straight writer's" subservience to the comedian and his interest in spectacle. Like Lewis's hypothetical movie about a bank teller, *The Ladies Man* really is just a series of gags within a house with little regard for diegetic time: Herbert moves seamlessly, for instance, between destroying a painting of Miss Wellenmellon to executing a ballroom dance with George Raft.

The fact that spatial association forms a more important structuring principle than the film's narrative is also suggested by the film's ending, which, like the endings of many slapstick comedies, calls into question its proposed narrative settlement. Importantly, the ending of *The Ladies Man* offers us a clear perspective on the place of character psychology in relation to the larger interest in space. Earlier in the film, Herbert has been asked to tend to Miss Wellenmellon's house pet, Baby. Those gags turn on Baby's visual absence (and aural presence): Lewis opens the door to Baby's room only to hear the loud roars of a jungle cat; he feeds Baby with a thirty-gallon pail of milk; he gives Baby an entire side of pork, which the animal then tosses out as a single, dinosaur-sized bone. Just prior to the film's conclusion, Baby escapes her room, and Herbert runs frantically around the set, hoping to avoid what he is certain is a ferocious animal. He eventually flees into the house's elevator cage, only to be told to look down—Baby is at his feet. Herbert collapses to the floor and discovers that Baby is none other than a small Bassett puppy with a spiked metal collar. This resolution of Lewis's phobic object (one that is metonymic for his fear of women)—the supposedly terrifying animal is, in reality, not terrifying at all; thus, Lewis's fear of women is similarly unjustified—provides a segue into the film's concluding scene.

The film's concluding scene is the most sentimental of the entire film. All of the women are seated in the dining room. As they eat, several of the women announce that they have tasks for Herbert—a broken high heel, a wonky television set, sheets that need ironing—and we are given to understand that, following the Baby incident, Herbert has decided to leave his job. Their laughter about Herbert provokes one of the women, Faye (Pat Stanley), to deliver a speech in defense of Herbert and his desire to leave. Herbert then comes downstairs with his suitcase in his hand. He announces that he is leaving, and he walks out, expecting, because the house has previously developed a ritual around his various attempts to leave, the women to come after him. No one does, and Herbert is plainly disappointed: his fear, we are given to understand, masks an underlying desire for maternal love. Finally, Faye comes to him and explains that the women simply want what is best for him. Her speech convinces him to stay and therefore to accept and transform his fear. And in this moment, his response moves past the broken cadence and practiced solecisms of The Idiot and into the natural speech of a rounder, more dramatic character: "I like it here very much, and I like everybody a lot," he says. "And I like to be needed. But honestly needed. And after what you just said, I wouldn't leave here for anything or anyone." This moment of resolution is then broken by the roars of Baby. The women scream and run wildly for the exits, and Herbert is left alone in the dining room, waiting for the return of the now domesticated object of his fears, the long-eared puppy with the loud growl. But instead of the dog, a lion crosses the room. Herbert walks toward the foreground; the camera dollies in toward his face; and he screams for his mother. The film thus closes on an image of Herbert's abjection, a regression beyond his earlier fear and into a kind of pure state of oedipal fear: women are, after all, even scarier than they initially seemed.

Of course, this sort of parodic or recursive ending is not exclusive of traditional patterns of narration. The gesture is in one sense parasitic upon the form that it parodies. (Some of Keaton's films, for instance, follow more typical narrative structures, yet also manage to call their settlements into question at their conclusions. And a similar pattern inheres in many romantic comedies, such as *The Philadelphia Story* [1940] and *Sullivan's Travels* [1941]. This fact suggests that these romantic comedies might be thought of as adjacent genres, sharing some of the characteristics with the physical comedy and others with, say, the melodrama.) But in *The Ladies*

Man, as in others of Lewis's films, the effect is to call into question the spectator's expectation of a resolute ending. If the typical protagonist of classical film, for instance, possesses a goal and then goes about achieving or failing to achieve that goal, the protagonist of *The Ladies Man* is revealed to have had, from the film's beginning, something like a goal without meaning. And in Lewis's film, this parodic meaninglessness is the natural accomplice of the film's overall interest in a spatial system whose coherence depends not upon the inner, psychological traits of Lewis's character but on the ways in which Lewis as a performer is able to make the space hang together by means of his body. The result is a confrontation with classical style: Lewis's continuity of space succeeds as a more efficient principle than the straightforward narrative for the spectacle of his humor. If, as David Bordwell puts it, "in classical fabula construction, causality is the prime unifying principle," Lewis's films employ not a principle of causality, but an aesthetic of spatial association, under- or overextended duration, and inner abjection, all focused around the desire to produce gags.[22]

Yet for all of this emphasis on spatial structure, it is not space alone that forms the content of the overall film but the way in which this space is made the content of a larger mediatization. Two-thirds of the way through *The Ladies Man*, the house becomes the center of a live television broadcast, the scenes around which form a seventeen-minute block of gag, song, and spectacle. The broadcast has no apparent narrative motivation: in a brief scene preceding the broadcast, the producers of a show called "Up Your Street" simply call on Miss Wellenmellon, who is famous as a retired opera star, and ask her to take part in their show. What follows is a series of gags that trade on Lewis's ability to careen disastrously first through the bulky television equipment that engulfs the house and then through a televised interview between Miss Wellenmellon, seated in her house, and the show's host, Westbrook Van Voorhis, who is situated in a studio in New York.

The latter situation results in the creation of an image of time, or more specifically, an image of simultaneity. The supposed conceit of "Up Your Street" is that it is filmed in non-studio locations with non-actors. As the announcer for the show, Del Moore (playing himself), opens the production: "May I once again welcome you to the show that doesn't come from a studio, a show that wasn't made in some far-off land, a show that can and does come from 'Up Your Street'!" But as Moore makes this announcement, the film cuts to an image of Van Voorhis in a New York television studio, a studio that is itself constructed so as to resemble a middle-class living room (Figure 6.6). This image is complex, to say the least: it is filmed in depth, with three or four layers of visual

Figure 6.6. Televised simultaneity (*The Ladies Man*).

information, each of which in turn corresponds to a different aspect of the show's production. In its background, the image registers the pro-filmic environment (Van Voorhis seated in his chair), but moving toward the foreground, the same image reveals a series of extrafilmic layers in front of the manufactured image of the show's host. One camera films Van Voorhis to frame right, and another films him in the foreground and to frame left. Two microphone booms, at different levels of depth, are extended over the set's open ceiling. A sound man sits at a console to the extreme left; Del Moore recites his announcement to the extreme right. Closest to the foreground, the frame empties itself of persons, leaving only a black and white monitor that displays the image produced by the first camera and a well-lit teleprompter that cycles through Moore's actual lines.

This construction in depth describes a larger image of simultaneous time. In addition to the sense of simultaneity created by the various layers of production (all of which, we are given to understand, contribute to the singular image of "Up Your Street" that is being seen by the show's imaginary viewers), an image of Van Voorhis appears in the black-and-white monitor in the lower portion of the frame. The composition creates a little feedback loop for the eye, which moves between pre- and pro-filmic levels of the production. Furthermore, the black and white image of Van Voorhis itself becomes the shot that instantiates a shot-reverse shot exchange with the image of Miss Wellenmellon in her California home.

It is during this block that *The Ladies Man* reveals the fact that the house itself is a set constructed for the purposes of filming (Figure 6.7). Although the camera had pulled away in the introductory sequence, the television production allows it to retreat even farther into the soundstage, further highlighting the stage-like structure of the individual rooms, revealing the edge of the house's wooden floor, and displaying a television camera and light at the limits of the frame. The image is also a figure for Lewis's production: some of the equipment visible as part of the television production, for example, was equipment that Lewis was actually using to produce *The Ladies Man*.[23]

In keeping with the general recursivity of the construction of this block, Lewis then uses this image of time to work out a gag about depth and the limits of the frame. As Miss Wellenmelon attempts to speak, across the airwaves, to Van Voorhis, Morty stumbles in and out of the frame, managing at first to get his suit cuff stuck on her carnation and then wandering through the hallways behind her, stopping frequently to stare into the camera. As the television show cuts between Miss Wellenmellon and Van Voorhis, Lewis parodies this sense of simultaneity by extending the distance behind Miss Wellenmellon, thus revealing that the sense of simultaneity relies upon a flattening of the frame. As occurs throughout Lewis's self-directed films, both the individual scenes here as well as the overall block take the form of *mise-en-abyme*, which the film uses to suggest the impossibility of personal authenticity. Authenticity, *The Ladies Man*

Figure 6.7. The house as set (*The Ladies Man*).

gives us to understand, is a casualty of a larger media environment in which individual utterances are swamped by the (usually plural) mediums in which these utterances take place. What is important in the scene with Van Voorhis, for example, is not his words or of those of Moore, but the larger televisual situation in which they take place. Thus, in the film as a whole, the sense of a continuity constructed through space rather than story seems to reflect upon a gap in the center of narrative meaning.

For these reasons, this block of scenes allows us to understand the larger structure of the film and its attempt to create spatial continuity. If, for Williams, the continuity of television is composed of "speed, variety, and miscellaneity," *The Ladies Man* offers a distinct image of filmic continuity where these values are transmuted into a single figure of spectacular space. *The Ladies Man* stages a confrontation between the two mediums. The spectacle of Lewis's film relies upon its color and the screen's wide frame—the house is the subject of *The Ladies Man* because it accentuates these exclusive, non-televisual traits of the cinema. By heightening this confrontation through these predominately visual elements of the medium, the film strains against—and breaks with—earlier conventions of filmic storytelling. That is, it is not simply that the film possesses generic motivation for its distinction from classical film form but that this distinction is the result of both the requirements of the genre (gag above story) and of its confrontation with the televisual (widescreen above small screen, multichromatic above bichromatic).

If *The Ladies Man* depends upon spatial continuity to build a filmic whole, *The Errand Boy* works by "mis-extending" ordinary duration. This structure is particularly clear in the film's ending, which is among the most recursive of all of Lewis's gags. Like Keaton in *Sherlock Jr.*, the closing sequence of *The Errand Boy* takes an interest in film and its screening, but its effect, and what it has to say about the medium that is its subject, is quite different. In Keaton's work, we experience Buster's struggle, fascination, and eventual absorption into the film frame, and although its conclusion suggests Keaton's ambivalence about the screened film (particularly as it relates to romantic encounter), the overall effect is one of celebration. Unlike the fascination and absorption that characterizes Keaton's encounter, the effect of Lewis's encounter with the film frame is one of alienation. He is stuck within it and transformed according to rules characterized by chance. Rather than articulate a relationship to the world of the film, which *Sherlock Jr.* construes as an intimacy with the self, *The Errand Boy* articulates a sense of distance from that world and its viewing, a lack of intimacy with the self onscreen.

This ending is composed of four scenes, and these are nominally connected by means of the film's narrative: (1) a conversation, in the

Paramutual property department, between Morty (Lewis) and a puppet named Magnolia; (2) a scene on the soundstage during the filming of a Paramutual melodrama; (3) a conversation among a group of producers and directors about the previous scene on the soundstage; and (4) Morty's exultant parade across the studio lot as one of the studio's newest stars. Scene (1) includes the story's *anagnorisis*, which, characteristically for Lewis, is not a moment of recognition of the identity of another, but of himself. After coming to the conclusion that he has failed at his job as an errand boy and hired tattle, Morty strolls through the prop department in search of a finger puppet with whom he has earlier communed. (Lewis's affinity for puppets and the nonhuman is a separate dimension of his distance from the adult world of reason.) The finger puppet is nowhere to be seen, but a second, bird-shaped puppet, Magnolia, appears to give him counsel. Morty tells Magnolia his story of leaving New Jersey for Hollywood (which suggests in part the story of the real Lewis, Jerome Levitch of Newark), but he is eventually stopped by his own sense of logic and propriety. ("Wait a minute," he says. "I just thought of something. . . . Puppets can't talk.") This then occasions a speech from Magnolia in which she elaborates an almost cognitivist theory of film spectatorship whereby viewers supply the frame in which a story or spectacle is to be turned into productive illusion: "Can you remember when you were a little boy and your parents took you to a puppet show and you'd think, 'They're almost live' or 'They made me believe they're live'? . . . Well it isn't any different now, especially when you want to believe what you see and hear." Hearing this, Morty comes to recognize, as he puts it, "It makes me feel good, just liking someone," and he leaves the prop department returned to himself. The overall sense here, despite its intensely infantile character, is one of redemption and self-understanding.

Morty's moment of recognition and redemption is, however, powerfully ironized by the scene that follows. An image of Magnolia fades into an image of a stone statue, over which a woman's voice soliloquizes, "Oh my love, my love . . . my love!" The camera tilts down and dollies out to reveal a woman speaking to a photograph of a man who, we come to understand, is her dead lover. After a long, melodramatic speech, she proceeds to kill herself on a sectional sofa. Offscreen, a loud voice abruptly announces, "Cut! Print that one!" and a director marches through the shot to join the woman, who is now revealed to be a studio actress. Both the soft, orchestral music that accompanies the actress's speech and the scene's maudlin tone recall that of Morty's turn with Magnolia, and the graphic match between the puppet and the statue consciously links the two scenes. By juxtaposing Morty's moment of recognition with the broad performance of a studio actress, Lewis destabilizes the tone of the entire sequence, undercutting the sentimentality of the previous scene and calling into question Morty's transformation.

But this juxtaposition also licenses a movement between worlds, between an apparent reality and its fictional counterpart, a distinction that the film also ironizes. After the director's entrance into the frame, the film cuts to reveal an entire studio soundstage with crew and cameras, where the actress receives broad applause for her, as she puts it, "rather tender" monologue. The head of the studio tells Morty to wheel out a cake and a giant magnum of champagne to celebrate the actress's birthday, at the same time instructing another executive to roll the cameras. After announcing that she would like to make "a sincere and honest toast" (adjectives that are always, in Lewis's work, lacking in stable reference) and following this announcement with a portion of the speech that accompanied her earlier suicide, the actress commands Morty to open the champagne. This sets off a long gag that centers around Morty's attempt to control the gushing champagne bottle (which is in reality connected to something like a fire hose), a Lewisian turn at *L'Arroseur arrosé* (Lumiere, 1896).

The gag is, to put it mildly, excessive. Morty spends more than a minute dousing the producers, the actress, and their crew. In contrast to the Magnolia scene and the previous section of scene (2), which are densely composed and built of long shot lengths (the average shot length of the Magnolia scene is 15.9 seconds, that of the actress's speech and toast is 19.5), the gag is built of brief shots of Morty's victims interspersed with similarly brief images of Morty failing to control the champagne. (The ASL of this portion of the scene is 4.7.) Despite this radical difference in cutting patterns, however, the effect is not that of speed and excitement. One has instead the sense that the gag is over- or mis-extended—that, like the film's *anagnorisis* and the actress's mawkish death that have set its stage, its humor is radically undercut by the irony the subtends the sequence. This is a gag about gags.

It is appropriate then that the gag is itself interrupted by the revelation that it is being screened. The camera dollies back to reveal the curtained edges of a film screen (Figure 6.8 on page 148), and then cuts to an auditorium, where two producers and a studio director are laughing at the same image. (The scene confirms a general rule for gauging the constantly modulating irony of Lewis's films: when characters onscreen think a gag is funny, it tends not to be, and when the same characters think a gag is not funny, it is. This rule also confirms something about the nature of physical humor more generally, the fact that it is predicated on a sense of spectatorial distance from both its action and the psychology of the characters within it. As Frank Krutnik has observed, "Lewis's

Figure 6.8. Mis-extended duration: a gag about gags *(The Errand Boy)*.

reactions are often so overextended that they outstrip the motivating context of the gag."[24]) Here, the revelation of the frame adds distance between the spectator and the gag, while at the same time displaying the fact that the gag is legible in multiple ways. What is perceivable as excess—a gag whose mechanism outlasts its actual humor—is at the same time understood by the onscreen director and producers as riotously funny.

Bazin saw something similar in Jacques Tati. In an essay on *Les Vacances de Monsieur Hulot* (1953), he argues that the film's gag-based structure helps to create a film *about* time. *Les Vacances*, he says,

> cannot be anything other than a succession of events at once wholly coherent and dramatically independent. Each one of the hero's adventures and misadventures should therefore begin with the caption "Mr. Hulot at some other time." Without a doubt, up to this point in this history of cinema, Time has never been the basic material, almost the very object, of a film. Even better and even more so than in films that experiment with "real time," *Les Vacances* illuminates the temporal dimension of human existence.[25]

As in other physical comedies, *Les Vacances* constructs a distinct constellation of spectatorial identification—viewers experience Mr. Hulot's sense of time as a relief from that experienced by the vacationers—and this constellation in turn creates critical reflection. Unlike *Les Vacances*, however, Lewis's concern with time and duration manages to turn a foregrounding of the temporal upon the medium itself so that it is not "the temporal dimension of human existence" that is illuminated but rather the time of Hollywood cinema: Lewis turns the time of the cinema itself into a joke.

This is palpable in scene (3), which continues with the director and producer attempting to convince Mr. Paramutual (the head of the studio) that Morty is a star. The grandest defense of Lewis is given, in close-up, by a man that Mr. Paramutual identifies as "Mr. New York Method Director." Long and seemingly felt, his speech is composed of epigrammatic nonsense: "Anyone in the world would give anything to do a performance," he says memorably, "because performing is nothing more than a form of expression." Here again the reigning sentiment of the film is powerfully undercut: the man is self-consciously acknowledged as a method actor and his speech is full of emotion with no apparent object: "Yes, Mr. Paramutual," he concludes about Morty's turn with the hose, "*that* was a performance." Apparently convinced by this monologue, Mr. Paramutual leaves the screening room to promote Morty. Scene (4) consists of the new star's victory lap around the Paramutual lot. He sits in the back of a convertible and the audience is treated to great crowds of studio workers, high and low, who have come to applaud and celebrate his power.

Read in the light of this intense ironization of sentiment and the real Lewis's considerable success at the time, the sequence is self-loathing. Rather than a triumphal turn around the studio lot and the rightful acknowledgment of his talents (the straight reading of the scene), the film's conclusion is entirely the result of a lucky accident. If Keaton's films consist of the acrobatics of a man who discovers his physical talents in the face of grand and impossible situations, Lewis's work consists of a series of exquisite failures in the face of repeated opportunities for redemption. Keaton accentuates the heroic beneath the mock-heroic; Lewis locates the pathos at the bottom of seemingly humorous abjection.

∽

Such is Lewis's ambivalence, both about himself and about the medium. But if Lewis's ambivalence registers a sense of cynicism and disenchantment about the cinema more generally, this affect helps to constitute the modernist potential of his work. If the effect of Keaton's absorption is a reenchantment of the film frame, the restoration of its power after the baring of its device, the effect of *The Errand Boy* is a sense of distanciation from that frame, an almost complete ironization of its power. This too has to do with the presence of television. Like the studio system around him, Lewis struggled with the medium of television, never feeling that he had been given a fair shot. He seems to have sensed that television contained an opportunity for a direct, less mediate connection to his audience, a connection he would come to cultivate in his telethon work. But the result of this struggle on film was a series of films whose formal composition, disfiguring pathos, and almost confrontational attitude toward their audiences inaugurated a new difference from the films of the studio era.

Scholars and historians of media have traditionally defined the relationship between modernist or avant-garde film works and those of the surrounding mass culture as "one of fundamentally incompatible registers," as Miriam Hansen put it.[26] This is no doubt in large part a result of the oppositional way in which the avant-garde has defined itself. It has also to do with the anti-intellectualism and marketing acumen of the American film industry, which has, for reasons of profit, welcomed descriptions of itself as classical, realist, and popular—i.e., universal. Lewis himself, for example, decried the (in retrospect, rather mild) success of the European art film of the 1960s, insisting that he would never make films that pandered to "the twenty sophisticates in the world."[27] This opposition, which has been rehearsed by everyone from Jarry to Jerry, is now one hundred and fifty years old. It has its origins in debates surrounding nineteenth-century painting, and in particular around critically reviled works such as Manet's *Olympia* that depicted the lives of the lower classes.

Throughout the twentieth century, both the popular cinema and the avant-garde both defied and perpetually reinscribed this opposition. With varying measures of criticality, the avant-garde absorbed the materials of mass culture, manipulating them as a means to its own ends. Joseph Cornell's *Rose Hobart* (1936) and Kenneth Anger's *Puce Moment* (1949), to take two examples, draw upon the materials of the studio cinema (Universal's B-feature *East of Borneo* [1931] and the aura of the Hollywood starlet, respectively) in order to fashion works that were intended for smaller, more sophisticated audiences and that reflected critically upon the nature of mass cultural consumption. And Andy Warhol's work, of course, takes the products of mass culture as its very substance, thus foregrounding the impossibility of any true ontological distinction between the two. Even Dziga Vertov is not particularly well served by the opposition, which precludes any sense of the humor and celebration of filmic illusionism in the Soviet filmmaker's work. Instead, these examples rely on a dialectical relationship between avant-garde and mass cultures, which is characterized by the twin poles of exchange and opposition.

Mass cultural products project an inverse image of this relationship, positioning themselves as universal, but managing all the while to incorporate aspects of high modernist sensibility into their more vernacular style. (This is true as well of advertising, as Tashlin's *Artists and Models* so thoughtfully points out.) Lewis's comment about the "twenty sophisticates in the world" is hardly atypical of Hollywood's attitude toward the avant-garde. In the late twenties, German Expressionism exerted an effect on Hollywood style—in particular on its set design and lighting—but the studios generally ignored the more radical innovations of Expressionist style. And much more recently, Thom Andersen's *Los Angeles Plays Itself* (2003) has documented the aggressive and reactionary quality of Hollywood's depiction of modernist architecture. (See, for instance, his account of Mel Gibson's destruction—with the help of a pickup truck, no less—of John Lautner's 1958 Russ Garcia House in *Lethal Weapon 2* [1989].) At least consciously, Hollywood's interest in the avant-garde tends toward the poles of consumption and instrumentalization (e.g., the aesthetic of German Expressionism was used, at least in part, to create product differentiation and thereby increase ticket sales) and populist denigration (e.g., Gibson's red-blooded destruction of the "effete" Russ Garcia House). Yet Lewis's work suggests that this relationship is more complicated than these examples indicate.

Understanding and contextualizing Lewis's films again raises the question of the classical and modern. The word *classical* has a range of overlapping meanings, several of which are operative in the domain of film history. The word can be used simply to refer to Greek and Roman antiquity, as when Maurice Bardèche and Robert Brassillach note, in their 1935 *History of Motion Pictures*, that, "while historical spectacles, and especially classical ones, were a specialty of the Italians, they sometimes explored the modern soul too."[28] It can also refer to, as the *Oxford English Dictionary* puts it, "an acknowledged standard or model" or to an object that is somehow "representative, typical; archetypal" or "traditional."[29] This is the way in Jean Renoir uses the phrase "classical cinema" in 1926 when he speaks of Charlie Chaplin, Ernst Lubitsch, and Clarence Brown as providing a "formula for [a cinema of] the future." Although these first two uses have an implicit periodizing function, the word can also serve to explicitly designate the movement or nature of history. As the *OED* puts it: "of or relating to a period considered the most highly developed of the civilization that produced it" or "designating such a period." In the domain of film history, this use is often ironic or ambivalent, as in scholarship that champions a modernist, or alternative, cinema in contrast to the classical style of the Hollywood studio era. And finally, and closely connected with this last use, is the sense in which the classical is understood as "characterized by adherence to established stylistic forms, and by harmony, balance, and restraint." This use is sometimes further specified by the word *neoclassical*.

This slipperiness of the idea of the classical has something to do with the durability of the construct of classical cinema in the discipline of cinema studies, which stresses first one connotation and then another, depending upon the broader theoretical and methodological commitments of the text in which the construct appears. And it is not unusual for film historians and theorists to slide between connotations depending upon the situation in which the construct is utilized, something that is made easy by the fact that these meanings overlap substantially.

More importantly for the subject at hand, the word *classical* has always been paired with the word *modern*. And unsurprisingly, the word *modern* shifts in tandem with its other half, designating sometimes a historical distinction between the present and the past that makes no judgment of value, sometimes an aesthetic form that breaks, even gently, with a classical model, and sometimes a historical break that describes major aesthetic and ideological rupture. In scholarship that stretches from the early 1970s to the present, the distinction has most commonly been invoked in this final sense, the classical cinema standing in for a dominant set of aesthetic norms (sometimes understood as realist, sometimes along neoclassical lines, and sometimes as simply durable in relation to other cinemas) and the modern for any cinema (or genre or even individual film) that breaks with these norms.

Lewis is for many reasons an interesting figure here, not least because of the complex institutional and formal (aesthetic) relationship with Hollywood industry that I have been describing but also because of the interest displayed in his work by members of the French New Wave. The eventual understanding of Lewis's work as engaged in critical reflection (an understanding that this chapter seeks to extend) is for this reason fascinating. Lewis himself was hardly avant-garde in sensibility, but it is also not case that we are belatedly or anachronistically reading this impulse into his work. What is clear from a book like *The Total Film-maker* is that Lewis has always—like Keaton and Chaplin before him—been interested in formal, technological, and stylistic questions about the cinema. He is thus legible as a kind of Godard without an intellectual culture of film to surround him; he is a modernist in an environment within which there exists no such space or designation.

The traditional opposition between realist and modernist film-making also ignores the ways in which popular American and European films have managed to inherit some dimension of modernism. In *The*

Classical Hollywood Cinema, Bordwell, Thompson, and Staiger conclude their book with the identification of "alternative modes of film practice," one of which they label "modernist."[30] Whereas the classical Hollywood cinema is defined by its interest in narrative, the authors of *The Classical Hollywood Cinema* argue that modernist cinema

> could be described as one in which spatial and temporal systems come forward and share with narrative the role of structuring the film. That is, narration is no longer the most important aspect of plot; other structures can compete for our attention. Hence these films often pose problems of how to unify themselves: a dynamic of unity and fragmentation is set up within the text.[31]

Though they acknowledge that the category is provisional, the authors suggest that it includes "most works of Ozu, Dreyer, Jacques Tati, Mizoguchi, Jacques Rivette, Robert Bresson, Eisenstein, Godard, Oshima, Straub/Huillet, Marguerite Duras, Yvonne Rainer, *et al.*"[32] But this description of the modernist cinema applies surprisingly well to Lewis's self-directed films, which structure themselves around systems of space (e.g., *The Ladies Man*), time (e.g., *The Errand Boy*), and "the fragment as a form of coherence" (e.g., *The Bellboy*).[33] The crucial contest here is the slapstick comedy's relationship to narrative, the description of which has been the most productive area of scholarship in the physical comedy. For this reason, I want to pause for a minute on the suggestion that modernist films "often pose problems of how to unify themselves," and that consequently "a dynamic of unity and fragmentation is set up within the text." It is worth thinking through how this formal question, and the formal dynamic that it creates, might be seen to operate in Lewis's work and how Lewis manages to solve what we could call "the unity problem." This will allow us to think about the broader comparison between Lewis's work (and the work of physical comedy in general) and that of more apparently modernist filmmakers such as Ozu, Dreyer, and Godard.

The Bellboy, Lewis's first self-directed feature, begins by actually foregrounding the problem of unification. In the film, Lewis plays an inept bellboy named Stanley who works at a plush Miami Beach hotel (The Fontainebleau, where the real Lewis frequently performed). *The Bellboy* is justly famous for the fact that, with the exception of an extended cameo as himself ("Joe Levitch"), Lewis plays the whole movie in pantomime. More importantly for the point at hand, however, the film itself has no discernible plot and is instead structured around a series of gags that take place in and around the environs of the hotel. That is to say, the film finds its structure not in a narrative dominant that uses temporal and spatial systems as vehicles for plot but in the unit of the gag, which is itself dependent upon a larger structuration of physical space. The various rooms and spaces of the hotel are the occasions for the creation of the gags, which the film stacks, one on top of the other, with no attention to narrative progression. The film forms an experiment for which *The Ladies Man* would become the realization.

The Bellboy is preceded by a prologue with a film executive named "Jack Emulsion," who delivers a monologue into the camera. After showing a series of illustrations of the "run-of-the-mill film fare" that Paramount has opted not to make, he explains:

> We chose what you're about to see, a film based on fun. And it's just a little different. Insofar as there is no story and no plot. That's right. I said, no story, no plot. It is actually a series of silly sequences. Or you might say, it is a visual diary of a few weeks in the life of a real nut.

Shawn Levy suggests that Lewis added the prologue to soothe actual Paramount studio executives who were indeed baffled by the film's lack of plot. (In *The Total Film-maker*, Lewis himself writes that "the execs had been concerned that the audience wouldn't understand why there was no plot. So I shot a piece of film opening on a supposed exec of the studio. His narration was, 'The picture you are about to see relates to nothing.'"[34]) But while it's possible to read the scene as an *apologia*, the joke seems less soothing than openly spiteful of the studio forces that had previously reined in Lewis's authorial drive. *The Bellboy* was, after all, Lewis's first self-directed film, financed with his own money and written and produced by him under astounding practical pressures.[35] In this light, the prologue is better understood as an outright declaration of independence.

More importantly, the scene suggests that Lewis's answer to the unity problem is that the film is "a series of silly sequences" that serve as "a visual diary of a few weeks in the life of a real nut." That is to say, the organizing principle behind *The Bellboy* is the quality of silliness as it pertains to the grotesque character of Stanley. And this principle is enough both to generate the series of gags that form the content of the film and to create a sense of unity between these gag-fragments.

In this sense, a version of the "undermining and transformation" of traditional narrative modes can be found in Lewis's work, which is invested throughout with an ambivalent irony about the terms of a classical film practice. Earlier, I claimed that, with some imagination, we might understand the films of Buster Keaton as realist in orientation because they are animated by an interest in the human relationship to the world. Keaton's work attempts to transform the subject's relationship to a universe of mechanical objects by acknowledging and thereby redeeming the separateness of consciousness and world. In contrast with this realist stance toward the world of things, Lewis's films have an entirely different ontological character. They do not attempt to depict nor attempt to come into contact with the world beyond the image, but to convey a sense of its distance. If Keaton's work is a series of images of the world—of *our* world, one could say—Lewis's films, one could say, depict *a* world—one among many. And it is a world very far from our own, with its own laws and its own peculiar emotional logic. The "formalism" of a film like *The Ladies Man* does not attempt to determine what it takes to make a film (it does not search for the limits of film as such), but instead reveals that the limits of its world may be incorporated into that world's meaning. It represents a vision of the world in which that world's meaning comes into being only upon its total ironization. That is to say, its specificity lies paradoxically in a sense of the cinema's plurality. It therefore declares that our world (the world beyond and before the frame) is itself plural, incapable of being beheld in a single vision.

Such an account helps to explain Lewis's interest in spatial *discontinuity*, as in the Miss Cartilage sequence in *The Ladies Man* or in Tashlin and Lewis's refusal to efface the movement between the "real world" exterior of the driveway and what is obviously a large stage set backyard in *Cinderfella* (1960). Such discontinuity has the effect of declaring the world onscreen as separate, the product of imagination, the phenomenon of one man's mind, an effect that will become particularly pronounced decades later in the turn to digital video. These formal mechanisms are also the source of some of the pathos in Lewis's films, the sense of simultaneous liberation and imprisonment that he projects through the character of The Idiot. However pedestrian its intellectual pedigree, in this way at least can Lewis's work be understood as modernist in orientation.

Of course, this account of Lewis's modernism only goes so far. However engaged the spectator of Lewis's film may be, it is absurd to endow a movie like *The Bellboy* with qualities of "the recognizable, the miraculous and the sympathetic," the aspects of critical response that Greenberg singles out as ethically productive in the reception of Picasso, or with the "process of intellection" that forms the center of Annette Michelson's understanding of Dziga Vertov.[36] These are simply not the values of Lewis's work nor those of Hollywood film in general. But if conventional accounts of the cinema's modernist inheritance stress the ways in which various modernist techniques of filmmaking have been watered down for popular consumption in the classical cinema, we can see in the relation of Lewis's work to his French admirers a movement in the opposite direction.

It's particularly interesting to consider the inheritance of Lewis's work by Godard. For several decades, Godard voiced his admiration for Lewis's work, first in his productions with Tashlin and then in the comedian's self-directed films.[37] If Godard's interest in Lewis can be understood in the context of French *auteurism* (the special 1967 issue of *Cahiers du Cinema* dedicated to Lewis is the best document of this), it can also be understood within the larger history of modernism and the slapstick comedy. Godard took up various of Lewis's ideas, some of which I have been describing as modernist in character, and employed them in a more political and self-consciously modernist context.

Godard's inheritance and redeployment of Lewis's ideas is particularly clear in *Tout Va Bien* (1972), Godard and Jean-Pierre Gorin's attempt to describe the political mood in their country in the aftermath of May 1968. Other writers have suggested that Lewis's cutaway set for *The Ladies Man* served as the inspiration for Godard and Gorin's sausage factory, the location within which the majority of the film occurs.[38] But while it is easy to see a simple physical resemblance (compare Figures 6.7 and 6.9), no one has articulated the nature of the transformation of

Figure 6.9. The sausage factory (*Tout Va Bien*).

Lewis's idea to its new purpose in Godard and Gorin's film. The issue is that it is not the set itself that forms the particular point of connection between the two films but Lewis's particular construction of space. In Lewis and his interest in creating new forms of continuity for the sake of the gag, Godard found a new means by which to structure a film not simply outside of the ideological constraints of classical narrative (a project upon which he had been working for many years) but to depict the ways in which space itself possesses an ideological valence.

One way to think about this is to consider the fact that the two films share Bordwell's problem of unification. Lewis needed to join together a series of disconnected gags, and the giant house served as a rationale for their unification. Godard needed a means by which he could depict the factory strike not as the result of one character's psychology but as the logical result of an economic situation, which itself took on spatial characteristics. In this comparison, the representation of economic relations takes the place of the gag: both constitute variables that destabilize an equation usually solved by means of narrative. Both gag and economic relation are fragments that threatened the larger coherence of the individual film.

If in *The Ladies Man* spatial continuity serves as a motivating force for the gag, in *Tout Va Bien* it becomes a way to express economic and ideological relations as a series of spatial constructions. Just as Lewis moves from gag to gag, Godard and Gorin track and cut between the various forces within the factory—from Susan (Jane Fonda), her husband (Yves Montand), and the factory boss (Vittorio Caprioli) in the executive office, for instance, to the insurgents who hold them hostage in the secretarial area, to the shop stairs on which the confrontation between the union and the insurgents is staged. The film, Godard said in an early interview, "shows the three social forces [union, management, leftists] in the same physical space. Instead of first describing the individuals, it first describes the masses, and the power structure of the masses."[39] Thus, if narrative is a means of describing individuals and their motivations, space becomes a means of describing a larger ideological structure within which these individual psychologies are contained. In both films, the cutaway set creates a distancing effect, which is recognizable as irony: Lewis's gag-centered reference to the mediatized nature of filmic space becomes Godard and Gorin's more Brechtian self-reflexivity.

These Lewisian spatial strategies were made more attractive to Godard by the ways in which they disavowed the goal-oriented protagonist of classical narrative. I have already discussed the ways in which *The Ladies Man* undercuts the supposed psychological progress of Herbert H. Heebert. The film's ending, for instance, is confirmation not only of the fact that *The Ladies Man* exists more for its gags than its story, but that these gags actually rely for their humor upon the ironic destabilization of that story. Irony provides the opening within which comedy may occur. Godard too takes up the tool of irony, but employs it to didactic ends, as in the final shot of the film, which tracks across an empty lot on a cloudy day while playing a song about it always being sunny in France. (The irony of *Tout Va Bien* is often funny too, albeit in a different register: a communist intellectual sells his book in a giant supermarket, for instance, and the film stages it such that his book is explicitly compared to toilet paper and bags of potatoes.) But Godard transposes the ironic, gag-based characterization of Lewis's film into a multiperspectival account of the factory strike. Rather than follow Susan as she tries to report on the striking workers, for instance, the film splinters into the actions and speeches of many characters each with his or her own individual goals, all of which are in turn connected to the overarching dispute about the factory and its representation. If Lewis's clowning turns on his fragmentary, dis-unified self, Godard's didacticism works according to a similar mechanism: he subjects the classical protagonist to an overwhelming centrifugal force, an almost world-encompassing irony, such that he becomes a series of multiple and contradictory persons, the inner lives of which have little bearing on their material condition.[40]

I don't mean to overstate these connections. There are many powerful and important formal differences between the two films, even accounting for their circumstances of production and their generic separation. Most notably, whereas Lewis's film has a predominately vertical structure (many of the gags rely on Herbert running up and down stairs; Lewis frequently positions the camera at a high angle in order to look down on the action of the house), Godard's film has an overwhelmingly horizontal orientation. Not only does *Tout Va Bien* refuse both high and low camera positions—employing instead the head- or chest-high angle of television journalism—the dominant movement both of the camera and of actors within individual scenes is from left to right and right to left. Whereas Lewis's film is everywhere concerned with depth as a means of motivating the individual gags and with displaying an overarching mediatization of space, *Tout Va Bien* seeks repeatedly to flatten its images, forgoing depth for a density of composition along its striking horizontal axis.

Seen another way, this is a matter of the ways in which the two films confront their respective viewers, a process that can be mapped as a series of intersections within their constructions of space. In *The Ladies Man*, the vertical composition of the house joins up with an interest in gagging-in-depth; the two axes (x and y) meet in the figure of Lewis. *The Ladies Man* confronts its viewer not by means of an alienation effect, but through the bumbling, anxious, not-quite-diegetic figure of Lewis himself. This separates it from both the classical cinema and the politically ambitious cinema of Godard. In *Tout Va Bien*, the horizontal orientation of the cutaway set as well as that of the long tracking shots that display that factory join up with the different horizontality of the speeches delivered to the camera (see Figure 6.10). These axes (x and z) meet not within filmic space but on the surface of the frame itself—at the place where the viewer comes into contact with the film.

Peter Wollen's famous account of *Vent d'Est* (1970) argues that Godard developed a "counter-cinema," which Wollen characterizes as forgoing the ordinary requirements of the classical cinema in favor of a series of contrarian principles, including that of "narrative intransivity." "The basic story, as much of it as remains," Wollen writes of Godard's work, "does not have any recognizable sequence, but is more like a series of intermittent flashes."[41] Although Wollen traces the origins of this structure to Brecht and Antonin Artaud (as well as to the picaresque novel—itself a genre of comedy), his characterization applies equally well to *The Ladies Man* and others of Lewis's self-directed films. It is in this second horizontality— the z axis—that *Tout Va Bien* separates itself fully from Lewis's strategy of spatial continuity, going on to confront the viewer on the plane of the screen itself. It is true that Godard's films are flagrantly intertextual, full of quotations across the history of Hollywood film, some of which are laudatory, some ironic, and some without apparent meaning. But in

Figure 6.10. A second horizontality (*Tout Va Bien*).

Lewis Godard found an idea of coherence through space the ambivalent use of which in *The Ladies Man* would take on a more political charge.

This movement from Lewis to Godard represents an interesting instance of movement between low and high cultures. More importantly, it represents a movement that functions not as low culture imitating its high counterpart—as it does in J. Hoberman's theorization of "vulgar modernism," for instance—but as the high taking up an instance of low modernism and redeploying its figures to new ends.[42] If Lewis's films did in fact meaningfully influence Godard (for there is no question that Godard responded to them) and if the modernism of Lewis's films does not simply result from their borrowing of "genuine" culture, but from their production of entirely new formal and aesthetic ideas, then it is clear that the relation between high and low, avant-garde and kitsch, is not a one-way street, but a relation of exchange, however dense and problematic. Furthermore, connecting Lewis's formal strategies for the conveyance of humor with Godard's investment in "the process of intellection" and in the popular cinema's radical potential allows us to claim some feature of modernism for Lewis's work. Lewis the man might hold conservative, even reactionary, political positions, but Lewis the filmmaker was a member of an unconscious avant-garde, an accidental auteur.

Godard was himself aware of the dynamics of this exchange, which he seems to have understood as taking a distinct shape within the medium of film. In his 1957 review of Frank Tashlin's *Hollywood or Bust* (1956), he alludes to an interesting sort of cinematic specificity, separating the modernism of the cinema from that of the literary tradition by means of its disinterest in boundaries of form and class. "The cinema," he wrote, "is too resolutely modern for there to be any question of it following any path other than an open one, a perpetual aesthetic inauguration":

> Its history differs all the more sharply from that of the theatre or the novel in that it is the exact opposite. Whereas literary experts nowadays praise a play or a book only in so far as it conclusively seals all exits round it (cf. James Joyce's *Ulysses* or Samuel Beckett's *Fin de Partie*), we on the other hand praise *To Catch a Thief, Elena et les hommes, Voyage to Italy* or *Et Dieu . . . crea le femme* because these films conclusively open new horizons.[43]

In the idea of "perpetual aesthetic inauguration" and the opening of new aesthetic horizons, we can discern the rudiments of the connection between physical comedy and film modernism. In Godard's little account, high modernist literature works by separating its address from the formal qualities of mass cultural products. It functions, that is, by invoking Greenbergian "difficulty." The cinema, for Godard, on the other hand, is plural, open, and mass cultural, all qualities that go toward constituting its specific modernity. Even the films of Jerry Lewis—created in large part for children and despised by the cultural bourgeoisie—have, when seen in the right light and harnessed to progressive ends, a modernist dimension. That Lewis himself would have shunned "the twenty sophisticates in the world" only reinforces the odd, almost accidental quality of his innovations. In the end, then, the movement from Lewis to Godard suggests the ambivalence of the vernacular Hollywood modern, which serves as the material for further modernizing impulses in the world cinema while at the same time displaying a lasting reactionary inertia. Nowhere is this ambivalence more apparent than in the figure of Lewis—the "witless genius," the idiot savant, the so-called total filmmaker.

Epilogue

The Apotheosis of Failure: *Jackass*

THIS BOOK HAS USED A SINGLE device within slapstick comedy to chart an ontology of film across a series of technological and institutional changes in American cinema, from the formation of the studio system to the coming of synchronized sound to the eventual dissolution of the system and certain of its formal and stylistic imperatives. This narrative begs the question of what has become of the medium now, in production, distribution, and reception environments that are characterized by the ubiquity of digital technologies. Might the comedy of self-reference have something to say about these newest possibilities of the cinema?

The "digital revolution" has raised questions regarding the putative truth status or value of digital images, changing patterns of cinema's distribution and reception, the changing relation between spectators' bodies and these images, and the perceived stability of the discipline's object of study. Perhaps unsurprisingly given this last concern, one striking feature of these conversations is the great variance in theoretical and critical burden that is placed upon the fact and nature of the digital turn, from William J. Mitchell's early pronouncement that digital images foreclose upon the basic truth claims of the analog image to John Belton's sense that "digital projection . . . does not, in any way, transform the nature of the motion-picture experience," a claim that Belton frames around the experience of reception but one that has been repeated in more formalist criticism.[1]

As I hope to demonstrate below, the changed rhetoric and meanings of slapstick comedy provide us with a slant version of Mitchell's early pronouncements: these comedies suggest that digital technologies have greatly transformed the nature and experience of the cinema, but that this change has occurred at a level that is more basic and thus more difficult to observe than was the case with earlier technological changes such as, say, the adoption of panchromatic film stock or the spread of widescreen formats. A further difficulty is that these changes to the viewing experience have occurred over a relatively long period of time, as would befit the cautious diffusion of digital technologies into the industry itself. Regardless, it is my claim here that these technologies have altered the cinema in a way that can be meaningfully described at an ontological level and that this change is best observed within and through the performance of critical judgment.

To this end, I want to look at the reiteration of a single gag across eighty years of film history, first on 35mm film in the heyday of the silent era and then on digital video in a feature film the form, style, and audience of which were derived from amateur digital video as well as the display of this video on cable television. The gag is famous: a man stands beneath the façade of a falling house, and he survives this fall by placing himself (or being placed) within the geometrical space of a second-story window. The original instance is that of Buster Keaton's *Steamboat Bill Jr.* (1928); the second is that of the conclusion of *Jackass Number Two* (Tremaine, 2006).[2] My claim is that Keaton's performance, with its vision of an automatic grace, of the body as redeeming something of the human, is a specifically filmic vision—that is, one that is inseparable from the ontology of analog film—and hence that the repetition of this gag in *Jackass* can make perspicuous something about the ontology of digital video, namely, the fate of the body against and within a technology of abstraction.

The virtuoso finale of *Steamboat Bill Jr.* consists of a series of gags within a howling cyclone. As the town of River Junction collapses around him, Buster wakes up in a hospital bed. He is exposed to the open air, the storm having swept away the roof and walls of a building. A great wind then picks up his bed and shuttles it first into a barn, where Buster peers up at a stable of donkeys, and then into the front lawn of a two-story home. The winds now at gale force, he takes shelter beneath the bed, only to have the house's lone inhabitant, an old man in an impressive beard, jump from a second-story window onto the mattress. The wind then hurtles the bed off-screen and Buster, stunned from the impact of the man's jump, stands alone in the storm. The film cuts from Buster rubbing his neck in medium long shot (Keaton's preferred distance for psychologization) to a much wider shot in which we see Buster framed by the frame of the house itself, his body a small point within the larger environment of the home and its yard. This staging sets up the gag in question: as Buster recovers from his injury, the house's facade becomes unmoored and falls, as if on a hinge, onto the ground below. Buster, of course, is unscathed: he has unwittingly positioned himself within the one open space of that facade, the window frame having fallen precisely, even mathematically, around his erect body.

The thrill of Keaton's gag stems both from its having been staged as an accident (Buster is merely, if also preternaturally, lucky not to have been injured) as well as from its display of this virtuoso stunt (we know that Keaton the director and performer has staged this event and risked his personal safety in the process). Like so many gags, its meaning relies upon the articulation of an ironic relation between the ideal and the real. This is not the display of an actual accident, but the image of one, and the fact and awareness of its having been staged is constitutive of our pleasure. The moment is made all the more beautiful here, as in all of Keaton's stunts, by the fact that Buster's body displays a kind of involuntary or automatic grace. As I suggested at the outset of this book, Buster instantiates an automatism that preserves the possibility of being human. His films are utopian in this way: Buster may live in a decidedly Fordist environment, one in which nature itself is figured as one vast set of mechanisms and within which there is increasingly little space for human being, but the character and body of Buster imagine this world as navigable through a beautifully passive action, a negative capability realized at the level of sinew and bone. He is an unacknowledged legislator of the mechanical world.

Needless to say, this house gag is done to much different effect in *Jackass Number Two*. Unlike the relatively tight narrative construction of *Steamboat Bill Jr.* but true to the stage origins of slapstick comedy (and similar, in part, to Kovacs's television work), the second installment of the *Jackass* film series consists entirely of a series of gags and stunts, one strung after the other in a ninety-minute program distinguished not by story but by an undulating pattern of affect.[3] *Jackass Number Two*, like the first film and like the show before them, moves its audiences and its performers between experiences of shock, disgust, awe, titillating laughter, and sadistic pleasure. As other writers (and one of the creators of *Jackass*) have noted, there is a clear, if also ambiguous, relation here between early-twentieth-century theatrical performance, the historical avant-garde, and the performances, style, and form of *Jackass*.[4] The *Jackass* films and television show repeatedly make plain the connection between slapstick comedy and Surrealism, from the obsessive interest in shock to the broadly antiauthoritarian aesthetic and attitude of its performers even to individual images, like the placing of a leech on a performer's eyeball that recalls the opening of *Un Chien Andalou* (1929).

The form of *Jackass Number Two* is entirely presentational, often done in direct address to the audience and without adhering to a narrative. (As Spike Jonze said of the third *Jackass* movie, "The great thing about doing our movie in 3-D is we're not trying to disappear into a narrative."[5]) In a way that recalls both turn-of-the-century live performance, the early cinema, and variety television work, the performers turn repeatedly to the camera to announce the names and substances of the individual gags, to record their own affective experiences, and to form a mimetic bond with their audience.[6] The movie's form is by no means random, however: it spaces its most outrageous stunts at strategic moments in the program—from an opening slow motion sequence in which the performers run from a herd of live bulls through a suburban neighborhood to a lengthy closing gag ("Terror Taxi") that has a distinct narrative structure—in a way that is reminiscent of the form of the vaudeville program one century earlier, here altered not to accommodate people entering and exiting the theater at different times but to keep them within with the promise of ever more extreme shock and humiliation.

Fascinatingly, the film ends with a song-and-dance number, a loose parody of Hollywood style, in this case a musical—replete with a broad staircase to nowhere, costumed women in kick lines, and synchronized swimming—all done to the "The Best of Times" from Harvey Fierstein and Jerry Herman's *La Cage aux Folles*. The joke is almost too complex to describe. Like the opening to the first film, which sends up the Hollywood action film, this musical number declares the film's parodic and oppositional relation to other Hollywood films, its satiric relation to social and sexual convention, and, perhaps more surprisingly, its place within a larger tradition of stage and film entertainment. Like much slapstick comedy, the finale has it both ways: neither wholly within the traditions of the stage or Hollywood musical nor wholly without, the number serves the purpose of actually ending the program on a "showstopper" while at the same time critiquing the need for formal closure. What is more, the song's lyrics ("The best of times is now / What's left of Summer / But a faded rose? / The best of times is now / As for tomorrow, well, who knows? / Who knows? Who knows?"), which in the musical describe the metaphysical justification for a love affair, here rather literally describe the justification for the stunts that we have witnessed over the past hour and a half. The relation is, in this sense, not parody at all but a fascinating association between a gay love affair and a series of taboo-breaking gags and their attempt to locate the physical and emotional limits of the body.

In *Jackass Number Two*, the homosexual setting and story of the original musical (a nightclub in St. Tropez; the love affair between its owner and one of his performers) is used as a pretext for putting the performers in drag (e.g., Steve-O dances with the synchronized swimmers in a gold lame bathing suit) and in costumes associated with certain forms of gay masculinity (e.g., Dave England and Ehren McGhehey dress in Halloween-store construction worker uniforms while they attempt to balance atop, and are consequently dumped from, an actually rotating concrete mixer). Of course, some of the performers play earlier gags in similar costumes, so that the musical number is not so much the excuse for these costumes but rather suggests an entire aesthetic world that is constructed for the physical and emotional humiliation of the performers. Yet the effect isn't exactly homophobic; it is better characterized as the capable destruction of taboo and the open celebration of a certain kind of homoeroticism, albeit one that is distinct from gay culture (and wholly recognizable to anyone who has spent time in or around fraternities). Indeed, the world of *Jackass* is relentlessly homosocial; it only seems able to imagine its odd utopia—a world devoid of work, responsibility, or authority—within and around men, as if the inclusion of women would introduce an Oedipal conflict that would inevitably send this world toward rule and law.

It is at the conclusion of "The Best of Times," and hence at the end of *Jackass Number Two* itself, that we reencounter Keaton's gag. The song and dance has moved from the initial MGM-looking staircase to a construction site to the synchronized swimmers to a burning apartment building and now, finally, to an *Oklahoma!*-like set, the male performers in cowboy costumes and some dancing extras in pioneer burlesque. After some half-hearted dancing, the camera dollies between the stars of the movie, crouched opposite each other in couples, before ending on Johnny Knoxville alone. (These pairings and the final appearance of Knoxville alone are ambivalent references both to the love affair of the original *La Cage aux Folles* and to Knoxville's status as the movie's headliner, a status that effectively prevents him from achieving even this heavily ironized image of coupling. In this sense, it recalls the ending to *College* [1927], Buñuel's favorite of Keaton's films, in which Buster "gets the girl" but which then treats us to a montage of his marriage that ends in twin gravestones.) Like Keaton, Knoxville stands before the facade of a building, which is this time marked "Saloon." He is also positioned in the space of a single, second-story window, which allows him to survive the house's collapse. Yet immediately after the conclusion of this stunt, a wrecking ball (with no diegetic source in the movie or in the preceding musical number, let alone in the *Oklahoma!* set) swings in from offscreen right, knocking him violently from the frame. The actor Rip Torn then marches through the foreground of the shot, wearing a red sequined coat and throwing party favors onto an empty stage.

While the broadly "Hollywood" setting of the final number, with its loose references to Busby Berkeley and to studio-era *mise-en-scene*, suggest that this is a self-conscious reference to Keaton, it is crucial to keep in mind several moments of difference with the original gag. Most obviously, in keeping with the tone of parody established by the musical number as a whole, the facade of this house does not belong to a larger, more or less complete diegetic environment. Instead, when the facade falls, we see, in addition to what is obviously a stage backdrop and various "Western" props, a floodlight and a director's chair, which seem to have been put there not for functional reasons relating to the production but to reinforce our knowledge that what we are seeing is staged. Unlike *Steamboat Bill Jr.*, there is no house behind the building's facade: it is shown to simply be plywood fascia without any attached structure, there solely for the staging of the gag.

This underscores the rather complex sense in which *Jackass* might be said to take place in our world. As others have noticed, it is crucial to the rhetoric of the *Jackass* television show and movies that they are *not* staged in a fictional universe; indeed, a good part (if not all) of the charge of the individual gags depends upon our sense that they occur in our world and are authentic in this way. This is one reason for the incessant use of musicians, athletes, and anonymous bystanders not as actors within this world but as witnesses to the acts depicted onscreen; these people are there to affirm that these gags and stunts did in fact happen, hence that there is reason and reality beneath our shock, pleasure, and disgust. Yet at the same time, the fact that many of these people come from the world of entertainment consequently provides—like the musical finale that is both staged showstopper and document of injury and humiliation—the movie with the sense that *our* world is itself staged or virtual.[7]

A further and, to my mind, more interesting formal difference here is the wrecking ball that tears Knoxville from the frame after the house has fallen. The meaning of Keaton's gag changes entirely here. Most obviously, this wrecking ball destroys the sense of graceful accident, and hence the image of an accidental utopia that is present throughout Keaton's films, in favor of a bald declaration of failure. Keaton survives the falling house by means of a luck that inheres to or within his body; Knoxville survives the falling house through dumb luck, only to be struck down in more spectacular fashion.[8] We could say that Keaton's films reimagine, or reconstitute, failure as success in the form of the accident, whereas *Jackass* imagines failure itself as a kind of happiness, or more minimally, as authenticity, a feeling that emerges at the boundary between the physical limits of the body and a powerful sense of sociability. Indeed, it is telling that, as is the case with all of the gags and stunts before it, when we see Knoxville hit by the wrecking ball, we hear the offscreen laughter of the other performers.

What might all of this tell us about the medium in which it was realized? Louise Peacock has noted that, unlike most slapstick film comedy, in *Jackass* "the pain is real but it is in some cases actively sought."[9] But why exactly is pain sought in moments like that of the wrecking ball? What does it achieve for its performers and their audience? Needless to say, the producers and performers of *Jackass* turned to digital video not out of any aspiration to identify the limits and possibilities of digital video (as might be claimed for certain instances of video art) but rather for financial reasons, to accommodate the improvised and mobile character of the performances, and—at least initially—to further signal the putatively countercultural nature of the television program and movies. Yet again, it is through such apparently "practical" or institutional concerns that we can begin to distinguish some of the background of ontological difference. Notably, the creators of *Jackass* are self-conscious about certain of these differences, from Johnny Knoxville's reported concern that the cameras used in *Jackass 3D* (2010) would obstruct the actors from establishing sufficient identification with each other and with their audiences to Tremaine's choice to use 35mm for the opening of the first *Jackass* movie in order to parody Hollywood form and style.[10] Tremaine has said that the opening of that film, which aims for the look and sound of a Hollywood action sequence (replete with a pretentious, Hans Zimmer–sounding aria), "was supposed to be the big Hollywood lie. We were trying to get the whole audience to think we'd just completely sold out. We shot this bit on film and we wanted everyone watching it to think that we just went completely Hollywood. . . . People ended up liking it, which was too bad."[11] This suggests, as Jorie Lagerwey has claimed, that for Tremaine, "inexpensive video equipment and its inherent technical 'liveness' (the image is captured directly and immediately on tape without the delay and distance implied in printing film) are linked with a populism and a 'reality' without which the *Jackass* project would fail."[12] In other words, the project of *Jackass* itself (like Keaton's work before them) is itself bound up with an exploration and realization of the possibilities of the medium in which it is instantiated, regardless of the intentions or exhibition contexts of the show and movies themselves.[13] When Johnny Knoxville survives the falling house but is crushed by a mysterious wrecking ball, he finds himself, in an important sense, against the limits of his medium itself. True to the calculated bathos of slapstick comedy, this isn't really even metaphor.

All of this bears productive relationship to the theorization of digital video, which has in large part turned around the question of its materiality. A first advance sought to characterize digital video (and consequently digital filmmaking and exhibition) as defined by its immateriality, at least in relation to analog film. This advance was then corrected by an emphasis upon the distinct materiality of digital artifacts, the fact, for instance, that despite their radical reproducibility, every movie encoded as a digital file is in an important sense distinct from every other by virtue of the particular magnetic disc upon which it is stored or the processes of transfer that brought it there in the first place.

While it is indisputable that digital artifacts are always and everywhere material objects, I want to take up the idea that the discourse of digital video functions according to an understanding or fantasy of its immateriality. Any phenomenology of digital video must necessarily take into account our experience (however unfounded) of the medium as immaterial. Many accounts of digital video that stress its materiality take this claim too far and underdetermine the relationship between its material bases and its discursive meanings or possibilities. As objections to much classical film theory never cease to stress, we cannot read the discursive possibilities of a medium directly from its material bases. Yet the two are not radically divorced: a medium achieves meaning by means of the discursive formations and historical *a prioris* that gather around and constitute it, and these formations and histories are themselves entangled within our often implicit or folk accounts of these media as materials. This is true even for what would seem to be a best case for the opposing position. While very few paintings would seem to directly rely upon pigment and canvas for their meanings, the background against which they achieve these meanings is inseparable from these physical features: Renaissance perspective, for instance, only achieves meaning insofar as it is achieved on two-dimensional canvas or paper; its surface is therefore understood as something that can receive or hold an inscription.

These two aspects of the reiteration of Keaton's gag—an altered relation to the depiction of our world and the sense in which failure functions as a sign of authenticity—suggest that *Jackass* both acknowledges and works against the characteristic abstraction of digital video (or, at a minimum, that the creators and performers of *Jackass* think of digital video as characteristically abstract) and its consequent and fraught relationship to human embodiment. Because these are hardly uncontroversial ways of taking up the subject and nature of digital video, I want to briefly put forth two reasons for thinking of digital video as abstracting and consequently as having a distinct relation to embodiment. The first derives from the relationship between the material substrate of digital video and our experience of it, the second from a more historical sense in which digital video has incorporated the philosophical and ideological burdens of certain ways of thinking about information.

Aden Evans has argued that "the digital has an ontology, a way of being, and products and processes generated through digital technologies bear traces of this way of being. The hallmark of the digital is to render abstraction materially operative, to bring abstraction into the concrete without it ceasing to be abstract."[14] This is, he argues, a basic characteristic of discrete code, the basis and power of which is its ability to treat any singular thing "as a reproducible arrangement of generalizable properties," or as a "discrete, isolable" entity "with independently determined, malleable properties."[15] In other words, what is distinct about entities on digital video is not their reproducibility or malleability, but rather the fact that they are represented against an infinite background of sameness, are legible only within the object ontology of the medium itself.

Evans's account of digital objects implicitly shares features with accounts like Mitchell's that try to chart the changed truth status of digital photography and cinema. Both accounts describe a totalizing force beneath the digital image, one that extracts a sameness from digital images beneath an apparent democratization of the technology. The pessimism of these accounts has been regularly contested, as in Mark Hansen's *New Philosophy for New Media* and Anna Munster's *Materializing New Media*, both of which insist upon the uniquely embodied forms of perception that are made available by digital art objects and to the possibilities for reimagining the philosophy and theory of media that these objects implicitly call forth.[16] For our purposes, however, it is notable that for both Hansen and Munster the utopian possibilities of the digital environment are realized in digital texts that specifically lay claim to status as art objects. This suggests, at least in part, that cinema and television, when they are produced and distributed by means of digital technologies, are middle, and in some sense melancholic, cases. The spectators who encounter these texts, whether in theaters wired for digital projection, at home on their couches, or holding their phones on a crowded train, are blocked from developing the richer proprioceptive relations toward these objects that are made available, at least in part, in museum contexts. The theatrical experience can seem, in this light, as if it were almost vestigial.

What does such abstraction mean for the experience and representation of embodiment? One rationale for Katherine Hayles's *How We Became Posthuman* is to chart, as she puts it, "how information lost its body"—that is, how we came to think of information as a fundamental, even transcendental entity that circulates within multiple material substrates.[17] Hayles's book is testament to the fact that there is nothing that necessitates such a belief, that it is a myth in Roland Barthes's sense. Yet it is undeniable that such a belief adheres, with varying degrees of plausibility, in everything from the intellectual origins of artificial intelligence research to ordinary PET scans to a teenager's experience of *Call of Duty*. To think of information as the immaterial substrate of everything that exists is to view all entities as "discrete" and "isolable," hence to subscribe to a vision of, as Hayles puts it, "unlimited power and disembodied immortality." This is a world in which bodies negatively signal particularity or finitude, are merely the "meat" that temporarily holds and expresses the underlying software of self.

Digital video is, in this sense, just another visualization technology. It always and everywhere converts the body into data. This seems to me to be one meaningful distinction between analog film and digital video: film converts the human body to silver halide and celluloid, yet these substances retain some of the meaning and value of nature per se; digital video converts the human body into information. Of course, as viewers, we do not experience these bodies as information any more than we experienced bodies on analog film as celluloid and silver halide crystals, but given the omnipresence of digital imaging technologies and the obvious relationship of these technologies to digital video, we do, in some sense, experience these images as data. They take place, or achieve representation, against this backdrop.

To return to *Jackass*, the doubled or recursive sense of world here, in which what is represented is continuous with our own world and experience yet also figures our world as itself staged or virtual, is mirrored in the ability of digital video to fracture and multiply experience, to express the infinite difference and iterability that stem from the principles of abstraction and sameness. The digital environment is thus characterized by a sense in which our world is itself definitively plural, such that we cannot well distinguish between our fantasies or projections and a shared real, and such that acknowledgment must be achieved through an experience of fantasy as itself shared. And all of this is further related to the radically different temporalities of film and digital video: the former always takes place in an imagined past; it is always an image of time that has passed (hence its relationship to nostalgia); digital video *can* signify the past (and often does), but behind its ability to signify different times lives an eternal present. We can sense this present both intra- and extratextually. Within individual films, past and future take on a subjunctive quality, as in the hagiography of Spielberg's *Lincoln* (2012), which is—on its surface—legible not as history but as one representation of it; while on streaming services such as Criterion's *FilmStruck* vast catalogues of cinema are shown to be contained within a single box or landscape, hence to be radically simultaneous.

Perhaps more interesting, however, is the shift in the nature and representation of embodiment, a shift made plain by the movement from lucky survival (and pain avoided) in Keaton's work to happy failure (and pain achieved) in *Jackass*. In keeping with the abstract and predominantly disembodied character of digital video, we might think of this difference as two attempts to acknowledge the real: the thrill and pleasure of Keaton's work is related to our understanding that this performer did just these things and did them gracefully, and it is a part of this grace that they are embedded in a fictional world; the thrill and pleasure of *Jackass* lies in our sense that the actors did in fact perform these acts and moreover that they did them in a spirit of nihilism ("The best of times is now / As for tomorrow, well, who knows?"). And to succeed as nihilism they must be accomplished in our world. Keaton was only once hurt badly on the set of a film (his neck broke as he was hit by the spigot from a railroad water tower), and we do not register this event in the finished film. The performers of *Jackass* are hurt repeatedly (to the point, sometimes, of requiring hospitalization) and these moments are the very heart of the movies and the television show. Indeed, they are most profound when they reveal themselves to be involuntary or beyond willed experience. (I think of the almost pornographic look of shock, a feeling that registers as a kind of out-of-body or post-conscious experience, on Ehren McGhehey's face after his co-stars use a Lamborghini to pull out one of his teeth in *Jackass 3D*.) Here, a sense of reality—one that is tied, crucially, to a perverse sense of pleasure—is indexed by sounds and images of pain.

In this sense, *Jackass*, like the movies of Keaton and Chaplin before it, takes place in a resolutely realist form: it succeeds when it testifies to the body's pliability and resilience in the face of material reality. But it is characteristic of these later gags-as-failure, like the wrecking ball in *Jackass Number Two*, that they are always signs of presence. This may be because, in the digital environment, the narrow avoidance of disaster, as it occurs in the original instance of Keaton's gag, for instance, no longer functions as an index of presence; presence is now more easily achieved through the registration of failure and pain. Signs of failure and pain indicate to us that the images and sounds we see and hear are not the product of fantasy or projection but instead are the results of physical limits that inhere within particular human bodies. The body on digital video is no longer a site at which we might achieve a utopian (if also sometimes melancholy) fusion of body and technology but rather a useful index for or arbiter of material reality itself, hence a kind of final hope for the human subject. That the same thrill and pleasure is to be found in the fail video, where stunts and gags like those in *Jackass* are democratized in a further attempt to testify to this shared reality, is further testament to this.[18]

If we think of the emphasis upon the ordinary body and its pain as a kind of response to abstraction, one in which pain is taken as an index of the irreducibility of experience, the question of skepticism takes a new turn. Here, technology seems to separate or make abstract the self, such that the self looks over and over again for new ways of conveying its existence. People on digital video have some sense of themselves being made "digital, abstract, reduced." And in such an environment, the self must insistently and even obsessively be made present. In other words, *Jackass* might be understood as attempting, through its ritual presentation of sado-masochistic experience, to testify to the presence of the human self. It is, in this sense, melancholically posthuman.

The gags in *Jackass* reflect a subjectivity that is, to quote Hayles, "constituted by the crossing of the materiality of informatics with the immateriality of information," hence they occur at the chiasmus between materiality and immateriality, at the site at which these terms become visible or materialized within the medium of digital video. They are images of the passage between "the materiality of informatics" (i.e., the "real," profilmic body) and "the immateriality of information" (i.e., the human image figured, on digital video, as information). And they are theoretical in the sense that they isolate this passage from "informatics" to "information" and then acknowledge it as an important discursive and material basis of the medium itself.

I will summarize then by saying that slapstick comedy in the digital environment operates against and in consciousness of the sense in which digital video abstracts and normalizes through the discourse and experience of immateriality. The gag, from *Jackass* to *Fail Blog*, is now definitively chiastic in the sense that it works at, and across, the boundaries of the medium of digital video, at the intersection of the material and the immaterial. It functions at the crossing of these polarities in the sense that it is irreducible—its meaning depends, in part, upon the sense that they constitute a singular moment of a singular body—yet at the same time it achieves this figuration against the backdrop of the normalization and abstraction of the medium itself. In this sense, we are returned to the concept and representation of ambivalence with which my account of Keaton was first concerned: these gags figure materiality—here in the form of the human body—against the backdrop of the immaterial, the human body in contact with the digital milieu. That we as viewers participate in or digest this ambivalence in the form of an oscillation between sadism and masochism suggests that our own orientation—toward the medium and toward our sense of world—is perverse, neither closer nor farther from the real than was its analog ancestor. We have, then, a new iteration of Bazin's "myth of total cinema," an asymptotic relation between representation and reality, a history that promises total connection but one that will always recede from reality in the face of our fear of presence.

Notes

Introduction. The Comedy of Self-Reference

1. In early trade journals of the film industry, the word *slapstick* is largely pejorative, a form and style of comedy to be overcome. Throughout this book, I use the phrases "slapstick comedy" and "physical comedy" interchangeably to describe a particular mode of film comedy, and without any connotation of value. As Louise Peacock has helpfully (and simply) defined it, "slapstick is a mode of performance that relies on broad physical comedy." See her *Slapstick and Comic Performance: Comedy and Pain* (New York: Palgrave, 2014), 27.

2. Stanley Cavell, *The World Viewed: Reflections on the Ontology of Film* (Cambridge: Harvard University Press, 1979), 124.

3. As one of the reviewers of this book helpfully pointed out, the concept of self-reference can be understood to characterize much of Cavell's engagement with Hollywood cinema and, in particular, to give foundation to his claim that certain movies inherit and express the tradition of Emersonian perfectionism. On this count, see especially the introduction to *Pursuits of Happiness: The Hollywood Comedy of Remarriage* (Cambridge: Harvard University Press, 1981), 13–14; "Words for a Conversation," 1–44.

4. Cavell, *Pursuits*, 13–14.

5. Cavell, *World Viewed*, 126.

6. Cavell, *Pursuits*, 99.

7. On the concepts of genre and mode, see Northrop Frye, *Anatomy of Criticism: Four Essays* (New York: Atheneum, 1969), 33–67.

8. See D'haeyere, "Slapstick on Slapstick: Mack Sennett's Metamovies Revisit the Keystone Film Company," *Film History* 26, no. 2 (2014): 82–111.

9. Buster Keaton quoted in *Buster Keaton: Interviews*, ed. Kevin M. Sweeney (Oxford, MS: University of Mississippi Press, 2007), 52.

10. Burke, "Comic Correctives," in *Reader in Comedy: An Anthology of Theory and Criticism*, ed. Magda Romanska and Alan Ackerman (New York: Bloomsbury, 2016), 269.

11. Bela Balázs, *Early Film Theory: Visible Man and* The Spirit of Film, trans. Rodney Livingstone (New York: Bergahn, 2011), 85–86.

12. Ibid., 86.

13. Balázs, *Theory of the Film*, trans. Edith Bone (New York: Dover, 1970), 21.

14. Hugo Munsterberg, *Hugo Münsterberg on Film: The Photoplay: A Psychological Study and Other Writings* (New York: Routledge, 2001), 175.

15. Neil Harris, *Humbug: The Art of P. T. Barnum* (Chicago: University of Chicago Press, 1991), 79. On the operational aesthetic and slapstick film comedy, see Tom Gunning, "Crazy Machines in the Garden of Forking Paths" in *Classical Hollywood Comedy*, ed. Kristine Brunovska Karnick and Henry Jenkins (New York: Routledge, 1995), 87–105.

16. René Clair, *Cinema Yesterday and Today*, trans. Stanley Appelbaum, ed. R. C. Dale (New York: Dover, 1972), 64; Siegfried Kracauer, *Theory of Film: The Redemption of Physical Reality* (Princeton: Princeton University Press, 1997), 62. Hansen's introduction to Kracauer's *Theory of Film* explicitly places Hollywood slapstick comedy at the heart of Kracauer's work on film and its engagement with the mimetic powers of the cinema. See Kracauer, *Theory of Film*, xxi–xxiv.

17. André Bazin, "Theater and Cinema," in *What Is Cinema? Vol. 1*, essays selected and translated by Hugh Gray (Berkeley: University of California Press, 2005), 121.

18. David Bordwell, Janet Staiger, and Kristin Thompson, *The Classical Hollywood Cinema: Film Style and Mode of Production to 1960* (New York: Columbia University Press, 1985), 20; Linda Williams, "Gender, Genre, and Excess," *Film Quarterly* 44, no. 4 (Summer 1991): 2–13.

19. Quoted in Rob King, *The Fun Factory: The Keystone Film Company and the Emergence of Mass Culture* (Berkeley: University of California Press, 2009), 112.

20. See for instance Maggie Hennefeld, *Specters of Slapstick and Silent Film Comediennes* (New York: Columbia University Press, 2018); Kristin Anderson Wagner, *Comic Venus: Women and Comedy in American Silent Film* (Detroit: Wayne State University Press, 2018); Steve Massa, *Slapstick Divas: The Women of Silent Comedy* (Albany, GA: BearManor, 2017); and Linda Mizejewski, *Pretty / Funny: Women Comedians and Body Politics* (Austin: University of Texas Press, 2014).

21. For the former idea, see Roger Scruton, "Photography and Representation," *Critical Inquiry* 7 (Spring 1981): 577–603; and for the latter, Kendall Walton, "Transparent Pictures: On the Nature of Photographic Realism," *Critical Inquiry* 11, no. 2 (Dec. 1984): 246–77.

22. Amie Thomasson, "The Ontology of Art," in *The Blackwell Guide to Aesthetics* (Malden, MA: Wiley-Blackwell, 2004), 88–90.

23. See for instance Rothman, *Hitchcock: The Murderous Gaze* (Cambridge: Harvard University Press, 1984) and the essays in his *The "I" of the Camera: Essays in Film Criticism, Theory, and Aesthetics* (New York: Cambridge University Press, 2004).

Chapter 1. Slapstick Spectators

1. On Dressler's career, see Massa, 230–36.

2. Richard C. Allen, *Vaudeville and Film 1895–1915: A Study in Media Interaction* (Ann Arbor: ProQuest Dissertations and Theses, 1975), 48–50.

3. Hennefeld has recently argued for the importance of female comedians in this environment, where the "wild corporeality" of the female performer acts "as an impetus for working through the industry's own social and aesthetic contradictions: those between debased early attractions and bourgeois ideals of narrative integration"; Hennefeld, *Specters*, 85–86. Interestingly, she also argues that the characteristic ambivalence of female performance led, in this sense, to the creation of movies that "represent meta-discourses for scholars to consider in rethinking the co-development of narrative film style, film industry cultural politics, and experiences of gender and laughter" (26).

4. Quoted in Simon Louvish, *Keystone: The Life and Clowns of Mack Sennett* (London: Faber & Faber, 2004), 26.

5. For Gunning's account of *The Drunkard's Reformation*, see his *D. W. Griffith and the Origins of American Narrative Film: The Early Years at Biograph* (Urbana: University of Illinois Press, 1994), 162–71.

6. On the production of *Tillie's Punctured Romance*, see Bo Berglund, "The Making of *Tillie's Punctured Romance*," *Griffithiana* 75 (2005). On its restoration, see Ross Lipman, "Tillie's Punctured Legacy: Observations on the Restoration of Chaplin's First Feature," *Early Popular Visual Culture* 7, no. 2 (July 2009): 127–43.

7. King, *The Fun Factory*, 128.

8. Ibid., 131.

9. Charles R. Condon, "A Six-Reel Keystone Comedy," *Motography* 12, no. 20 (Nov. 14, 1914): 657.

10. See, for instance, the chapter "Technology, Style and Mode of Production," in Bordwell, Staiger, and Thompson, 243–61.

Chapter 2. Buster Keaton's Theory of Film

1. Vertov quoted in Michael North, *Machine-Age Comedy* (New York: Oxford University Press, 2009), 38.

2. Aragon, "On Décor," in Richard Abel, *French Film Theory and Criticism: A History/Anthology, 1907–1939* (Princeton: Princeton University Press, 1993), 165.

3. Bunuel, "Buster Keaton's *College*," in *The Shadow and Its Shadow: Surrealist Writings on the Cinema*, ed. Paul Hammond (San Francisco: City Lights, 2007), 61.

4. In what follows, I try to refer to Buster Keaton the filmmaker as "Keaton" and Buster Keaton, the character as he appears on screen, as "Buster." I stick to this practice despite the fact that in most of Keaton's films the Buster character has a distinct name (e.g., Johnnie Gray in *The General*). Over the course of these films, of course, Buster does become a character, or, more accurately, a "type." This fact is further borne out by the films themselves, in some of which Buster's fellow actors can been seen mouthing the name "Buster" rather than that of the character identified in the credits.

5. Noël Carroll, *Comedy Incarnate: Buster Keaton, Physical Humor, and Bodily Coping* (Malden, MA: Blackwell, 2007), 70. Alex Clayton makes the similar argument about Buster's ride on the cowcatcher in *The General*: "Keaton's heroism at this moment consists in marrying the aptitudes of a fully conscious human agent with

the steadfast virtues of the machine: foresight teamed with fortitude, initiative met with precision, swiftness of thought at pace with the movement of a crankshaft." See his *The Body in Hollywood Slapstick* (Jefferson, NC: McFarland, 2007), 98.

6. Carroll, *Comedy Incarnate*, 70–81.
7. North, *Machine-Age Comedy*, 39.
8. Gilberto Perez, *The Material Ghost: Films and Their Medium* (Baltimore: Johns Hopkins University Press, 1998), 94.
9. Ibid., 89.
10. Gunning, "Crazy Machines," 102.
11. Gunning, "Buster Keaton or the Work of Comedy in the Age of Mechanical Reproduction," *Cineaste* 21, no. 3 (June 1995): 15.
12. Bazin, "The Ontology of the Photographic Image," in *What Is Cinema*, Vol. 1, 12.
13. Arthur Pound, *The Iron Man in Industry: An Outline of the Social Significance of Automatic Machinery* (Boston: Atlantic Monthly Press, 1922).
14. Ernest W. Burgess, "The New Community and Its Future," *Annals of the American Academy of Political and Social Science* 149, no. 1 (May 1930): 158–59.
15. John M. Clark, "The Empire of Machines," *Yale Review* 12, no. 1 (Oct. 1922): 136.
16. Frank T. Carlton, "The Machine and Management," *The Scientific Monthly* 22, no. 3 (March 1926): 253.
17. William C. Bagley, "Educational Determinism," *Bulletin of the American Association of University Professors* 8, no. 5 (May 1922): 12.
18. Gerben Bakker, "How Motion Pictures Industrialized Entertainment," *Journal of Economic History* 72, no. 4 (Dec. 2012): 1036.
19. Hyacinth Dubreuil, *Robots or Men?: A French Workman's Experience in American Industry* (New York: Harper and Brothers, 1930), 16–17.
20. "One has to hand this to the Americans: with slapstick films they have created a form that offers a counterweight to their reality: if in that reality they subject the world to an often unbearable discipline, the film in turn dismantles this self-imposed order quite forcefully," *Frankfurter Zeitung*, January 29, 1926 (as quoted in Hansen's introduction to Kracauer, *Theory of Film*, xl, fn. 39).
21. Ernest F. Lloyd, "The American Automatic Tool," *Journal of Political Economy* 27, no. 6 (June 1919): 465.
22. Ibid., 460.
23. Ibid., 460–61.
24. Ibid., 461.
25. Thorstein Veblen, *The Theory of Business Enterprise* (Charles Scribner's Sons, 1915), 6.
26. Terry Smith, *Making the Modern: Industry, Art, and Design in America* (Chicago: University of Chicago Press, 1993), 8.
27. Gunning, "Buster Keaton," 75.
28. That Keaton's career was a casualty of this absorption is another story. Still, *The Cameraman* was widely praised at MGM—so much so that for years afterward, the studio used it as an exemplary film in its training of other directors. See "Commentary," *The Cameraman*, DVD. Directed by Edward Sedgwick and Buster Keaton, 1928 (Atlanta: TCM Archives, 2004).

29. North has an interesting reading of the monkey. See *Machine-Age Comedy*, 49–52.
30. David Bordwell, *Narration in the Fiction Film* (Madison: University of Wisconsin Press, 1985), 157.
31. See Jonathan Enfield, "'A More Glittering, a Grosser Power': American Film and Fiction, 1915–1941," PhD diss., University of Chicago, 2005, 105.
32. John W. Ward, "The Meaning of Lindbergh's Flight," *American Quarterly* 10, no. 1 (Spring 1958): 3.
33. Cavell, *The World Viewed*, 105.
34. David Rodowick provides a compelling account of Cavell's definition of film's automatisms, and he connects this account to an engaging discussion of the nature of mediums more generally. See his *The Virtual Life of Film* (Cambridge: Harvard University Press, 2007), 41–49.
35. Cavell, *The World Viewed*, 106.
36. Carroll, *Comedy Incarnate*, 36.
37. Michael Fried, *Courbet's Realism* (Chicago: University of Chicago Press, 1990), 285.
38. Annette Michelson, "'The Man with the Movie Camera': From Magician to Epistemologist," *Artforum* 10, no. 7 (March 1972): 69.

Chapter 3. Redeeming Vision

1. As William Rothman eloquently writes, "Chaplin seems always to be performing for an audience whose love he craves, whereas Keaton characteristically seems unconscious of having an audience." See *The "I" of the Camera*, 44.
2. "Chaplin's Latest, 'Shoulder Arms,' Sure Fire Comedy," *Atlanta Constitution*, Nov. 12, 1918, 14.
3. Baudelaire, "On Laughter," quoted in James Leo Cahill, "How It Feels to Be Run Over: Early Film Accidents," *Discourse* 30, no. 3 (Fall 2008): 289.
4. Scholarship that reads Wittgenstein's discussion of aspect perception as having primarily to do with the phenomenology of vision includes Richard Allen, *Projecting Illusion: Film Spectatorship and the Impression of Reality* (New York: Cambridge University Press, 1995); Allen, "Looking at Pictures," in *Film Theory and Philosophy*, ed. Richard Allen and Murray Smith (New York: Oxford University Press, 1999); Malcolm Turvey, *Doubting Vision: Film and the Revelationist Tradition* (New York: Oxford University Press, 2006); and Edward Branigan, *Projecting a Camera: Language-Games and Film Theory* (New York: Routledge, 2006).
5. Avner Baz, "What's the Point of Seeing Aspects?" *Philosophical Investigations* 23, no. 2 (April 2000): 99.
6. Cavell, *Claim of Reason*, 370.
7. Baz, 98.
8. Wittgenstein, *Philosophical Investigations*, trans. G. E. M. Anscombe (Malden, MA: Blackwell, 2001), §430.
9. I pass over *The Circus* (1928), which was released in the first year of the widespread adoption of synchronized sound and which had a soundtrack that consisted of a score written by Chaplin. It also includes an opening song that

Chaplin himself sang, making it—and not the ending of *Modern Times*, as many have suggested—the first time that Chaplin's voice was heard onscreen. Still, as production notes suggest, Chaplin felt that he did not yet have to wrestle with the issue of synchronized sound, a fact that is manifestly not the case for *City Lights* or for *Modern Times*.

10. Rothman, *The "I" of the Camera*, 44. Rothman's "The Ending of *City Lights*" is, to my mind, the definitive reading of the sequence. My reading tries to extend Rothman's insight, as he puts it, that "a passionate wish and a palpable terror are at the heart of Chaplin's films: the wish and terror of overcoming the barrier for which film is a metaphor, the wish and terror of making or allowing a dream to become real" (*The "I" of the Camera*, 46).

11. Ibid.

12. Cavell briefly remarks that "the genre of remarriage invites us to speak of putting together imagination and perception in terms of putting together night and day—say dreams and responsibilities. Each of its instances has its own realization of this project. But the sublimest realization of it in film is Chaplin's *City Lights*." See *Pursuits of Happiness*, 101.

13. Rothman, *The "I" of the Camera*, 53.

14. Charles Chaplin, "Pantomime and Comedy," *New York Times*, Jan. 25, 1931, X6.

15. Frank Nugent, "Heralding the Return, After an Undue Absence, of Charlie Chaplin in 'Modern Times,'" *New York Times*, Feb. 6, 1936, 23.

16. Anon., "'Modern Times,'" *Film Daily*, Feb. 6, 1936: 6.

17. On these movies and this comparison, see Lee Grieveson, "The Work of Film in the Age of Fordist Mechanization," *Cinema Journal* 51, no. 3 (Summer 2012): 25–51.

18. Mikhail Bakhtin, *Rabelais and His World* (Bloomington: Indiana University Press, 1984), 19–20.

19. As Alex Clayton argues, "Far from rendering the machine an augmentation of the body's powers, the visual arrangement thus emphasizes the *loss* of the body, its fragmentation and replacement by mechanical procedure." See *The Body in Hollywood Slapstick*, 100–101; emphasis in text.

20. In a fragment of 1935, Benjamin writes that Chaplin's "unique significance lies in the fact that, in his work, the human being is integrated into the film image by way of his gestures—that is, his bodily and mental posture. The innovation of Chaplin's gestures is that he dissects the expressive movements of human beings into a series of minute innervations." See "The Formula in Which the Dialectical Structure of Film Finds Expression," in *The Work of Art in the Age of Its Technological Reproducibility and Other Writings on Media*, ed. Michael W. Jennings, Brigid Doherty, and Thomas Y. Levin; trans. Edmund Jephcott, Rodney Livingstone, Howard Eiland et al. (Cambridge: Belknap Press of Harvard University Press, 2008), 340.

21. Bernhard Stricker, "Experience Missed or Lost?: Cavell's Concept of the Ordinary and Walter Benjamin on the 'Loss of Aura,'" *Conversations: The Journal of Cavellian Studies* 4 (2016): 22.

Chapter 4. Bodies of Silence, Bodies of Sound

1. To take another silent comedy, Harold Lloyd's late feature *Speedy*, which was released just a few months before *The Cocoanuts*, has an ASL of 4.4. For all of these figures, see http://www.cinemetrics.lv/database.php.
2. Bordwell, Staiger, and Thompson, 304, 307–308.
3. Donald Crafton, *The Talkies: American Cinema's Transition to Sound, 1926–1931*, History of the American cinema, vol. 4. (New York: Charles Scribner's Sons, 1997), 28.
4. Ibid., 47.
5. Rick Altman, "Sound Space," in *Sound Theory/Sound Practice*, ed. Altman (New York: Routledge, 1992), 55.
6. Frank Krutnik has brought attention to this fact, as well as to the fact that the gag plays with the relationship between body and voice. "This joke [with the phonograph] is directed not only at early sound-on-disc film systems but also at the phantasmic wholeness of the represented self in early sound cinema, an illusion based on concealing the split between the recorded image and recorded voice." See Krutnik, "Mutinies Wednesdays and Saturdays: Carnivalesque Comedy and the Marx Brothers," in *A Companion to Film Comedy*, ed. Andrew Horton and Joanna E. Rapf (Hoboken: Wiley, 2012), 105. See too Alex Clayton's reading of this scene and its relation to technologies of synchronized sound in *The Body in Hollywood Slapstick*, 124–27.
7. Bordwell, Staiger, and Thompson, 33–34.
8. George Seaton, Bert Kalmar, Will Johnstone, and Harry Ruby, *The Marx Brothers: Monkey Business; Duck Soup; and, A Day at the Races* (London: Faber, 1993), 81.
9. For this reading of *Intolerance*, see Hansen, *Babel and Babylon*, 170.
10. Bakhtin, 306.
11. Ibid., 307.
12. Quoted in Altman, "Sound Space," 49.
13. Ibid., 59.
14. Ibid., 60.
15. Seaton et al., 64–65.
16. Crafton, *The Talkies*, 447.
17. Ibid., 459.
18. Henry Jenkins, *What Made Pistachio Nuts?: Early Sound Comedy and the Vaudeville Aesthetic* (New York: Columbia University Press, 1992), 54.
19. Bakhtin, 320.
20. The question of whether Harpo cannot talk or simply refuses to talk is important for the understanding of his character and its comedy. See Patricia Mellencamp's allusion to this question in her "Jokes and Their Relation to the Marx Brothers," in *Cinema and Language*, ed. Stephen Heath and Patricia Mellencamp (Frederick, MD: University Publications of America, 1983), 74.
21. Seaton et al., 119–20.

22. Bakhtin, 316–17.
23. Kracauer, it turns out, articulates a little theory of the relationship between Groucho's verbal excesses and Harpo's mute destruction: "Whatever Groucho is saying disintegrates speech all around him. He is an eruptive monad in the middle of self-created anarchy. Accordingly, his verbal discharges go well with Harpo's slapstick pranks, which survive from the silent era. . . . Harpo is a residue of the past, an exiled comedy god condemned or permitted to act the part of a mischievous hobgoblin. Yet the world in which he appears is so crowded with dialogue that he would long since have vanished were it not for Groucho, who supports the spectre's destructive designs. As dizzying as any silent collision, Groucho's word cascades wreak havoc on language, and among the resultant debris Harpo continues to feel at ease." See his *Theory of Film*, 132.
24. Miriam Hansen, "The Mass Production of the Senses: Classical Cinema as Vernacular Modernism," *Modernism/modernity* 6, no. 2 (April 1999): 62.
25. Ibid., 64.

Chapter 5. Hollywood, Television, and the Case of Ernie Kovacs

1. Thomas Schatz, *Boom and Bust: The American Cinema in the 1940s*. History of the American cinema, vol. 6. (New York: Charles Scribner's Sons, 1997), 1–10.
2. Ibid., 462–65.
3. Crafton, "The View from Termite Terrace: Caricature and Parody in Warner Bros. Animation," *Film History* 5, no. 2 (June 1993): 212–17.
4. Paul Monaco, *The Sixties, 1960–1969*. History of the American cinema, vol. 8 (New York: Charles Scribner's Sons, 2001), 463.
5. Ibid., 40.
6. Bordwell, Staiger, and Thompson, 330–38.
7. Ibid., 330.
8. Peter Lev, *Transforming the Screen, 1950–1959*. History of the American cinema, vol. 7 (New York: Charles Scribner's Sons, 2003), 108.
9. Lyn Spigel, *Make Room for TV: Television and the Family Ideal in Postwar America* (Chicago: University of Chicago Press, 1992), 32.
10. Ibid., 133.
11. Raymond Williams, *Television: Technology and Cultural Form* (New York: Routledge, 2003), 11.
12. Ibid., 19.
13. Ibid.
14. Ibid., 86–91.
15. Ibid., 107.
16. Spigel, 165.
17. On the surreal, highly presentational address of the former show, see David Marc, *Comic Visions: Television Comedy and American Culture* (Malden, MA: Blackwell, 1997), 18–20.

18. Diane Rico, *Kovacsland: A Biography of Ernie Kovacs* (New York: Harcourt Brace Jovanovich, 1990), 43–54.

19. Fascinatingly, Kovacs and Keaton starred together in a critically reviled television Western, *Medicine Man* (1962), in which, true to form if also typecast, Kovacs played a snake-oil salesman and Keaton his mute Native sidekick. See Rico, 299.

20. Ibid., 158.

21. Ibid., 286–87, 305–307.

22. Ibid., 63.

23. Spigel has shown that the series, as well as Kovacs's own "no dialogue" show of 1957, and the reprise of this show as one of the ABC specials, capitalized on public anxiety and anger about the loud vulgarity of network television. See *TV by Design*, 178–212.

24. Rico, 279.

25. There is one variation in this form. The final special, which was released after Kovacs's death, opens with Kovacs's himself playing with the oscilloscope image, as if it were somehow present in the studio, and then synchronizes its blackout gags to a piece of classical music. Near the conclusion of the episode, we are treated to a series of blackout gags, which are again synchronized with "Die Morität."

26. Bruce Ferguson, "The Importance of Being Ernie: Taking a Close Look (and Listen)," in *Illuminating Video: An Essential Guide to Video Art*, ed. Sally Jo Fifer and Doug Hall (New York: Aperture, 1990), 352.

27. See Michel Chion, *Audio-Vision: Sound on Screen*, translated by Claudia Gorbman (New York: Columbia University Press, 1994), 63–65.

28. Robert Rosen, "Ernie Kovacs: Video Artist," in *Transmission*, ed. Peter D'Agostino (New York: Tanam Press, 1985): 144.

29. Sharon Guthrie, "'A Body Oozin' Life': Resurrecting 'The Ballad of Mack the Knife,'" *Journal of Popular Music Studies* 19, no. 2 (May 2007): 159–60.

30. Ibid., 158–60.

31. Spigel identifies the recording as that of Wolfgang Neuss. See *TV by Design*, 195. Interestingly, Neuss (who was a German comedian) recorded a version that omits two stanzas, the refrain, and the ending from the original Brecht-Weill version.

32. See, for example, Kovacs's instructions for his "Office Symphony," a sound-to-sight sketch in which office supplies and furniture function in synchronization with Juan Garcia Esquivel's "Jalousie": "In time to the music, this pen must drop gobs of ink out of the point. The phone, which will be located directly in back of the pen must have the dial work briefly, only one full turn will be needed in synchronization to the music in short movements, a kind of syncopated beat, the ear-piece and talking-piece of the phone must be made to rock back and forth in time to the music while remaining on the cradle it raises on one end, drops, raises on the other end, and drops . . . but also must be completely controlled mechanically. To the right of the phone is an old-fashioned pencil sharpener." As quoted in Spigel, *TV by Design*, 194.

33. See La Rosa, 33, where the artist Skip Blumberg calls Kovacs one of the "very few creative and experimental performers" of early television.

34. Cavell, *The World Viewed*, 26.

35. Christian Metz, *Film Language: A Semiotics of the Cinema* (Chicago: University of Chicago Press, 1991), 96.

Chapter 6. Nouvelles Blagues

1. For a wonderful account of this anxiety, see Scott Bukatman, "Paralysis in Motion: Jerry Lewis's Life as a Man," *Camera Obscura* 17 (May 1988): 195–205.

2. Monaco, 2.

3. The translation belongs to Paul Willemen, and it appears in Johnston and Willemen, *Frank Tashlin* (Edinburgh: Edinburgh Film Festival, 1973), 89.

4. See Louis Menand, "Unpopular Front: American Art and the Cold War," *New Yorker*, Oct. 17, 2005.

5. Journalist Harriet Van Horne of the *World-Telegram* applied the phrase "witless genius" to Lewis in her review of Lewis's 1957 television work. Despite (or perhaps because of) its fundamental ambivalence, Lewis himself was fond of the phrase and continued, for years, to use it in his own promotional materials. See Shawn Levy, *King of Comedy: The Life and Art of Jerry Lewis* (New York: St. Martin's Press, 1997), 228–29.

6. Clement Greenberg, *Art and Culture: Critical Essays* (New York, Beacon Press, 1961), 10.

7. As Murray Pomerance has written, "Lewis is a primitive and therefore also a modernist. In his apparently unathletic movement . . . he may make us wonder at our adoration for the proportionate, domesticated, and subjugated etiolations against which we measure him." See his *Enfant Terrible!: Jerry Lewis in American Film* (New York: New York University Press, 2002), 4. The word *Tashlinesque* was coined by Godard in his 1957 review of *Hollywood or Bust*. See "*Hollywood or Bust*," in *Godard on Godard: Critical Writings by Jean-Luc Godard*, trans. and ed. Tom Milne (New York: Da Capo Press, 1986), 57–59.

8. Caroline Jones, *Eyesight Alone: Clement Greenberg's Modernism and the Bureaucratization of the Senses* (Chicago: University of Chicago Press, 2006), 330.

9. Greenberg, *Art and Culture*, 3.

10. Ibid.

11. Ibid., 208.

12. Ibid.

13. Interestingly, Tashlin's files at the Margaret Herrick Library make it clear that he was conscious of the relation between these jokes and the state of the industry at the time (Frank Tashlin Papers, Fairbanks Center for Motion Picture Study, Margaret Herrick Library).

14. See Miriam Hansen, "Modernism, Medium-Specificity, and Mayhem: Frank Tashlin's *Artists and Models*." Lecture presented at the University of Chicago, May 8, 2009.

15. Donald Crafton, "Pie and Chase: Gag, Spectacle, and Narrative in Slapstick Comedy," in *Classical Hollywood Comedy*, ed. Kristine Brunovska Karnick and Henry Jenkins (New York: Routledge, 1995), 109.
16. Chris Fujiwara, *Jerry Lewis* (Urbana: University of Illinois Press, 2009), 15.
17. Levy, 259–60.
18. "Commentary," *The Ladies Man*, DVD, directed by Jerry Lewis, 1961 (Hollywood: Paramount Pictures, 2004).
19. Fujiwara, 18. The phrase "hanging there and groping there" belongs to Lewis and comes from the interview that appears at the end of Fujiwara's book.
20. Ibid.
21. Jerry Lewis, *The Total Film-maker* (Random House, 1971), 187.
22. Bordwell, *Narration in the Fiction Film*, 157.
23. "Commentary," *The Ladies Man*, DVD.
24. Krutnik, "Jerry Lewis: The Deformation of the Comic," *Film Quarterly* 48, no. 4 (Fall 1994): 24.
25. André Bazin, "Monsieur Hulot and Time," trans. Bert Cardullo. *Bright Lights Film Journal* 64 (May 2009); http://www.brightlightsfilm.com/64/64bazintati.php.
26. Hansen, "The Mass Production of the Senses," 62.
27. Monaco, 152.
28. Maurice Bardèche and Robert Brassilach, *The History of Motion Pictures*, trans. and ed. Iris Barry (New York: Arno Press, 1972), 51.
29. "classical, adj. and n." OED Online, June 2018; http://www.oed.com.unco.idm.oclc.org/view/Entry/33881?redirectedFrom=classical&; accessed Aug. 1, 2018.
30. Bordwell, Staiger, and Thompson, 378–85.
31. Ibid., 381.
32. Ibid., 382.
33. Fujiwara, 15.
34. Lewis, 32.
35. Levy, 246–47.
36. See Michelson, 60.
37. See Godard's 1957 review "*Hollywood or Bust*," in *Godard on Godard*, 57–59, as well as "A Struggle on Two Fronts: A Conversation with Jean-Luc Godard," *Film Quarterly* 22, no. 2 (Winter 1968–69): 20–35; and "The Carrots Are Cooked: A Conversation with Jean-Luc Godard," *Film Quarterly* 37, no. 3 (Spring 1984): 13–19. For interest in Lewis among other members of the New Wave, see *Cahiers* 197 (1967–68), a special issue that was devoted to Lewis's films, and in particular Jean-Louis Comolli's article on Lewis and "the double."
38. See, for instance, Dana Polan, "Being and Nuttiness: Jerry Lewis and the French," *Journal of Popular Film & Television* 12, no. 1 (Spring 1984): 44; Monaco, 152; and J. Hoberman's liner notes for the Criterion DVD release of *Tout Va Bien*, DVD, directed by Jean-Luc Godard and Jean-Pierre Gorin, 1972 (New York: Criterion Collection, 2005).

39. "Interview with Jean-Luc Godard," *Tout Va Bien*, DVD.

40. For thoughtful accounts of the psychological dysfunction and disunity of Lewis and his characters, see Frank Krutnik, *Inventing Jerry Lewis* (Washington, DC: Smithsonian Institution Press, 2000), 4–7 and 140–64; and Shaviro, *The Cinematic Body* (Minneapolis: University of Minnesota Press, 1993), 119–24.

41. Peter Wollen, "Godard and Counter-Cinema: *Vent d'Est*," in *The European Cinema Reader*, ed. Catherine Fowler (New York: Routledge, 2002), 75.

42. J. Hoberman, "Vulgar Modernsim," *Artforum* 20, no. 6 (Feb. 1982): 71–76.

43. Godard, *"Hollywood or Bust,"* 58.

Epilogue. The Apotheosis of Failure

1. William J. Mitchell, *The Reconfigured Eye: Visual Truth in the Post-Photographic Era* (Cambridge: MIT Press, 1992); John Belton, "Digital Cinema: A False Revolution," *October* 100 (Spring 2002): 104.

2. Among other places, the gag also appears in *Project A, Part II* (Chan, 1987) and *Deadpan* (McQueen, 1997), both of which were shot on film, I believe. (McQueen's movie was later transferred to video for exhibition.)

3. It may be objected that the *Jackass* movies and television series do not merit comparison with Keaton, whose virtuosic performances and remarkable talent as a filmmaker set him apart from the work of performers like Johnny Knoxville. But it's worth remembering that most slapstick film performance and filmmaking began life as objects of low cultural standing. And I make no claim to the aesthetic achievements of the *Jackass* franchise. What is at stake instead is the relation between this performance and the medium of digital video.

4. On this count, see Jorie Lagerwey, "*Jackass* for President: Revitalizing an American Public Life Through the Aesthetic of the Amateur," *Spectator* 24, no. 1 (Spring 2004): 86–97. Spike Jonze has himself put *Jackass* in this lineage, noting his own interest in the work of performance artists such as Chris Burden, who shot himself with a handgun twenty years before Johnny Knoxville repeated the gag on amateur video. See Dennis Lim, "Another Dimension of Idiocy," *New York Times*, Dec. 8, 2010; http://www.nytimes.com/2010/10/10/movies/10jackass.html.

5. Quoted in Lim, "Another Dimension of Idiocy."

6. On the distinct structure of spectatorship created by *Jackass*, see Scott Richmond, "'Dude, That's Just *Wrong*': Mimesis, Identification, *Jackass*," *World Picture* 6 (Winter 2011); http://www.worldpicturejournal.com/WP_6/Richmond.html.

7. In keeping with its origins as an episodic show on MTV, this has partly to do with *Jackass*'s membership in the genre of reality TV.

8. It's worth noting that the extra features of the DVD—which it seems appropriate to suggest constitute part of the original text of the movie—contain an outtake in which the house actually falls on Knoxville. See "Outtakes," *Jackass Number Two*, DVD, directed by Jeff Tremaine (Hollywood: Paramount/MTV, 2006).

9. Peacock, 148.

10. See Lim, "Another Dimension of Idiocy."
11. Quoted in Lagerwey, 90.
12. Ibid.
13. Interestingly, *Jackass 3D* was screened in 2010 at The Museum of Modern Art in New York. The relationship between *Jackass*, American performance art, and the institutionalization of avant-garde practice is the subject of Isher-Paul Sahni, "More than Horseplay: *Jackass*, Performativity, and the MoMA," *Studies in Popular Culture* 35, no. 2 (Spring 2013): 69–94.
14. Aden Evans, "Web 2.0 and the Ontology of the Digital," *Digital Humanities Quarterly* (2012); http://www.digitalhumanities.org/dhq/vol/6/2/000120/000120.html, section 9.
15. Ibid., sections 3 and 20.
16. Mark Hansen, *New Philosophy for New Media* (Cambridge: MIT Press, 2006); Anna Munster, *Materializing New Media: Embodiment in Information Aesthetics* (Lebanon, NH: University Press of New England, 2006).
17. Katherine N. Hayles, *How We Became Posthuman: Virtual Bodies in Cybernetics, Literature, and Informatics* (Chicago: University of Chicago Press, 1999).
18. As Clayton argues, "*Jackass* serves as a testament to the resilience of the body, its genuine capacity to bounce back." See *The Body in Slapstick Comedy*, 175.
19. Hayles, 93.

Bibliography

Abel, Richard. *French Film Theory and Criticism: A History/Anthology, 1907–1939*. Princeton: Princeton University Press, 1993.
Allen, Richard. "Looking at Pictures." In *Film Theory and Philosophy*, edited by Allen and Smith. New York: Oxford University Press, 1999.
———. *Projecting Illusion: Film Spectatorship and the Impression of Reality*. New York: Cambridge University Press, 1995.
Allen, Richard C. *Vaudeville and Film 1895–1915: A Study in Media Interaction*. Ann Arbor: ProQuest Dissertations and Theses, 1975.
Altman, Rick, ed. *Film Sound: Theory and Practice*. New York: Columbia University Press, 1985.
———. "Sound Space." In *Sound Theory/Sound Practice*, ed. Altman. New York: Routledge, 1992.
Anderson Wagner, Kristen. *Comic Venus: Women and Comedy in American Silent Film*. Detroit: Wayne State University Press, 2018.
Animal Crackers. DVD. Directed by Victor Heerman, 1930. Universal City, CA: Universal Studios, 1998.
Anonymous. "'Modern Times.'" *Film Daily*, February 6, 1936, 6.
Arnheim, Rudolf. *Film as Art*. Berkeley: University of California Press, 1966.
Artists and Models, DVD. Directed by Frank Tashlin, 1955. Los Angeles: Paramount, 2007.
Bagley, William C. "Educational Determinism." *Bulletin of the American Association of University Professors* 8, no. 5 (May 1922): 373–84.
Bakhtin, M. M. *Rabelais and His World*. Bloomington: Indiana University Press, 1984.
Bakker, Gerben. "How Motion Pictures Industrialized Entertainment." *Journal of Economic History* 72, no. 4 (December 2012): 1036–63.
Balazs, Bela. *Early Film Theory:* Visible Man *and* The Spirit of Film. Translated by Rodney Livingstone. New York: Bergahn, 2011.
———. *Theory of the Film*. Translated by Edith Bone. New York: Dover, 1970.
Baz, Avner. "What's the Point of Seeing Aspects?" *Philosophical Investigations* 23, no. 2 (April 2000): 97–121.
Bazin, André. *What Is Cinema? Vols. I and II*. Essays selected and translated by Hugh Gray. Berkeley: University of California Press, 2005.

———. *Bazin at Work: Major Essays and Reviews from the Forties and Fifties*. Edited by Bert Cardullo; translated by Alain Piette and Bert Cardullo. New York: Routledge, 1997.

———. "Monsieur Hulot and Time." Translated by Bert Cardullo. *Bright Lights Film Journal* 64 (May 2009); http://www.brightlightsfilm.com/64/64bazintati.php.

The Bellboy. DVD. Directed by Jerry Lewis, 1960. Hollywood: Paramount Home Entertainment, 2004.

Belton, John. "Digital Cinema: A False Revolution." *October* 100 (Spring 2002): 98–114.

Benjamin, Walter. *Walter Benjamin: Selected Writings, Volume 3: 1935–1938*. Edited by Michael W. Jennings. Cambridge: Harvard University Press, 2006.

———. *The Work of Art in the Age of Its Technological Reproducibility and Other Writings on Media*. Edited by Michael W. Jennings, Brigid Doherty, and Thomas Y. Levin; translated by Edmund Jephcott, Rodney Livingstone, Howard Eiland et al. Cambridge: Belknap Press of Harvard University Press, 2008.

Berglund, Bo. "The Making of *Tillie's Punctured Romance*." *Griffithiana* 75 (2005).

Bergson, Henri. *Laughter: An Essay on the Meaning of the Comic*. Translated by Cloudsley Brereton. Rockville, MD: Arc Manor, 2008.

Bordwell, David. *Narration in the Fiction Film*. Madison: University of Wisconsin Press, 1985.

———, Janet Staiger, and Kristin Thompson. *The Classical Hollywood Cinema: Film Style and Mode of Production to 1960*. New York: Columbia University Press, 1985.

Branigan, Edward. *Projecting a Camera: Language-Games and Film Theory*. New York: Routledge, 2006.

Bukatman, Scott. "Paralysis in Motion: Jerry Lewis's Life as a Man." *Camera Obscura* 17 (May 1988): 195–205.

Burgess, Ernest W. "The New Community and Its Future." *Annals of the American Academy of Political and Social Science* 149, no. 1 (May 1930): 157–64.

"The Butcher Boy." DVD. Directed by Roscoe "Fatty" Arbuckle, 1917. New York: Kino Video, 2001.

Cahill, James Leo. "How It Feels to Be Run Over: Early Film Accidents." *Discourse* 30, no. 3 (Fall 2008): 289–316.

The Cameraman. DVD. Directed by Edward Sedgwick and Buster Keaton, 1928. Atlanta: TCM Archives, 2004.

Carlton, Frank T. "The Machine and Management." *The Scientific Monthly* 22, no. 3 (March 1926): 252–57.

Carroll, Noël. *Comedy Incarnate: Buster Keaton, Physical Humor, and Bodily Coping*. Malden, MA: Blackwell, 2007.

———. "Notes on the Sight Gag." In *Comedy / Cinema / Theory*, edited by Andrew Horton, 25–42. Berkeley: University of California Press, 1991.

Cavell, Stanley. *Cavell on Film*. Edited by William Rothman. Albany: State University of New York Press, 2005.

———. *The Claim of Reason: Wittgenstein, Skepticism, Morality, and Tragedy*. New York: Oxford University Press, 1999.

———. *Contesting Tears: The Hollywood Melodrama of the Unknown Woman.* Chicago: University of Chicago Press, 1996.

———. *Must We Mean What We Say?: A Book of Essays.* New York: Cambridge University Press, 1976.

———. *Pursuits of Happiness: The Hollywood Comedy of Remarriage.* Cambridge: Harvard University Press, 1981.

———. *The World Viewed: Reflections on the Ontology of Film.* Cambridge: Harvard University Press, 1979.

Chaplin at Keystone: An International Collaboration of 34 Original Films, DVD. Los Angeles: Flicker Alley, 2010.

Chaplin, Charles. "Pantomime and Comedy." *New York Times*, January 25, 1931, X6.

"Chaplin's Latest, 'Shoulder Arms,' Sure Fire Comedy." *Atlanta Constitution*, November 12, 1918, 14.

The Chaplin Revue, DVD. Burbank, CA: Warner Home Video, 2004.

Chion, Michel. *Audio-Vision: Sound on Screen.* Translated by Claudia Gorbman. New York: Columbia University Press, 1994.

———. *The Voice in Cinema.* Translated by Claudia Gorbman. New York: Columbia University Press, 1999.

CineMetrics. "*The Cameraman.*" Last modified December 27, 2010; http://www.cinemetrics.lv/database.php.

———. "*The Cocoanuts.*" Last modified November 16, 2011; http://www.cinemetrics.lv/database.php.

———. "*Speedy.*" Last modified December 10, 2007; http://www.cinemetrics.lv/database.php.

City Lights, DVD. Directed by Charles Chaplin, 1931. New York: Criterion, 2013.

Clair, René. *Cinema Yesterday and Today.* Translated by Stanley Appelbaum; Edited by R. C. Dale. New York: Dover, 1972.

Clark, John M. "The Empire of Machines." *Yale Review* 12, no. 1 (October 1922): 132–43.

Clayton, Alex. *The Body in Hollywood Slapstick.* Jefferson, NC: McFarland, 2007.

The Cocoanuts. DVD. Directed by Joseph Santley and Robert Florey, 1929. Universal City, CA: Universal Studios, 2004.

Cohen, Ted. *Jokes: Philosophical Thoughts on Joking Matters.* Chicago: University of Chicago Press, 1999.

College. DVD. Directed by James W. Horne, 1927. New York: Kino on Video, 2001.

Comolli, Jean-Louis. "Chacun Son Soi." *Cahiers du Cinema* no. 197 (January 1967): 51–54.

Condon, Charles R. "A Six-Reel Keystone Comedy." *Motography* 12, no. 20 (November 14, 1914): 657–58.

Cops. DVD. Directed by Buster Keaton and Eddie Cline, 1922. New York: Kino on Video, 2001.

Crafton, Donald. "Pie and Chase: Gag, Spectacle, and Narrative in Slapstick Comedy." In *Classical Hollywood Comedy*, edited by Kristine Brunovska Karnick and Henry Jenkins, 106–19. New York: Routledge, 1995.

———. *The Talkies: American Cinema's Transition to Sound, 1926–1931.* History of the American cinema vol. 4. New York: Scribner's, 1997.

———. "The View from Termite Terrace: Caricature and Parody in Warner Bros. Animation." *Film History* 5, no. 2 (June 1993): 204–30.

D'haeyere, Hilde. "Slapstick on Slapstick: Mack Sennett's Metamovies Revisit the Keystone Film Company." *Film History* 26, no. 2 (2014): 82–111.

Dardis, Tom. *Keaton, the Man Who Wouldn't Lie Down*. New York: Scribner's, 1979.

Deleuze, Gilles. *The Movement-Image*. Translated by Hugh Tomlinson and Barbara Hammerjam. Minneapolis: University of Minnesota Press, 1986.

The Disorderly Orderly. DVD. Directed by Frank Tashlin, 1964. Hollywood: Paramount Home Entertainment, 2004.

Dubreuil, Hyacinth. *Robots or Men?: A French Workman's Experience in American Industry*. New York: Harper and Brothers, 1930.

Duck Soup. DVD. Directed by Leo McCarey, 1933. Universal City, CA: Universal Studios, 2004.

Eisenstein, Sergei. *Film Form: Essays in Film Theory*. New York: Harcourt, 1969.

Enfield, Jonathan. "'A More Glittering, a Grosser Power': American Film and Fiction, 1915–1941." PhD diss., University of Chicago, 2005. Proquest (3168339).

Ernie Kovacs: The ABC Specials. DVD. Directed by Ernie Kovacs, 1961. Los Angeles: Shout! Factory, 2012.

The Errand Boy. DVD. Directed by Jerry Lewis, 1961. Hollywood: Paramount Home Entertainment, 2004.

Evans, Aden. "Web 2.0 and the Ontology of the Digital." *Digital Humanities Quarterly* (2012); http://www.digitalhumanities.org/dhq/vol/6/2/000120/000120.html.

Ferguson, Bruce. "The Importance of Being Ernie: Taking a Close Look (and Listen)." In *Illuminating Video: An Essential Guide to Video Art*, ed. Sally Jo Fifer and Doug Hall. New York: Aperture, 1990.

Flaig, Paul. "Lacan's Harpo." *Cinema Journal* 50, no. 4 (Summer 2011): 98–116.

Frank Tashlin Papers, Fairbanks Center for Motion Picture Study, Margaret Herrick Library, Beverley Hills, CA.

Fried, Michael. *Art and Objecthood: Essays and Reviews*. Chicago: University of Chicago Press, 1998.

———. *Courbet's Realism*. Chicago: University of Chicago Press, 1990.

Frye, Northrop. *Anatomy of Criticism: Four Essays*. New York: Atheneum, 1968.

Fujiwara, Chris. *Jerry Lewis*. Urbana: University of Illinois Press, 2009.

Gaines, Jane, ed. *Classical Hollywood Narrative: The Paradigm Wars*. Durham: Duke University Press, 1992.

Garcia, Roger, ed. *Frank Tashlin*. Locarno: Éditions du Festival international du film de Locarno in collaboration with the British Film Institute, 1994.

Godard, Jean-Luc. "The Carrots Are Cooked: A Conversation with Jean-Luc Godard." *Film Quarterly* 37, no. 3 (Spring 1984): 13–19.

———. "Hollywood or Bust." In *Godard on Godard: Critical Writings by Jean-Luc Godard*, translated and edited by Tom Milne. New York: Da Capo, 1986.

———. "A Struggle on Two Fronts: A Conversation with Jean-Luc Godard." *Film Quarterly* 22, no. 2 (Winter 1968–69): 20–35.

The Gold Rush. DVD. Directed by Charles Chaplin, 1925. New York: Creative Design Art, 2003.

Gordon, Rae Beth. *Why the French Love Jerry Lewis: From Cabaret to Early Cinema*. Stanford: Stanford University Press, 2001.

Greenberg, Clement. *Art and Culture: Critical Essays*. New York: Beacon Press, 1961.

Grieveson, Lee. "The Work of Film in the Age of Fordist Mechanization." *Cinema Journal* 51, no. 3 (Summer 2012): 25–51.

Gunning, Tom. "Buster Keaton or the Work of Comedy in the Age of Mechanical Reproduction." *Cineaste* 21, no. 3 (June 1995): 14–16.

———. "Crazy Machines in the Garden of Forking Paths." In *Classical Hollywood Comedy*, edited by Kristine Brunovska Karnick, and Henry Jenkins, 87–105. New York: Routledge, 1995.

———. *D. W. Griffith and the Origins of American Narrative Film*. Urbana: University of Illinois Press, 1994.

———. "Response to Pie and Chase." In *Classical Hollywood Comedy*, edited by Kristine Brunovska Karnick and Henry Jenkins, 120–23. New York: Routledge, 1995.

Guthrie, Sharon. "'A Body Oozin' Life': Resurrecting 'The Ballad of Mack the Knife.'" *Journal of Popular Music Studies* 19, no. 2 (May 2007): 157–78.

Hammond, Paul. *The Shadow and Its Shadow: Surrealist Writings on the Cinema*. San Francisco: City Lights, 2007.

Hansen, Mark. *New Philosophy for New Media*. Cambridge: MIT Press, 2006.

Hansen, Miriam Bratu. *Babel and Babylon: Spectatorship in American Silent Film*. Cambridge: Harvard University Press, 1991.

———. "The Mass Production of the Senses: Classical Cinema as Vernacular Modernism." *Modernism/modernity* 6, no. 2 (April 1999): 59–77.

———. "Of Mice and Ducks: Benjamin and Adorno on Disney." *South Atlantic Quarterly* 92, no. 1 (Winter 1993): 27–61.

———. "Modernism, Medium-Specificity, and Mayhem: Frank Tashlin's *Artists and Models*." Lecture presented at the University of Chicago, Chicago, IL, May 8, 2009.

Harris, Neil. *Humbug: The Art of P. T. Barnum*. Chicago: University of Chicago Press, 1991.

Hatherley, Owen. *The Chaplin Machine: Slapstick, Fordism, and the International Communist Avant-Garde*. Chicago: Pluto Press, 2016.

Hayes, N. Katherine. *How We Became Posthuman: Virtual Bodies in Cybernetics, Literature, and Informatics*. Chicago: University of Chicago Press, 1999.

Hellzapoppin'. DVD. Directed by H. C. Potter, 1941. Los Angeles: Reel Vault, 2015.

Hennefeld, Maggie. *Specters of Slapstick and Silent Film Comediennes*. New York: Columbia University Press, 2018.

Hillier, Jim, ed. *Cahiers Du Cinéma: The 1950s: Neo-Realism, Hollywood, New Wave*. Cambridge: Harvard University Press, 1985.

Hoberman, J. *Vulgar Modernism: Writing on Movies and Other Media*. Philadelphia: Temple University Press, 1991.

Horton, Andrew, ed. *Buster Keaton's Sherlock Jr.* New York: Cambridge University Press, 1997.
Hutcheon, Linda. *A Theory of Parody: The Teachings of Twentieth-Century Art Forms.* New York: Methuen, 1985.
Jackass Number Two. DVD. Directed by Jeff Tremaine, 2006. Los Angeles: Paramount, 2006.
Jackass 3D. DVD. Directed by Jeff Tremaine, 2010. Los Angeles: Paramount, 2011.
Jenkins, Henry. *What Made Pistachio Nuts?: Early Sound Comedy and the Vaudeville Aesthetic.* New York: Columbia University Press, 1992.
Johnston, Claire, and Paul Willemen, eds. *Frank Tashlin.* Edinburgh: Edinburgh Film Festival, 1973.
Keaton, Buster. *My Wonderful World of Slapstick.* New York: Doubleday, 1960.
King, Rob. *The Fun Factory: The Keystone Film Company and the Emergence of Mass Culture.* Berkeley: University of California Press, 2009.
Kivy, Peter, ed. *The Blackwell Guide to Aesthetics.* Malden, MA: Wiley-Blackwell, 2004.
Knopf, Robert. *The Theater and Cinema of Buster Keaton.* Princeton: Princeton University Press, 1999.
Kracauer, Siegfried. *The Mass Ornament: Weimar Essays.* Edited and translated by Thomas Y. Levin. Cambridge: Harvard University Press, 1995.
———. *Theory of Film: The Redemption of Physical Reality.* Princeton: Princeton University Press, 1997.
Krutnik, Frank. *Inventing Jerry Lewis.* Washington: Smithsonian Institution Press, 2000.
———. "Jerry Lewis: The Deformation of the Comic." *Film Quarterly* 48, no. 4 (Fall 1994): 12–26.
The Ladies Man. DVD. Directed by Jerry Lewis, 1961. Hollywood: Paramount Pictures, 2004.
Jones, Caroline. *Eyesight Alone: Clement Greenberg's Modernism and the Bureaucratization of the Senses.* Chicago: University of Chicago Press, 2006.
La Rosa, Melanie. "Early Video Pioneer: An Interview with Skip Blumberg." *Journal of Film and Video* 64, no. 1–2 (Spring-Summer 2012): 30–41.
Lagerwey, Jorie. "*Jackass* for President: Revitalizing an American Public Life Through the Aesthetic of the Amateur." *Spectator* 24, no. 1 (Spring 2004): 86–97.
Lastra, James. "Buñuel, Bataille, and Buster, or, the Surrealist Life of Things." *Critical Quarterly* 51, no. 2 (July 2009): 16–38.
———. *Sound Technology and the American Cinema: Perception, Representation, Modernity.* New York: Columbia University Press, 2000.
Lev, Peter. *Transforming the Screen, 1950–1959.* History of the American cinema, v. 7. New York: Charles Scribner's Sons, 2003.
Levinson, Jerrold, ed. *The Oxford Handbook of Aesthetics.* New York: Oxford University Press, 2005.
Levy, Shawn. *King of Comedy: The Life and Art of Jerry Lewis.* New York: St. Martin's Press, 1997.
Lewis, Jerry. *The Total Film-maker.* New York: Random House, 1971.
Lim, Dennis. "Another Dimension of Idiocy." *New York Times,* December 8, 2010; http://www.nytimes.com/2010/10/10/movies/10jackass.html.

Lipman, Ross. "Tillie's Punctured Legacy: Observations on the Restoration of Chaplin's First Feature." *Early Popular Visual Culture* 7, no. 2 (July 2009): 127–43.
Lloyd, Ernest F. "The American Automatic Tool." *Journal of Political Economy* 27, no. 6 (June 1919): 457–65.
Los Angeles Plays Itself. DVD. Directed by Thom Andersen, 2003. New York: Burton/Floyd Inc.; Submarine Entertainment, 2007.
Louvish, Simon. *Keystone: The Life and Clowns of Mack Sennett*. London: Faber & Faber, 2004.
Marc, David. *Comic Visions: Television Comedy and American Culture*. Malden, MA: Blackwell, 1997.
Massa, Steve. *Slapstick Divas: The Women of Silent Comedy*. Albany, GA: BearManor, 2017.
McKay, John. "Walter Benjamin and Rudolf Arnheim on Charlie Chaplin." *Yale Journal of Criticism* 9, no. 2 (Fall 1996): 309–14.
Mellencamp, Patricia. "Jokes and Their Relation to the Marx Brothers." In *Cinema and Language*, edited by Stephen Heath and Patricia Mellencamp. Frederick, MD: University Publications of America, 1983.
Menand, Louis. "Unpopular Front: American Art and the Cold War." *New Yorker*, October 17, 2005.
Metz, Christian. *Film Language: A Semiotics of the Cinema*. Chicago: University of Chicago Press, 1991.
Michelson, Annette. "'The Man with the Movie Camera': From Magician to Epistemologist." *Artforum* 10, no. 7 (March 1972): 60–72.
———. "Review: What Is Cinema?" *Artforum* 6, no. 10 (1968): 68–72.
Mitchell, William J. *The Reconfigured Eye: Visual Truth in the Post-Photographic Era*. Cambridge: MIT Press, 1992.
Mizejewski, Linda. *Pretty / Funny: Women Comedians and Body Politics*. Austin: University of Texas Press, 2014.
Modern Times. DVD. Directed by Charles Chaplin, 1936. New York: Criterion, 2010.
Monaco, Paul. *The Sixties, 1960–1969*. History of the American cinema, v. 8. New York: Charles Scribner's Sons, 2001.
Monkey Business. DVD. Directed by Norman Z. McLeod, 1931. Universal City, CA: Universal Studios, 2004.
Morgan, Daniel. "Rethinking Bazin: Ontology and Realist Aesthetics." *Critical Inquiry* 32, no. 3 (Spring 2006): 443–81.
Munster, Anna. *Materializing New Media: Embodiment in Information Aesthetics*. Lebanon, NH: University Press of New England, 2006.
Münsterberg, Hugo. *Hugo Münsterberg on Film: The Photoplay: A Psychological Study and Other Writings*. New York: Routledge, 2001.
The Navigator. DVD. Directed by Buster Keaton, 1924. New York: Kino Lorber, 2012.
Neale, Stephen, and Frank Krutnick. *Popular Film and Television Comedy*. London: Routledge, 1990.
North, Michael. *Machine-Age Comedy*. New York: Oxford University Press, 2009.
Nugent, Frank. "Heralding the Return, After an Undue Absence, of Charlie Chaplin in 'Modern Times.'" *New York Times*, February 6, 1936, 23.

Our Hospitality. DVD. Directed by Buster Keaton and John G. Blystone, 1923. New York: Kino on Video, 2001.

Paulus, Tom, and Rob King, eds. *Slapstick Comedy*. New York: Routledge, 2010.

Peacock, Louise. *Slapstick and Comic Performance: Comedy and Pain*. New York: Palgrave, 2014.

Perez, Gilberto. *The Material Ghost: Films and Their Medium*. Baltimore: Johns Hopkins University Press, 1998.

Polan, Dana. "Being and Nuttiness: Jerry Lewis and the French." *Journal of Popular Film & Television* 12, no. 1 (Spring 1984): 42–46.

Pomerance, Murray. *Enfant Terrible!: Jerry Lewis in American Film*. New York: New York University Press, 2002.

Pound, Arthur. *The Iron Man in Industry: An Outline of the Social Significance of Automatic Machinery*. Boston: Atlantic Monthly Press, 1922.

Richmond, Scott. "'Dude, That's Just *Wrong*': Mimesis, Identification, *Jackass*." *World Picture* 6 (Winter 2011); http://www.worldpicturejournal.com/WP_6/Richmond.html.

Rico, Diane. *Kovacsland: A Biography of Ernie Kovacs*. New York: Harcourt Brace Jovanovich, 1990.

Road to Utopia. DVD. Directed by Hal Walker, 1946. Los Angeles: Universal Home Pictures Entertainment, 2002.

Rodowick, D. N. *The Virtual Life of Film*. Cambridge: Harvard University Press, 2007.

Romanska, Madga, and Alan Ackerman, eds. *Reader in Comedy: An Anthology of Theory and Criticism*. New York: Bloomsbury, 2016.

Rosen, Philip, ed. *Narrative, Apparatus, Ideology: A Film Theory Reader*. New York: Columbia University Press, 1986.

Rosen, Robert. "Ernie Kovacs: Video Artist." In *Transmission*, edited by Peter D'Agostino, 143–49. New York: Tanam Press, 1985.

Rosenbaum, Jonathan. "Tashlinesque." In *Frank Tashlin*, edited by Roger Garcia. Locarno: Éditions du Festival international du film de Locarno in collaboration with the British Film Institute, 1994.

Rothman, William. *Hitchcock: The Murderous Gaze*. Cambridge: Harvard University Press, 1984.

———. *The "I" of the Camera: Essays in Film Criticism, Theory, and Aesthetics*. New York: Cambridge University Press, 2004.

———, and Marian Keane. *Reading Cavell's* The World Viewed: *A Philosophical Perspective on Film*. Detroit: Wayne State University Press, 2000.

Sahni, Isher-Paul. "More than Horseplay: *Jackass*, Performativity, and the MoMA." *Studies in Popular Culture* 35, no. 2 (Spring 2013): 69–94.

Schatz, Thomas. *Boom and Bust: The American Cinema in the 1940s*. History of the American cinema, v. 6. New York: Charles Scribner's Sons, 1997.

Scruton, Roger. "Photography and Representation." *Critical Inquiry* 7, no. 3 (Spring 1981): 577–603.

Seaton, George, Bert Kalmar, Will Johnstone, and Harry Ruby. *The Marx Brothers: Monkey Business; Duck Soup; and, A Day at the Races*. London: Faber, 1993.

Seven Chances. DVD. Directed by Buster Keaton, 1925. New York: Kino on Video, 2001.

Shaviro, Steven. *The Cinematic Body*. Minneapolis: University of Minnesota Press, 1993.
Sherlock Jr. DVD. Directed by Buster Keaton, 1924. New York: Kino on Video, 2001.
Smith, Terry. *Making the Modern: Industry, Art, and Design in America*. Chicago: University of Chicago Press, 1993.
Speedy. DVD. Directed by Ted Wilde, 1928. Los Angeles: New Line Home Entertainment, 2005.
Spigel, Lynn. *Make Room for TV: Television and the Family Ideal in Postwar America*. Chicago: University of Chicago Press, 1992.
Stricker, Bernhard. "Experience Missed or Lost?: Cavell's Concept of the Ordinary and Walter Benjamin on the 'Loss of Aura.'" *Conversations: The Journal of Cavellian Studies* 4 (2016): 4–25.
Sweeney, Kevin M., ed. *Buster Keaton: Interviews*. Oxford: University of Mississippi Press, 2007.
Talbot, William Henry Fox. *The Pencil of Nature*; http://www.thepencilofnature.com.
The Three Stooges Collection, Vol. 4: 1943–1945. DVD. Los Angeles: Sony Home Pictures Entertainment, 2008.
Tout Va Bien. DVD. Directed by Jean-Luc Godard and Jean-Pierre Gorin, 1972. New York: Criterion Collection, 2005.
Trahair, Lisa. "Being on the Outside: Cinematic Automatism in Stanley Cavell's *The World Viewed*." *Film-Philosophy* 18 (2014); http://www.film-philosophy.com/index.php/f-p/article/view/1034.
———. *The Comedy of Philosophy: Sense and Nonsense in Early Cinematic Slapstick*. Albany: State University of New York Press, 2007.
Turvey, Malcom. *Doubting Vision: Film and the Revelationist Tradition*. New York: Oxford University Press, 2006.
Ulmer, Gregory L. "'A Night at the Text': Roland Barthes's Marx Brothers." *Yale French Studies* no. 73 (January 1987): 38–57.
Ure, Andrew. *The Philosophy of Manufactures: or, An Exposition of the Scientific, Moral, and Commercial Economy of the Factory System of Great Britain*. London: Charles Knight, 1835.
Veblen, Thorstein. *The Theory of Business Enterprise*. New York: Charles Scribner's Sons, 1915.
Walton, Kendall. "Transparent Pictures: On the Nature of Photographic Realism." *Critical Inquiry* 11, no. 2 (December 1984): 246–77.
Ward, John W. "The Meaning of Lindbergh's Flight." *American Quarterly* 10, no. 1 (Spring 1958): 3–16.
Weis, Elisabeth, and John Belton, eds. *Film Sound: Theory and Practice*. New York: Columbia University Press, 1985.
Williams, Linda. "Gender, Genre, and Excess." *Film Quarterly* 44, no. 4 (Summer 1991): 2–13.
Williams, Raymond. *Television; Technology and Cultural Form*. New York: Routledge, 2003.
Wittgenstein, Ludwig. *Philosophical Investigations*. Translated by G. E. M. Anscombe. Malden, MA: Blackwell, 2001.

Wollen, Peter. "Godard and Counter-Cinema: *Vent d'Est*." In *The European Cinema Reader*, edited by Catherine Fowler, 74–82. New York: Routledge, 2002.

Index

ABC Specials (1960–1961), 14, 185n25; form of, 115–17; and interest in synchronization, 119–20; representation of women in, 121–23; and sight-to-sound pieces, 116–17, 121; use of music in, 118
abstract expressionism, 129–30
acknowledgment, 4, 47, 48, 50–52, 53, 55, 60, 63, 68, 70, 72, 77, 89, 123, 125, 126, 135, 172; negative, 90. *See also* Cavell, Stanley
agreement, 3, 46, 57–59, 60–61
Allen, Gracie, 10, 111
Allen, Steve, 113
ambivalence, 30, 31, 35–36, 40–41, 51–52
anagnorisis. *See* moment of recognition
Andersen, Thom, 151
Anger, Kenneth, 150
Animal Crackers (1930), 82, 95
Aragon, Louis, 27
Arbuckle, Fatty, 31, 33
Artists and Models (1955), vii, viii, 106, 127–36, 151
aspect perception. *See* seeing as
At Twelve O'Clock (1913), 17
automation, 27, 30–36, 69, 70; and aesthetic experience, 32–33; definition of, 34; in "The American Automatic Tool," 33–36

automatism, 13, 28–30, 34, 36, 37, 41, 41–44, 48, 51, 52, 134, 135, 165; and human behavior, 28–30, 42; in Stanley Cavell, 42–44, 181n34
avant-garde, 39, 50, 132–33, 150–52, 160, 165; Hollywood relationship to, 151
Avery, Tex, 105, 131

Bacall, Lauren, 106
Bacall to Arms (1946), 105
Balázs, Béla, 6
Ball, Lucille, 10, 111
Bardéche, Maurice, 151
Barrymore, John, 80–81
Baudelaire, Charles, 56, 123
Baz, Avner, 57, 181n5
Bazin, André, 7, 8, 31, 48, 50, 175; and "the myth of total cinema," 175
Bellboy, The (1960), 104, 108, 138, 153–55
Belton, John, 163, 188
Benjamin, Walter, 7, 30, 126, 182n20
Berkeley, Busby, 168
Berle, Milton, 113
blackout gags, 114–16
Blanchot, Maurice, 137
Bogart, Humphrey, 106
Bordwell, David, 9, 24, 41, 80, 92, 98, 142, 153, 157

Brassillach, Robert, 151
Braun, Karl Ferdinand, 123
Brecht, Berthold, 115, 120, 123, 159, 185n31
Broad City (2014–2019), 10
Buñuel, Luis, 28, 138
burlesque, 15, 16, 17
Burns, George, 111

Cahiers du Cinéma, 126, 156
Cameraman, The (1928), vii, 4, 13, 30, 37–44, 48, 79, 114
Carroll, Noël, 28, 179n
Cass, John L., 90
Cavell, Stanley, 2–4, 11, 12, 42–44, 47, 48, 53, 59, 124, 177n; and acknowledgment, 4; comedies of remarriage, 3, 12; idea of criticism in, 3; and skepticism, 2, 43; *The World Viewed*, 2, 42–44, 76, 124
Chaplin, Charles, ix, x, 4, 6, 8, 9, 13, 16, 19–22, 48, 53–64, 67–72, 74–76, 82, 85, 89, 125, 126, 151, 152, 173; Béla Balázs on, 6; and synchronized sound, 68–69, 181n9; and relation of performer to audience, 54, 57, 62–63, 68, 75
Chevalier, Maurice, 4, 82, 83
Chion, Michel, 119
Cinderfella (1960), 155
city symphony, 39
classical Hollywood cinema, 9, 12, 18, 24, 39–41, 52, 90–91, 95, 96, 98–99, 103, 137, 142, 145, 152–53; meaning of "classical" in, 151–52; relation to modernism, 99, 151–52; and representation of the human body, 98, 136
CinemaScope, 108
Cinerama, 108
City Lights (1931), vii, 4, 13, 48, 60, 62–72, 74, 76, 77, 85; closing scenes of, 63–68
Cocoanuts, The (1929), 79, 80, 82, 88–90, 99, 183n; representation of telephonic sound in, 88–89

Coffee with Kovacs, 112
Colbert, Claudette, 2
College (1927), 36, 39, 167
comedy, slapstick. *See* slapstick comedy
commedia dell'arte, 15
commodification, 126, 130
continuity, 7, 18, 145, 155
Cops (1922), 28
Cornell, Joseph, 150
Crafton, Donald, 80, 105, 136
Crosby, Bing, 14, 104

DeMille, Cecil, 5
Detroit, 32–33
"Die Moritӓt von Mackie Messer" (song), vii, 116, 118, 120–23
Disorderly Orderly, The (1964), 136
Don Juan (1926), 81, 83
Dressler, Marie, 10, 15, 16, 19
Drunkard's Reformation, A (1909), 13, 17–18, 21–22
Dubreuil, Hyacinthe, 32
Duck Soup (1933), vii, 82, 91–92, 96, 98

East of Borneo (1931), 150
Eisenstein, Sergei, 71
Electric House, The (1922), 29
Ernie in Kovacsland (1951), 112
Errand Boy, The (1961), viii, 137, 145–49, 153; duration of gags in, 145, 147–48; ironization of sentiment in, 146, 149; revelation of the film screen in, 147–48
Evans, Aden, 171

Fail Blog, 174
Family Jewels, The (1965), 138
Fatal Hour, The (1908), 17
female comedians, 10, 179n3
Fey, Tina, 10
film: and desire, 47–48, 55, 60, 62, 65, 67–68, 71–72, 77; and fantasy, 31, 43, 47, 64–65, 67–70, 72, 88, 172; and intimacy, 51, 53, 57, 60,

61, 62, 145; and privacy, 47, 53, 63, 72
First Auto, The (1927), 87–88
Ford, Henry, 28
French New Wave, 152
Fujiwara, Chris, 136, 138

Gable, Clark, 2
General, The (1926), 1, 29–30, 39, 46, 48
genre, 3–4, 9
George Burns and Gracie Allen Show, The (1950–1958), 111
German Expressionism, 151
Girl Can't Help It, The (1956), 108
Gish, Lillian, 19
Godard, Jean-Luc, 14, 152, 153, 156–60, 161; interest in Jerry Lewis, 156–58; relation to classical Hollywood cinema, 157–59
Gold Rush, The (1925), 58–62, 68, 74–76
Greenberg, Clement, ix, 130–35, 160
Griffith, D. W., 4, 13, 17, 18, 20–24
Gunning, Tom, 18, 22, 29
Guthrie, Sharon, 120

Hansen, Mark, 171
Hansen, Miriam, 99, 136, 150, 178n16, 183n9
Harris, Neil, 7
Hayles, Katherine, 171
Heidegger, Martin, 57
Hellzapoppin' (1941), vii, 2, 14, 101–106, 113; and self-reference, 102–103
Help! Help! (1912), 17, 24
His Girl Friday (1940), 2
Hoberman J., 160
Hollywood or Bust (1956), 160
Hollywood Steps Out (1941), 105
Hope, Bob, 14, 104
Horse Feathers (1932), 82
House Un-American Activities Committee (HUAC), 107
Howard, Shemp, 102

I Love Lucy (1951–1957), 111
Intolerance (1916), 88
It Happened One Night (1934), 2
It's Time for Ernie (1951), 112, 114

Jackass Number Two (2006), 14, 164–70, 172–74, 188n8; and authenticity, 168–69; and embodiment, 172–73; falling house gag in, 167–69; form of, 166; and homosociality, 166–67; use of 35mm in, 169; use of digital video, 169–70; and representation of pain, 173
Jenkins, Henry, 95
Johnson, Chic, 2, 102
Jones, Caroline, 131

Keaton, Buster, 1, 2, 5, 10, 16, 25, 27, 28, 29, 30, 31, 32, 33, 37, 40, 42, 44, 46, 47, 48, 50, 51, 52, 53, 54, 57, 63, 69, 70, 75, 79, 82, 85, 104, 105, 125, 126, 141, 145, 149, 152, 155, 164, 165, 167, 168, 169, 170, 173, 174, 179n, 181n, 185n, 188n; ambivalence of, 35–36, 40–41, 51–52; as automaton, 28; and falling house gag, 164–65; heroic reading of, 28; and ironization of romance, 36, 40, 41, 51, 167; and nineteenth-century settings, 35; and realism, 44, 48–50; relation to machine technologies, 27–29, 37–40; relation to modernism, 28; and synchronized sound, 79–80; as victim, 29
Keystone Film Company, 4, 10, 16–17
King, Rob, 21
kitsch, 130, 132–33, 160
Kovacs, Ernie, vii, 14, 103, 112–15, 125–26, 136–37, 165; and Berthold Brecht, 115; Dutch Masters' specials, 115; early television work, 112–14; radio work of, 112; *Zoomar* (novel), 112

Kovacs on Music (1959), 114
Kracauer, Siegfried, 31
Krutnik, Frank, 147

L'Age d'Or (1930), 138
Ladies Man, The (1961), viii, 1, 12, 125, 137–45, 153–60; authenticity in, 144–45; images of television in, 142–43; and the Lewisian "block," 137; pedagogical image in, 139; set of, 144; vertical structure of, 158–59
Lagerwey, Jorie, 169
Lang, Fritz, 28
Lethal Weapon 2 (1989), 151
Lewis, Jerry, viii, ix, 1, 3, 12, 90, 104–109, 112, 115, 122–61; form of self-produced films, 136–37; interest in duration, 12; invention of video assist, 108; relation to the accidental, 130, 133–35; relation to high modernism, 126–29, 135, 152–54; relation to television, 125–26, 149–50; and *The Total Film-maker*, 152, 154
Lloyd, Ernest, 33–35
Lone Ranger, The (1949–1957), 121
Lonely Villa, The (1909), 17
Los Angeles Plays Itself (2003), 151
Lost in Space (1965–1968), 129
Louis, Morris, 133
Love Me Tonight (1932), 84
Lubitsch, Ernst, 80, 151

Mabel's Dramatic Career (1913), 4
"Mack the Knife," 120
Mamoulian, Rouben, 84
Man with the Movie Camera, The (1929), 50
Mansfield, Jayne, 131
Marriage Circle, The (1924), 80
Martin, Dean, 112, 127–29, 135
Marx Brothers, The, x, 3, 12, 13, 14, 62, 77–99, 104, 119, 125
Marx, Groucho, 86–88, 92–93

Marx, Harpo, 83–84, 88–90, 183n20; as grotesque body, 95–99; as mute, 89–90
Mary Tyler Moore Show, The (1970–1977), 104
mechanization, 9, 27, 28, 30, 32, 35, 36, 106
medium-specificity, 6–7, 108, 132–34, 160
Metropolis (1927), 28
Metz, Christian, 124
Michelson, Annette, 50
Micro-Phonies (1945), 105
Mill, John Stuart, 53
Min and Bill (1930), 15
minstrelsy, 15
mise-en-abyme, 2, 65, 83, 92, 105, 118, 144, 166, 168
Mitchell, William J., 163
Modern Times (1936), vii, ix, 62, 9, 13, 69–77, 82, 85, 182n; and cinema as surveillance, 70–72; images of the film screen in, 71–73; interest in temporality in, 70–72, 76; representation of automation in, 69–71; reviews of 69–70; and seeing as, 75; use of sound in, 71–74, 76–77
modernism, 43, 123, 126, 130, 133, 150–51, 152–54; and kitsch, 132; vulgar, 160
moment of recognition, 67–68, 146–47
Monkey Business (1931), 3, 4, 82–85, 87, 88, 90, 92, 98, 99; reference to gangster cycle, 92; representation of phonographic sound in, 82–85; representation of radio sound in, 85–88
Monty Python, 117
Moore, Del, 142–43
Motion Picture Production Code, 90
Munster, Anna, 171
Münsterberg, Hugo, 6

Namuth, Hans, 130
National Board of Censorship, 18
Navigator, The (1924), 29, 37, 39
Noland, Kenneth, 133
Normand, Mabel, 10, 16, 19
North, Michael, 28

Olsen, Ole, 2, 102
One Hour with You (1932), 80
One Week (1920), 36
O'Neill, Eugene, 95
ontology of film, 1, 10–14, 25, 44, 46, 47, 51, 77, 82, 95, 114, 115, 126, 163, 164, 171; and film theory, 8; historical, 10–11; and synchronized sound, 82
operational aesthetic, 7, 101
Orphans of the Storm (1921), 4
oscilloscope, vii, 116, 117, 118, 121, 122, 123–24, 184n25

package-unit system, 107
pantomime, 15, 16, 62, 69, 74, 75, 77, 112, 119, 137, 153
Paramount decree, 107
parody, 25, 41–42, 51, 83, 86, 95, 106, 108, 113, 130, 135, 166, 169
Patsy, The (1964), 3, 107–108, 125, 138
Peacock, Louise, 169
Perez, Gilberto, 29
Philadelphia Story, The (1940), 2, 48, 141
Pollock, Jackson, ix, 129–30; and Frank Tashlin, 130–35
producer-unit system, 107
Puce Moment (1949), 150

RCA (Radio Corporation of America), 80, 81, 90
Renoir, Jean, 50, 151
Rico, Diane, 115
Road to Utopia (1945), 104
Rockwell, Norman, 129
Rose Hobart (1936), 150

Rothman, William, 12, 63, 64, 68, 181n1, 182n10

Schatz, Thomas, 101
Seduction of the Innocent, 120
seeing as, 13, 57–59, 62, 69, 181n4, 181n5; and articulation of experience, 58–59; and ethical judgment, 56–57, 61–62
self-reference, 1–2, 4–5, 25, 101, 103–106; in burlesque, 16
self-reflexivity, 2, 4, 111, 157
Sennett, Mack, 12, 16–17, 20, 24
Seven Chances (1925), 29, 36
Sherlock Jr. (1924), vii, 1, 4, 5, 13, 30, 37, 42. 44–53, 82, 103, 145; display of moving image in, 44–46
Shoulder Arms (1918), 54–57, 62, 63, 75
Silents Please (1960–1962), 115
slapstick comedy, 5, 174–75; and classical cinema, 12; and classical film theory, 5–8; as genre and mode, 3–4; history of, 15–16; and modernity, 9–10; and narrative, 16–21, 22–25, 136–38, 141–42, 153–54; and ontology of cinema, 1–2; and philosophy, 1, 5, 8; and realism, 7–8
spectatorship, 9, 16, 21–23, 33, 43, 44–45, 56, 146, 188n6
Spigel, Lyn, 109, 111, 185n31
Staiger, Janet, 9, 24, 107, 153
Steamboat Bill Jr. (1928), 28, 37, 164–65, 168
Strange Interlude (1932), 95
studio system, 2, 9, 10, 11, 14, 24, 25, 40, 90, 95, 101, 106, 125, 126, 131, 150, 163
Sullivan's Travels (1941), 141
Surrealism, 135
Swooner Crooner (1944), 105
synchresis, 105; broadcast, 119, 125
synchronization of sound, 14, 79–82, 84, 87, 89, 94, 119, 121, 123;

synchronization of sound *(continued)* and average shot lengths, 79–80; competing technologies of, 80–82; and dialogue, 16, 68, 69, 74, 76, 79, 82, 87–90, 93–96, 105, 112; and film style, 80–82; and the human voice, 81, 83–84, 93–94; and intelligibility, 88; and non-diegetic music, 84

Tashlin, Frank, ix, 12, 105, 106, 108, 126, 129, 130–36, 151, 155, 156, 186n13; and the "Tashlinesque," 130
Taylor, Frederick, 28
television, 1, 10, 12, 14, 71, 74, 76, 81, 101, 102, 104, 106, 108–12, 114, 119, 122–26, 133, 136, 141, 144, 150, 166, 168, 169, 171, 173; as broadcast, 114; as flow, 110–11; and hyperrealism, 109; and liveness, 114–15, 123–24; as mass medium, 109–10; as mobile privatization, 110; relationship to Hollywood cinema, 109, 123–24; and self-reference, 111–12; as subtext of comedy, 109; vaudeville performers interest in, 111
Ten Commandments, The (1923), 5
Termite Terrace, 105–106
Thomasson, Amie, 11
Three Stooges, The, 14, 102, 105
Tillie's Punctured Romance (1914), vii, 3, 4, 12, 15, 16, 17, 19–25; and film spectatorship, 16, 20–22; plot of, 19; "A Thief's Fate," 20–22

Tout Va Bien (1972), 156–60; horizontal structure of, 158–60; z-axis of, 158–59
travesty, 4, 16, 17, 19–21, 24–25

Un Chien Andalou (1929), 165
Uncle Josh at the Moving Picture Show (1902), 106

Vacances de Monsieur Hulot, Les (1953), 148–49
vaudeville, 4, 10, 15, 16, 17, 31, 95, 98, 103, 111, 112, 117, 119, 166
Veblen, Thorstein, 33, 35, 70
Vent d'Est (1970), 159
Vertov, Dziga, 27, 50, 150, 155, 179
video, digital, 155, 163, 169, 170–74; abstraction of, 173–74; and analog film, 172; and embodiment, 171–72; materiality of, 170–71
VistaVision, 108

Warhol, Andy, 150
Wertham, Fredric, 129
Will Success Spoil Rock Hunter? (1957), 109
Williams, Bert, 15
Williams, Raymond, 109, 136
Wittgenstein, Ludwig, 3, 13, 57, 59, 61, 62

Your Show of Shows (1950–1954), 104

Zola, Émile, 17

Also in the series

William Rothman, editor, *Cavell on Film*

J. David Slocum, editor, *Rebel Without a Cause*

Joe McElhaney, *The Death of Classical Cinema*

Kirsten Moana Thompson, *Apocalyptic Dread*

Frances Gateward, editor, *Seoul Searching*

Michael Atkinson, editor, *Exile Cinema*

Paul S. Moore, *Now Playing*

Robin L. Murray and Joseph K. Heumann, *Ecology and Popular Film*

William Rothman, editor, *Three Documentary Filmmakers*

Sean Griffin, editor, *Hetero*

Jean-Michel Frodon, editor, *Cinema and the Shoah*

Carolyn Jess-Cooke and Constantine Verevis, editors, *Second Takes*

Matthew Solomon, editor, *Fantastic Voyages of the Cinematic Imagination*

R. Barton Palmer and David Boyd, editors, *Hitchcock at the Source*

William Rothman, *Hitchcock: The Murderous Gaze, Second Edition*

Joanna Hearne, *Native Recognition*

Marc Raymond, *Hollywood's New Yorker*

Steven Rybin and Will Scheibel, editors, *Lonely Places, Dangerous Ground*

Claire Perkins and Constantine Verevis, editors, *B Is for Bad Cinema*

Dominic Lennard, *Bad Seeds and Holy Terrors*

Rosie Thomas, *Bombay before Bollywood*

Scott M. MacDonald, *Binghamton Babylon*

Sudhir Mahadevan, *A Very Old Machine*

David Greven, *Ghost Faces*

James S. Williams, *Encounters with Godard*

William H. Epstein and R. Barton Palmer, editors, *Invented Lives, Imagined Communities*

Lee Carruthers, *Doing Time*

Rebecca Meyers, William Rothman, and Charles Warren, editors, *Looking with Robert Gardner*

Belinda Smaill, *Regarding Life*

Douglas McFarland and Wesley King, editors, *John Huston as Adaptor*
R. Barton Palmer, Homer B. Pettey, and Steven M. Sanders, editors, *Hitchcock's Moral Gaze*
Nenad Jovanovic, *Brechtian Cinemas*
Will Scheibel, *American Stranger*
Amy Rust, *Passionate Detachments*
Steven Rybin, *Gestures of Love*
Seth Friedman, *Are You Watching Closely?*
Roger Rawlings, *Ripping England!*
Michael DeAngelis, *Rx Hollywood*
Ricardo E. Zulueta, *Queer Art Camp Superstar*
John Caruana and Mark Cauchi, editors, *Immanent Frames*
Nathan Holmes, *Welcome to Fear City*
Homer B. Pettey and R. Barton Palmer, editors, *Rule, Britannia!*
Milo Sweedler, *Rumble and Crash*
Ken Windrum, *From El Dorado to Lost Horizons*
Matthew Lau, *Sounds Like Helicopters*
Dominic Lennard, *Brute Force*
William Rothman, *Tuitions and Intuitions*
Michael Hammond, *The Great War in Hollywood Memory, 1918–1939*

www.ingramcontent.com/pod-product-compliance
Ingram Content Group UK Ltd.
Pitfield, Milton Keynes, MK11 3LW, UK
UKHW010710070625
2136IPUK00007B/23